"A timely contribution to a vital debate about the past and future of our cities — this is a story that needs to be told."
Christine Berry, co-author of *People Get Ready*

"Rose's compelling evocation of Manchester as a symptomatic 'rentier city' will provide a crucial reference point for all those seeking a less exploitative and socially polarised urban future."
Neil Gray, editor of *Rent and its Discontents*

"*The Rentier City* takes an unflinching look at the city Manchester has become, compared to what it could have been; assessing and analysing the costs of gentrification, the power of the developer lobby and the weaknesses of the urban left. This is a landmark study of the social and political processes that have made turned Britain into a country ruled by and for landlords."
Jeremy Gilbert, Professor of Cultural and Political Theory, University of East London

"A detailed, eye-opening investigation and analysis of the state of Manchester's housing, economy, and everyday experience, with a refreshing focus on the grassroots, providing a welcome dose of reality to relentless Manchester boosterism."
Dave Haslam, author of *Manchester, England*

"Finally, here's the antidote to the decades of Mad Fer It Urban Boosterism that have beset Greater Manchester. This book deserves a place in the pockets of all those in the northern metropolis who refuse to participate in the self-congratulatory rituals of Manctopia."
Owen Hatherley, author of *Red Metropolis*

T0037848

"Written by an author grounded in the struggles of his adopted city, *The Rentier City* is much more than a cautionary tale about 'Manc-hatten'; it is a dystopian window into the global urban age in construction and a call to arms to rebel before it's too late."

Stuart Hodkinson, author of *Safe as Houses*

"Since I studied in Manchester in 1986-90, the city's property infrastructure has been decimated by private developers working in tandem with city enablers. Sites of social communing and public housing have been transformed into high-cost, low-taste developments, including the Haçienda. Has any other city ever lost so much of its soul in such a short space of time? In *The Rentier City*, Isaac Rose, whose commitment to housing activism and community politics runs deep, has provided us with a searing account of this history."

Tim Lawrence, author of *Love Saves the Day*

"As a born and bred Mancunian I've been waiting for a book like this for some time! A wonderful, rich, yet accessible, account of the rise, fall and neoliberal resurrection of rentierism in Manchester over the longue durée. A must read for anyone interested in the past, and concerned about the present and future of this paradigmatic city."

Loretta Lees, co-author of *Planetary Gentrification*

Those who fight against a system are the ones who get to really understand how it works. Isaac Rose is a leading activist against the rentier version of Manchester. His book is more than just a history of one city, it's a forensic dissection of the whole rentier city system and how it came to be.

Keir Milburn, author of *Generation Left*

"In this sharp, impassioned study, Isaac Rose shines a light on the endlessly nuanced, utterly venal yet irrepressibly soulful northern metropolis that is modern-day Manchester. This is an essential, searing and vital piece of writing."

Alex Niven, author of *The North Will Rise Again*

"Isaac Rose, like Engels before him, takes us behind the shiny façade of the creative city to reveal the mechanisms of capital accumulation and population displacement that drive the city. *The Rentier City* gives the lie to the heroic Manchester story and helps us talk about reclaiming the city for the common good."

Justin O'Connor, author of *Culture is not an Industry*

"In this remarkable analysis of 300 years of urbanization in Manchester, Isaac Rose articulates how capitalism is always switching gears to siphon value from the city at the expense of working class lives. An important and hopeful book, written in the spirit of resistance against the wreckage of rentier extraction, and an indispensible contribution to our understanding of neoliberal urbanism."

Tom Slater, Professor of Urban Studies, Columbia University

"This is a gripping, un-put-down-able story of the UK's most shocking city. Stripping bare the relationship between capital, property and the organisation of space, it never loses its focus on the power of resistance as well as the pain of defeat."

Vron Ware, author of *Return of a Native*

"A remarkable achievement... *The Rentier City* is destined to become the definitive account of how and why Manchester has neoliberalised, while also suggesting how a different city trajectory can be realised."

Paul Watt, Department of Sociology, LSE

THE RENTIER CITY

THE RENTIER CITY

Manchester and the Making of the Neoliberal Metropolis

Isaac Rose

Published by Repeater Books

An imprint of Watkins Media Ltd

Unit 11 Shepperton House

89-93 Shepperton Road

London

N1 3DF

United Kingdom

www.repeaterbooks.com

A Repeater Books paperback original 2024

1

Distributed in the United States by Random House, Inc., New York.

Copyright Isaac Rose © 2024

Isaac Rose asserts the moral right to be identified as the author of this work.

ISBN: 9781915672186

Ebook ISBN: 9781915672193

All rights reserved. No part of this publication may be reproduced, stored in a retrieval system, or transmitted, in any form or by any means, electronic, mechanical, photocopying, recording or otherwise, without the prior permission of the publishers.

This book is sold subject to the condition that it shall not, by way of trade or otherwise, be lent, re-sold, hired out or otherwise circulated without the publisher's prior consent in any form of binding or cover other than that in which it is published and without a similar condition including this condition being imposed on the subsequent purchaser.

Printed and bound in the United Kingdom by TJ Books Limited

For my father, a Manchester lad

Contents

Leave your contracts in your pockets
They will not be honoured here

Bertolt Brecht, *The Handbook for City Dwellers*

Introduction

Under capitalism there is a perpetual struggle in which capital builds a physical landscape appropriate to its own condition at a particular moment in time, only to have to destroy it, usually in the course of a crisis, at a subsequent point in time.

David Harvey, *The Urban Process Under Capitalism*

One Morning in Collyhurst

In 1969 Manchester City Council commissioned the artist William Mitchell to make a work called *Four Estates*. Mitchell was a London-born sculptor, artist and inventor noted for his striking moulded designs in concrete. Previous works in Manchester included a 1962 mural in the entrance to the CIS Tower, then Britain's tallest building, and a bas-relief on the Humanities Building at the University of Manchester, named after Ellen Wilkinson, local communist and suffragette. He had also created an unrealised plan to illuminate the city's main square with a building-sized sign made of thousands of lightbulbs triggered by photoelectric cells. *Four Estates* was Mitchell's first public commission in the city — a set of four little totems, designed as focal points in the Council's new public housing estates. The one at the Hulme Crescents is long gone. But three remain, in Rusholme, Newton Heath and at the centre of Eastford Square, Collyhurst, about a mile north of the city centre.[1]

In June 2023 the eyes of the city were on Eastford Square. By this point it had gained an unenviable reputation as

Manchester's "biggest eyesore". Once a thriving community, tenants had started to be decanted 14 years previous, in preparation for the (ultimately failed) PFI scheme to redevelop the area. While the "square" had indeed once been a square, bound on three sides by blocks of flats, by 2023 all that remained was a single shuttered row of shops and maisonettes. For months, the media had been anticipating its imminent demolition, approved in March that year. Pat Karney, ward councillor for 44 years, had been tweeting a countdown. Only the presence of bats — and Noel Gallagher's desire to use the site as a location in the music video of his new single "Council Skies" — had delayed D-day. On the 9th June, the cameras assembled, and the demolition began.

In concrete, Mitchell's works capture something of the breezy optimism of postwar modernity; the belief that a better world could be built. Today, many of them are lost, demolished with buildings that have fallen out of favour. Speaking to critic Natalie Bradbury in 2011, Mitchell expressed a stoicism towards the loss of his works, but felt it was important that some remained "to give an idea of what the time was like and the type of things you could do".[2]

Today, the Collyhurst totem sits marooned at the centre of the largest redevelopment zone in Britain. Covering 155 hectares, equivalent to around a third of Manchester's existing city centre, the area, known as Victoria North, will see the delivery of 15,000 new homes over the next 15 years. Its total development value is estimated at £4bn.[3] To create the delivery vehicle, Manchester City Council entered an arrangement with Far East Consortium, a Hong Kong-based investment fund known for its developments across the western Pacific.

The plan for the area is residential-led regeneration. Work has already begun, with a spate of demolitions and the start of construction of 244 houses in "Collyhurst Village". Most are for private sale, though 100 will be social homes. A further 30 social homes are planned elsewhere in the neighbourhood but taken together the total committed social housing fails to make up for the stock lost through the last decade's demolitions, around 550 units in all. The final shape of the district is yet to emerge, but its general contours are already visible. Two months after the Eastford Square demolition, the Council's Planning Committee approved two detailed parts of the masterplan for Red Bank, around 5,000 homes. Only 70 were guaranteed affordable (not necessarily indicating social rent), with a potential further 650 affordable homes "subject", in that all-too-common phrase, "to viability".[4]

The fate of William Mitchell's totem and the square around it captures in microcosm something of the great transition that has happened in our cities over the last half century: the vast shift in housing provision from public good to private gain. If its construction in the late 1960s represented the high tide of public housing, provided by a Council which also commissioned art in the modernist style, then its demolition today, after a decade of disinvestment, marks a dramatic — and public — repudiation of this modernist legacy.

The Rentier City

This timeline fits into a fairly standard historiography of the origin of neoliberalism, one which traces the growing contradictions in the social democratic postwar settlement, and the ideological and political assault upon that consensus by Thatcher's New Right in the 1980s. Her totemic policy was Right to Buy, which brought about the decomposition of the situation at the end of the 1970s, in which around a third of all people in Britain were tenants in public housing. This

Mitchell's totem

process of neoliberalising space can be seen as accumulation by dispossession, the enclosure of what had once been public goods — a vast redistribution of resources from public to private hands.

However, if we consider the origins of the public housing privatised by Thatcher and the motivations behind those that built it, then another story comes into view. Public housing programmes, pioneered by municipal authorities from the late nineteenth century onwards, were aimed primarily at ending the degradation of working people's lives in what were called "the slums". These neighbourhoods were the legacy of the built environment of rapidly industrialising Victorian Britain. They were the domain of the private landlord and the product of the land speculator — the original rentier city. Their replacement by public housing and the introduction of rent controls in the modern era represents, then, among other things, *the euthanasia of the rentier*. This longer timeframe allows us to see the dynamics unfolding in our cities today in a new light: as the *return* of the rentier city.

But what is the meaning of this term "rentier"? In short, a rentier is an economic actor who receives rent purely by virtue of controlling something valuable. That "something" is an "asset" — valuable precisely because control over it endows its owner with the capacity to generate future income. The asset may take many forms, including land, housing or infrastructure, as well as intangible things like intellectual property or even contracts.

Today rentier capitalism plays an increasingly important structural role within the capitalist system as a whole. In his book *Rentier Capitalism*, Brett Christophers argues that the UK is increasingly *the* paradigmatic rentier economy,[5] demonstrating how all major sectors of the UK's economy are imbricated with "rentierism". Christophers explores a wide range of assets, however the classic forms of rentier capitalism — those which have been with us for the longest time — are financial and land rents. Christophers argues that the rise of the rentier is the deliberate result of the changes wrought by Thatcher in the 1980s, which systematically expanded the market for the private ownership of assets and in the long-term encouraged monopoly control. Right to Buy (enshrined in 1980 Housing Act), the "Big Bang" in the financial sector (1986) and the 1988 Housing Act, which created the legal framework for the return of the private rented sector, are all major milestones in this journey. If we were to ask — as Jeremy Gilbert and Alex Williams do in their book *Hegemony Now* — who won the twentieth century, then in Britain we would have to point to the landlord and land speculator.[6] These two forms of rentier — of land and housing — are the forces at the forefront of reshaping the geography of our cities.

We have become accustomed to thinking of capitalism mainly as a system for the production of commodities. Surplus value is extracted from the labour that is brought together with raw materials to produce *things*. But this is only one possible circuit for capital. Across the 1970s and 1980s, the Marxist geographer David Harvey expounded in detail a theory of the secondary circuit of capital reproduction.[7] If the primary circuit is the production of commodities, then the secondary circuit is investments in the built environment, or urbanisation. Crucially, he argued, capital can "switch" from the primary to the secondary circuit in the aftermath of a profitability crisis in the sphere of production. As the primary circuit begins to slow down, as it has done in the Global North since the late 1970s, the secondary circuit increases in relative importance within the overall money-making economy. Where investments in the built environment take the form of rental assets (as opposed to say, public or private "statement" buildings) then the growing importance of the secondary circuit develops in tandem with increased rentierisation.

Paradigmatic City

This book contends that the city of Manchester, England, is a very good place to understand these shifting dynamics. As is well known, Manchester was the birthplace of industrial capitalism, the "shock city" of the nineteenth century. Its factories and spatial layout were the great inspiration behind the theories of Marx and Engels, both of whom had personal knowledge of the city. It was governed above all by the circulation of capital through the production of commodities. This was a process with global reach, with the central commodity, cotton, a product of the Atlantic slave economy and the city's labour force drawn in large part from the colony of Ireland.

But capital also circulated through the production of the built environment — both the building of the slum housing for the working class and the suburbs for the bourgeoisie were the product of speculation on land and housing. Over the course of the twentieth century this dynamic altered, as the state replaced private actors in the provision of working-class housing. The rentier was, in large part, euthanised.

The collapse of this industrial economy in the middle of the twentieth century saw the de-linking of the city from the global circulation of capital. What followed was a sort of interregnum between two regimes of accumulation. The last thirty years have seen the re-integration of the city into the global economy; only now capital circulates in Manchester not through the primary circuit of commodity production, but through the secondary circuit of real estate and land. Through the history of Manchester, we can trace the transition from original industrial city to exemplary rentier city. It has become a machine for the extraction of rent into pension funds and off-shore bank accounts. It is the poster child for neoliberal urbanism.

Manchester Today

Manchester today is a city of renters — 61% of the population rent, with just over half of that number renting from a private landlord.[8] For comparison, in London, just under half rent, the remainder made up by owner-occupiers. The proportion of renters in Manchester is also higher than other comparable British regional cities too, with only Glasgow (55% renters) coming close.[9]

This city of renters is set to continue for the foreseeable

future. We can expect a huge growth in the number of corporate landlords. These are the owners of new build-to-rent developments, which have grown significantly nationwide in the last ten years. By the end of 2022, build-to-rent accounted for almost a quarter of a million units built or under construction in the UK, and is predicted by Savills to reach 1.25 million units by the end of the decade. London is the largest market for this kind of development, accounting for around half of all completed built-to-rent properties in the UK. But Manchester is second, with its city core (including parts of Salford and Trafford) accounting for 17% of the total number.[10] Considering the population of London is 8.6 times greater than Manchester, Salford and Trafford combined (and much of the Salford and Trafford population centres are away from the regional core) we can see how the *relative* mass of this property class is far higher in Manchester than in the capital.

This is the story of a breath-taking post-crash recovery in the property market. It is also the story of its concomitant housing crisis. The figures here are stark. Research published in summer 2023 showed rents had increased on average by 20% across the city. The previous year they had risen by a similar amount. Another recent study has shown that the rent burden is so high in Manchester that it outstrips London for unaffordability, due to the city's lower wages.[11] Rent rises and a lack of available social housing are driving homelessness. Research for the Smith Institute published in 2022 has shown that the City of Manchester has the highest number of households assessed as homeless in the country — 17.8 per thousand households — higher than any London borough. The next two highest are neighbouring Salford and Wigan, before Brent gets a look in from the capital.[12] Temporary accommodation is increasingly no longer temporary, and almost 3,000 households were trapped in it in 2022.

But this crisis was manufactured. The development regime has created the conditions for the boom. Public subsidy has poured into private development. Cheap land disposals have favoured developers. "Section 106" money for social projects has gone uncollected, and the planning regime has contorted itself again and again to ram through developments. Social housing targets were repeatedly unmet. Had the Council followed its own target of making 20% new builds affordable, then the city would have around 9,000 extra affordable homes by now. In 2022, Jennifer Williams, in the *Manchester Evening News*, asked whether Manchester had "rebuilt London's housing crisis". To which we might ask: has it actually built something worse?

Understanding *how* this came about can be difficult. There is a well-worn narrative, employed by the city's boosters, that has congealed into a powerful mythos about the "Manchester miracle". The same touchstones appear again and again: a Sex Pistols gig in 1976 at the Free Trade Hall, Joy Division and Ian Curtis, Factory Records, Tony Wilson and the Haçienda. The move from culture to property-led regeneration; guitar bands and synthesizers as the spark that set the renaissance alight. These moments have been repeated enough times that they have taken on the appearance of truth. But this narrative occludes far more than it reveals. The true story must be looked for elsewhere.

The trends that have unfolded in Manchester over the last 40 years, as it has moved from being an industrial to post-industrial city, are not unique to it. The benefit of exploring Manchester is not that it provides a singular case study of neoliberal urbanisation, but rather that the picture which emerges is of a city government that has been unusually effective at applying the tenets of neoliberal urbanism. By understanding *this* city, we have a sound basis from which to grasp wider patterns in the economy.

The Two Souls of Manchester

Throughout this story we will trace the pendulum as it swings between the two competing political traditions of Manchester. On the one hand is the working-class tradition of at times vigorous social reform, at other times outright sedition. Chartism, industrial syndicalism, socialism, communism, suffragism, Black radicalism and anti-imperialism all have powerful histories within Manchester. It is this history that is often deployed, as surface-level rhetoric at least, in portrayals of Manchester as the archetypal "radical" city.

On the other hand, however, Manchester makes a fair claim to be the original *laissez-faire*, liberal city. A city of colonialism, Anti-Corn Laws, suburban development corporations, the Manchester Men and Indian cotton. It is the city of Bright, Cobden and Gladstone, the latter of whom owed his family's wealth to some of the most extensive sugar plantations in Jamaica and Guyana. Manchester's history of liberalism is in fact so important that the Germans even had their own word for the city's particular nineteenth-century elite ideology: *Manchestertum* or "Manchesterism". Its proponents were known as the *Manchesterschule*.

Today's *Manchesterschule* are the developers and their boosters. They exhibit the same hypocrisies as their forebears did, the presented veneer of their cause's nobility a cover for deep exploitation and injustice. Indeed, noting how imbricated the original Manchester Liberals were both with the circulation of capital through the built environment at home, and the extraction of colonial rents abroad, we can see how *laissez-faire* liberalism has always, to some extent, had a rentier component.

The Contents of this Book

This is not a book about the housing crisis. There is little need for another one. Rather, it is a sustained exploration of the political economy and development of one city over the *longue durée*. The departure point is Doreen Massey's observations about place. Places, she argues, have always been constructed out of the articulations of social relations which are not only internal to that locale, but which link to them elsewhere. Of such places and their pasts, she writes: "their 'local uniqueness' is always already a product of wide contacts; the local is always already a product of 'global' forces, where global in this context refers not necessarily to the planetary scale, but to the geographical beyond, the world beyond the place itself".[13]

This book is structured in three parts, ordered roughly chronologically. The first section is an examination of the sweep of the city's history, from c. 1750-1950. In two chapters it examines the trajectory of the city's development, both in its "shock" and modern periods. The shock period was the original industrial, productive city. It was also a city whose built environment was largely created by private speculation. The twin results of this were the slum and the suburb, Little Ireland and Victoria Park. The modern period was in many ways formed as a reaction to this — the second chapter traces, following Marshall Berman, a "dialectic of modernity" at play in Manchester. It is an era that is often skipped over in many tellings of the city's history, but it is a crucial one. The scope of this first section is broad but provides the essential backdrop to the transitions of the 1980s.

The second part covers the period between the disintegration of the postwar consensus and the victory of the new neoliberal hegemony — the interregnum between two regimes of accumulation. It explores the alternative routes out of the contradictions of the 1970s posed by the New Right and a New Urban Left and traces the story of how the former defeated the latter. The third and final part examines the Manchester of today — the model neoliberal city — and the re-integration of its economy into the *secondary* circuit of global capital. This narrative will also trace how the city's contemporary housing crisis was a crisis by design. These three sections are paced differently, and to an extent exhibit shifts in style. Taken together, it is hoped, they provide a new understanding of how the present condition came about.

The geographic scope centres upon the City of Manchester, which has expanded its boundaries multiple times across the last three centuries. Today it is stretched along a north-south axis — a peculiar, elongated geography. Home to 550,000 individuals, it is the core city of the wider "Greater Manchester" region of 2.8 million, which consists of the core conurbation of Manchester, Salford and parts of Trafford and Tameside, and then a series of outlying townships — Rochdale, Oldham, Bolton and Bury to the north, Stockport and Altrincham to the south, and Wigan to the west. This geography is a legacy of the spatial patterning of industrialisation.

At times in the narrative, "Manchester" may stretch slightly beyond its city limits to include parts of the wider region. This is in part dictated by the city's development — just as in the late nineteenth century parts of Salford were drawn into the economic orbit of the city through the construction of the "Manchester" docks, today the property boom stretches across the city centre of Manchester and sections of its neighbouring boroughs. There is, regrettably, no sustained engagement with the internal dynamics of those boroughs. Aside from this being the necessary requirement of the dictates of length, it also belies the fact that Manchester has always been the economic dynamo of the region, a "diligent spider" setting the tempo of its neighbours. The focus remains on the core city, with its neighbours appearing only periodically in the narrative.

Author's Note
I didn't grow up in Manchester — my parents left the city in the late 1980s. But Manchester was always the metropolitan centre to which we orientated, visiting family who still lived here or, indeed, the new, "European-style" city centre. But, for nearly a decade now, I've called the city home. During this time two things have been impossible to ignore — the rapidity of the changing city skyline and the rising rents. These things feel intuitively connected. But many are well paid to convince you that they're not related — "data gurus", online "supply guys" and property developer shills. In Manchester particularly, a very local brand of boosterism has been militant in its Panglossian narrative.

Today, housing is the number one issue in Manchester — as it is becoming so nationwide. Not everybody in the city accepts the narrative of the boosters, nor do they want their city sold off to the highest bidder. This is not just a small group of activists shouting from the sidelines, but a much wider anger over how urban development is playing out in the city. For many years I have been part of a wide network of people who have tried to critique — and resist — the development machine. This is no outsider's account. Rather it is an attempt to tie together all the different critiques that have been put forward and narrativise them in a single volume, situating it within a wider historical frame than is usual for commentators on the city. It also, I hope, indicates towards a more general argument about the transitions within the wider political economy and particularly in our cities over the past forty years.

I must extend thanks to all who spoke to me, reviewed parts of the text or discussed the ideas within this work over many hours across many years. But in the end, the final analysis — and any mistakes — are entirely my own.

Part 1

The Primary Circuit

Chapter 1
Shock City

If Engels had lived not in Manchester but in Birmingham, his conception of "class" and his theories of the role of class in history might have been very different. In this case Marx might not have been a communist but a currency reformer. The fact that Manchester was taken to be the symbol of the age in the 1840s was of central political importance in modern world history.

Asa Briggs, *Victorian Cities*

The most radical street in shock city Manchester was Cropper Street. Situated off the Rochdale Road, as it made its way out of Ancoats and New Cross towards Middleton, it consisted of 83 homes along a couple of terraces. At that time, it was just outside the city limits, on the peripheries, surrounded by fields. This marginality was a great boon to its radical politics.[1]

On 10th March 1817, around 500 unemployed spinners and weavers assembled in St Peter's Field, at the town's centre. 1816, the "year without a summer", had seen crop failures, hunger and poverty stalk the land. Many turned to machine-breaking, striking at the perceived roots of their oppression. On that day, the petitioners planned a march to London to call for government intervention. Carrying blankets on their backs to sleep under, they became known as the "Blanketeers". A few hundred set off from Manchester. Pursued by cavalry, clashes erupted in Ardwick, on its south-eastern edge. At Stockport, many were arrested; one local labourer was shot dead by a dragoon. A handful carried on, but harried by soldiers, the march fizzled out by Derby. Fearful of insurrection, the authorities formed the Manchester and Salford Yeomanry, who two years later at St Peter's Field would charge a crowd of 60,000, killing 18 and injuring over 400.

Cropper Street was home to the highest density of Blanketeers. At number 38 lived John and Edward Philips; at 65 was John Pendleton; at 69, Spencer Ashton; 61, John Gibson; and 36, James Scowcroft. All were young weavers in their twenties, likely mates; all were arrested in 1817. Two years later, at least a dozen of those injured at Peterloo also lived on Cropper Street. One, Ann Bickerstaff at 63, was "carried off the field for dead". She was 22.

It remained a political hotbed for the next three decades. In February 1831 a petition was presented to Parliament calling for the abolition of slavery. Its signatories included, among others, "inhabitants of Cropper Street, Manchester". By 1841 it was the home of Chartists. One of them, Daniel Donovan, lived at number 69. He was an Irish weaver, originally from Cork, and president of the Powerloom Weavers' Union that headed the Great Strike of 1842. His neighbour was Maurice Donovan, the Union's secretary. Daniel's political life would culminate in 1848 when he was tried for treason in Liverpool as one of the leaders of the Irish Confederates. Cropper Street was a radical locale, a neighbourhood of resistance in rapidly industrialising Manchester, close to the great steam-powered factories of Ancoats. It was cosmopolitan, with English, Irish and Scottish workers all crammed together. It was home to the working-class weavers, spinners and artisans who would power radical politics in these turbulent decades.

How did this built environment create such political

formations? How, indeed, was this built environment produced? Here, we will consider the formation of the "shock city", paying particular attention to the arrangement of productive forces which created both the world's first industrialised economy, and the world's first recognisably industrial city — laid out in a pattern of concentric rings, with an inner band of working-class districts surrounding the commercial core, and a belt of suburbs beyond. The formation of this built environment was the consequence of the power of rentiers to produce space in the industrial era. From the speculative landlords who built the slums to the investors who funded the first suburbs, land and capital came together in a particularly novel way in industrial Manchester. This story complements the more well-known one of the city's manufacturing revolutions. But first we must take a wide-angle view and ask why the city came to be where it did in the first place.

Rainy City

For generations of the city's writers and filmmakers, the rain bestowed upon Manchester a noirish quality, its gloom a reflection of the manifold crises shot through its social fabric. It was, however, this very rain that determined the location of early industrial production on the Lancashire plain. As historian of political ecology Howard Platt writes:

> more than any other single causal factor, ecological conditions shaped the location of textile production, both the long preceding period of hand methods, and the emerging era of inanimate power and factory mechanisation. As early as the thirteenth century, the area had attracted spinners and weavers from both home and

abroad because the site, topography and climate combined to provide them with rain, and plenty of it.[2]

Situated at the confluence of three rivers and contained on three sides by hills, the city lay at the heart of a natural amphitheatre. The rain clouds which rolled in regularly from the North Atlantic were forced to precipitate by the high peaks of the Pennines. The Pleistocene rivers, carved by retreating ice, distributed the runoff throughout the region. In the city, 125 feet above sea level, annual average rainfall stood at 35 inches. This number increased with elevation. On average, across the entire fluvial region, 50 inches fell every year. It was twice as wet as the London region and was matched in England only by the inaccessible and remote mountains of the Lakeland, one hundred miles to the north. Somewhere in Lancashire it rained every other day, with two thirds ending as runoff: 22,570 gallons of rain per acre for each inch of rain, 650bn gallons of water running down yearly throughout the entire 587,000 acre river system.[3] The area was wet, full of "mosses"; in Engels' words, an "obscure, ill-cultivated swamp".[4]

This rainfall had a deep impact on early patterns of settlement. The textile workers, taking full advantage of its tendency to increase with elevation, built their villages up into the valleys. The damp air increased the durability and plasticity of the fibres they were spinning and weaving, lowering the likelihood of breakages. Textile production in the pre-industrial period spread out deep into the hinterland. In the towns, a similar effect was sought by spinning in unflagged basements, with their damp, humid atmospheres — the origins of the region's notorious underground dwellings. For obvious reasons, hilltop spinning was preferred.

So, from early on, Manchester had established itself as an

important centre in a wider manufacturing region. In 1365 a high stone bridge was constructed across the Irwell. All traffic from the north was routed across it through the town. From at least the sixteenth century there were links with Ireland, a trade and migration axis that would become increasingly important.[5] By the seventeenth century Manchester had come to replace Chester as the apex of the hierarchy of towns in the region. This was the town that saw the first clashes of the Civil War. 150 years later it was recognised as a nationally significant centre of textile production. By 1750 pure cottons were being produced and the region's woollen production declined. In 1773, the town's population stood at 43,000, a twenty-fold increase over the preceding two centuries. It was the centre of one of England's most densely populated regions.[6]

The land was owned by aristocrats. Families such as the Egertons, the Traffords and the Moseleys (who were also Lords of the Manor) held wide tracts across the region. These old feudal networks oversaw an archaic system of governance, a "weak citadel" that meant that the region was comparatively ill-governed, an ideal place for a *laissez-faire* outsized factory town to emerge.[7] In time, the weakness of the old regime's institutions enabled the rising bourgeoisie to seize total control of the city. But this was to come. At the end of the eighteenth century the Moseleys and their class retained their sway. It would be in the following century that the old regime would topple as the city became the world-historic ground-zero of industrial capitalism.

Atlantic Capitalism
The received historical narrative of industrialising Britain, at least until very recently, has tended to depict an arc of development firmly bound within the internal dynamics

of the country alone. It's a story that has focussed on local innovations, national dynamics of urbanisation and national actors. But this reading is wrong. We cannot grasp the industrialisation of Manchester and Lancashire (and therefore Britain) without understanding its integration into a wider global history of imperialism, mercantilism and transatlantic slavery. Manchester's proximity to the slave port of Liverpool was crucial. The city's merchants were responsible for between 50-75% of all British slave ship sailings and were the central importer of slave-picked cotton well into the nineteenth century. It wasn't only rain that came in off the Atlantic, but wealth, plundered, coerced and extracted from across the colonised world.

The rise of cotton as the central commodity of industrialising Lancashire was a pillar of Britain's colonial empire. Sven Beckert, in his global history of cotton, forces us to recalibrate our understanding of cotton's rise, away from a story of "technical or organisational advance" towards the simpler truth of Britain's "ability and willingness to project capital and power across vast oceans".[8] The organisation of violence enabled Britain to reorganise global cotton production, ending India's historic hegemony and forcefully asserting the centrality of Lancashire. This was a double movement: the suppression of India's production of finished cottons by restrictive tariffs on import into Britain, a demand of Lancashire's cotton manufacturers from the late eighteenth century; and the development of a European-controlled source of raw cotton in the slave plantations of the Caribbean. By 1715 Caribbean cotton imports overtook the older sources, with 1.5 million pounds imported. This dominance would be maintained until the end of the century, when production in the American South took over as the principal source of raw cotton — a position held until the close of the nineteenth century.[9]

The industrialisation of Britain was predicated upon the plantation economy. In *Capitalism and Slavery*, Eric Williams draws attention to the importance of the triangular trade to "the entire productive system" of industrialising England. He placed particular emphasis upon the importance of profits from the Caribbean sugar plantations, particularly those in Jamaica, in funding the infrastructure and corporations of the metropolitan economy. The relationship between the plantation frontier in the Americas and industrial production in Europe was complex and mutually reinforcing.[10] Industrialising mass markets were not simply the outcome of expanding market exchanges, but of two regimes of exploitation — plantation slave labour and factory wage labour, developing in concert. The long duration plantation economies of sugar and cotton were interdependent with urbanisation and industrialisation. Cotton worked in factories in Lancashire was picked by slaves in the Caribbean and American South — "behind Manchester stood Mississippi".[11]

We should also consider the colonial roots of factory production itself. The first "factories" were in fact the plantations. This argument was first made by C.L.R. James in *The Black Jacobins*, where he describes the enslaved on the plantations as "closer to the modern proletariat than any group of workers in existence at the time".[12] Later, in *Sweetness and Power*, American anthropologist Sidney Mintz develops this, characterising the plantation as a "synthesis of field and factory" where the hallmarks of industrial production first emerged.[13] The processing of sugar cane, its milling, grinding and boiling, as well as its harvesting, required specialised labour, disciplined, synchronised and subjected to the rhythms of clock time. Calling attention to the separation of slaves from their tools, and production from consumption, Mintz completes our argument that the origins of industrialisation are indelibly tied to the ruptures of the plantation economy.

British rentierism also traces its origins to the colonial past. In their magisterial study, *British Imperialism*, the historians P.J. Cain and A.G. Hopkins show how, over five centuries, it was the landed and financial interests which drove Britain's colonial empire. They termed this "gentlemanly capitalism". Over a century ago, J.A. Hobson castigated the rentier class, holed up in the southern counties, whose incomes were "dissociated from any present exertion of their recipients" and whose character "has been formed in our despotic Empire, and whose incomes are chiefly derived from the maintenance and furtherance of this despotic rule".[14] The development of Britain as an industrial and financial centre was built upon the violent expropriation of assets — land, natural resources and human labour — from across the world. Its financial sector pioneered the transformation of these people and lands into financial assets, items of property that could be valued, borrowed against and monetised. This imperial nexus structured and continues to structure our cities.

Lancashire's Early Industrialisation

One place we can begin to unravel these threads is in Cheshire. In the early 1780s, Samuel Greg, a local businessman, set out from Manchester on his horse in search of water. He was looking for an ideal location for a factory, one that could take advantage of recent advances in water power. He found it on the steep banks of the River Bollin, 12 miles south of Manchester. Here he founded Quarry Bank Mill for the purpose of spinning cotton. He financed it with the profits from his family's sugar plantations in Dominica, the largest of which had well over 100 slaves. Here we find the condensed truth of Lancashire's industrialisation. And though most of the Gregs' contemporaries, including people like Richard Arkwright, had no direct ownership of Caribbean slave plantations, they nevertheless still required slave-picked cotton as the essential raw material for their factory processes. The industrial revolution, driven by one commodity above all else, would have been impossible without the underpinnings of slavery.[15]

Quarry Bank Mill was built to hold water frames, an efficient spinning machine and recent technological breakthrough. The water frame was one of a string of inventions that had begun to reduce the bottleneck in cotton cloth production — weavers wove faster than spinners spun. Whereas in the 1750s the production of one pound of cotton yarn required 500 hours of work, by the 1790s the same quantity of yarn could be produced in just one or two hours.[16] Great waterwheels drove the machines that spun the threads, while outworker handweavers turned them into cloth. The bottleneck had been released.

Water power created a centrifugal dynamic of settlement. As the waterwheel had to be near rivers, handloom weavers clustered around these factories which were strung along the rivers of the Mersey-Irwell basin. Early mechanised spinning took place in remote locations up green valleys, in what were sometimes referred to as "colonies". Samuel Greg had *to leave the town* in search of water. By 1787, the entire basin sustained 200 spinning factories. Léon Faucher, a French liberal and author of *Manchester in 1844: Its Present Condition and Future Prospects* who wrote on the industrialisation of Lancashire in the 1840s, describes the spatial patterning of water powered industrialisation:

> At the commencement of manufactures, when the spinning of cotton and of wool ceased to be a domestic occupation, the spinners, seeking prime movers, established themselves along the water courses; and, as hydraulic force results from the amount of the fall of water, they were compelled to observe a respectful distance from each other; each of them instead of attracting himself to a nucleus already formed, became a new centre, around which the operatives grouped themselves just as did the peasants in the older time, under the protection of the feudal castle.[17]

There was a proliferation of small factory outposts; spinners clustered around the water wheels, handloom weavers living nearby. They were semi-proletarianised, supplementing their income with agricultural work, granting them a degree of independence and power over their employers. But the natural locations of the watercourses didn't always correspond with sources of labour, so factory owners had to move their workers to the factories from Derby or Manchester, building housing and employing forced labour and apprentices. For the bosses, it was a considerable expense.

Steam power changed this. While initially water had the edge, the technical improvements of Watt's engine saw steam start to assert itself as the favoured prime mover in cotton production. But its principal advantage wasn't its motor power, but the effect it had on the balance of class power. By permitting production to be moved closer to centres of population, the disposability of the workforce increased, and the bosses gained the upper hand.[18] The *spatial* impacts of this switch would be revolutionary: populations, economic activity, commodity production all began to agglomerate in urban centres; a centrifugal dynamic of settlement became centripetal. Faucher commented:

> The invention of the steam engine has, for a time, reversed the natural course of things. The manufacturer, instead of going to the prime movers, have forced the prime movers to come to them; and as coal abounds in almost every part of England, they have fixed their location with a view only to take advantages of the opportunities presented by the large commercial towns, for the purchase of material and the sale of their product.[19]

Coal had been present in Manchester since the opening of mines in East Manchester in 1740. It was plentiful from 1761, when the Duke of Bridgewater opened his canal to bring coal on barges from his mines into the heart of the city and its fireplaces and bakeries. Watt would transform its purpose into the inanimate source of motor power for a million machines. Manchester thus assumed its classic form — the *ur*-city for productive industrial capitalism. Through its factories, capital assembled the requisite raw materials and labour for commodity production, the classic "primary circuit" of capital and the creation of surplus value.

Fossil Urbanisation

The first place to employ steam power in Manchester was Drinkwater's Mill in Piccadilly, which enlisted a Watt engine in 1789. Over the following decades steam power took off. The largest industrialists to use the technology were McConnell

27

and Kennedy, who built a seven-storey mill in Ancoats in 1797, and A&G Murray, who opened an eight-storey factory on the Rochdale Canal one year later. By 1802, 111 factories powered by steam had opened in the city.[20] Productivity soared, the number of spindles increasing sixfold. By 1814 McConnell and Kennedy and the Murrays owned the two largest spinning factories in the city, with 170,000 spindles between them. In *Capital*, Marx describes these "organised systems of machines" in vivid terms:

> Here we have, in the place of the isolated machine, a mechanical monster whose body fills whole factories, and whose demonic power, at first hidden by the slow and measured motions of his gigantic members, finally bursts forth in the fast and feverish whirl of his countless working organs.[21]

As steam took command, Manchester's population exploded. In 1773 the city's population was just 22,500. By the 1840s the population of Manchester and Salford combined had hit 400,000, second only to London. Manchester's productive forces were a whirlpool, drawing in new populations from the surrounding countryside. Very few went specifically to work in the cotton mills, most were just looking for any job. But they found themselves amid the heaving pools of labour that factory production had conjured up. Of greatest importance, as a reservoir of reserve labour was Ireland. Irish labourers were pushed to Manchester in great numbers, by famine, state coercion, an iniquitous land system and the decline of handicraft employment, all deliberate outcomes of England's colonial rule. One Newton Heath silk manufacturer, James Taylor, described the process of searching for labourers in the colony:

The moment I have a turn-out and am fast for hands, I send to Ireland for ten, fifteen or twenty families, as the case may be. I usually send to Connaught, and I get the children, chiefly girls, of farmers and cottiers. The whole family comes — father, mother and children. I provide them with no money.[22]

From its early days Manchester was an immigrant city. The Irish were its original immigrant community, but they were soon joined by others. Poor Europeans, from Germany and Italy, came in the middle of the century. Later, many Eastern European Jews, fleeing pogroms in the Russian Empire, would settle in the city, forming tight communities around Cheetham Hill. The impact of these cycles of immigration in the city's culture, politics and social movements, and the composition of its working class, would be immense. The city's working class was cosmopolitan.

As the city grew as a mercantile centre, it also began to attract a class of wealthy foreign merchants, such as the Germans, who came to Manchester to take up roles in the textile trade and later the sciences and arts. Over time they were to have a huge influence on the city, establishing cultural institutions like the Hallé orchestra and developing key residential districts like Whalley Range and shaping its bourgeois civic life. Both Ernest Simon, the force behind Wythenshawe, and Tony Wilson could trace German ancestry.

The region became the most densely populated place in the world. This rapid concentration of productive forces and spatial crystallisation of wage labour broke the traditional urban form that had endured since the Middle Ages. The insertion of steam-powered commodity production into cityspace formed an entirely new type of city: the world-historic ground zero of industrial urbanism.

Have You Seen Manchester?

"The Age of Ruins is past", proclaims Sidonia to Coningsby in Disraeli's 1844 novel *Coningsby, or the New Generation*. "Have you seen Manchester?" The city — the "shock city", in Asa Briggs' phrase — attracted waves of observers across the first half of the nineteenth century. They came to gawp, unable to look away from the horrors and splendours of the industrial city in the throes of its violent birth.

An eyewitness from Rotherham in 1808 was shocked by the environmental degradation: "the town is abominably filthy, the steam engine pestiferous, and the water of the river as black as the stygian lake".[23] Thomas Carlyle, visiting the city in the autumn 1838, was overwhelmed:

> At five in the morning all was still as sleep and darkness. At half-past five all went off like an enormous mill-race or ocean-tide. The Boom-m-m, far and wide. It was the mills that were all starting then, and greasy drudges by the million taking post there. I have heard few sounds more impressive.[24]

Dickens too was a regular visitor, and aspects of the city are represented in the fictional "Coketown" of *Hard Times*. Elizabeth Gaskell's novels *Mary Barton* and *North and South*, both based in Manchester, became sensational bestsellers. Astute reviewers quickly grasped their significance. "When people on Turkey carpets with their three meat meals a day are wondering why working men are turning Chartist and Communist", wrote one reviewer in the staunchly Tory *Fraser's Magazine*, "let them read *Mary Barton*!" Londoners were eager for any information about the shock city. Angus Reach, a journalist for the *Morning Chronicle*, wrote a series of dispatches from the manufacturing districts in 1849. They are among the most detailed eyewitness reports of the time, described later by E.P. Thompson as "the most impressive survey of labour and poverty at mid-century which exists".[25]

Alexis de Tocqueville visited in 1835 and was shocked by the wealth drawn from so much human misery:

From this foul drain the greatest stream of human industry flows out to fertilise the whole world. From this filthy sewer pure gold flows. Here humanity attains its most complete development and its most brutish, here civilisation works its miracles, and civilised man is turned back almost into a savage.[26]

Another French liberal, Léon Faucher, in his valuable study *Manchester in 1844: Its Present Condition and Future Prospects*, surveyed the "curious topography" of industrial Lancashire, characterising Manchester as a "diligent spider" squatting at the centre of a web, sending forth railways, roads and canals towards its auxiliaries:

An order is sent from Liverpool in the morning, is discussed by the merchants in the Manchester exchange at noon, and in the evening is distributed among the manufacturers in the environs. In less than eight days, cotton spun at Manchester, Bolton, Oldham or Ashton is woven in the sheds of Bolton, Stalybridge or Stockport, dyed and printed at Blackburn, Chorley or Preston and finished, measured and packed at Manchester. By this division of labour amongst the towns and amongst the operatives in the manufacturers, the water, coal and machines work incessantly. Execution is almost as quick as thought. Man acquires, so to speak, the power of creation, and he only has to say, "let the fabrics exist" and they exist.[27]

Germans also hoped to learn from the city how they might progress their own country's development. Karl Friedrich Schinkel, the Prussian architect, stayed one night in the town in July 1826 and sketched the Ancoats factories of McConnell and Kennedy, awestruck at their size and might. Reflecting later in a letter to a friend, he wrote:

One sees buildings standing where three years ago there were still fields, but these buildings appear as blackened with smoke as if they had been in use for a hundred years. It makes a dreadful and dismal impression: monstrous shapeless buildings, put up only by foremen without architecture, only least that was necessary and out of red brick.[28]

Perhaps the most famous and influential of all these observers was a young countryman of Schinkel's, Friedrich Engels. He had been sent, aged just 22, by his father who owned a mill in Weaste, Salford, hoping, perhaps, that the business would knock some sense into his son. Instead, young Engels absconded, partnering with Mary Burns, a working-class Irish woman who guided him through the living districts of the immigrant proletariat. From these experiences, along with his study of works by Elizabeth Gaskell and the physician J.P. Kay, Engels gathered the materials for his first book, *The Condition of the Working Class in England*. In the dedicatory message, "to the Working Classes of Great Britain", he wrote:

I have lived long enough amongst you to know something about your circumstances… I have studied the various official and non-official documents as far as I was able to get hold of them — I have not been satisfied with this, I wanted more than mere abstract knowledge of my subject, I wanted to see you in your own homes, to observe you in your everyday life, to chat with you on your conditions and grievances, to witness your struggles against the social and political power of your oppressors.[29]

On his perambulations through the city, he discovered a set of truths. He saw the patterning of its spatial order. This he termed the "hypocritical plan", the extreme class segregation in the city. The avenues and villas of the bourgeoisie (people whose "fashionable talk and tiresome etiquette" he had spurned) were another world to the districts of the working class. "I have never seen so systematic a shutting out of the working class from the thoroughfares, so tender a concealment of everything which might affront the eye and the nerves of the bourgeoisie."[30] Page after page he unveiled more of the degraded conditions in which the working class lived, in filthy courts and ruined basements. He insisted on a structural, systemic understanding of these conditions — their origins "not in minor grievances, *but in the capitalistic system itself*".[31] These conditions, condemning thousands to death by disease, poverty and overwork, he castigated as "social murder". But he also saw in the city the potential for the system's abolition. The book brims over with exuberance and confidence in the coming social revolution. A few years later in the preface to the first English edition, he would reflect that his prophecies had borne the stamp of "youthful ardour". But what Engels saw in Manchester many others would see across the world in the coming decades.

Engels was the first to weave together an analysis of capital accumulation, class struggle and urban development, in a nascent Marxist urbanism.[32] Our understanding of the dynamics of the city owe him a huge debt. He added to *The Condition of the Working Class in England* in 1872, penning a pamphlet entitled *The Housing Question*, in which he dwelt upon capitalism's "secondary evil". Here he explained how the increasing value of land caused by mass urbanisation and the Industrial Revolution resulted in the inflation of the cost of housing for the worker. This forced repeated demolitions of working-class housing and the expulsion of working-class tenants from the valuable land of the central core to the outskirts. Engels named this bourgeois solution of demolition and expulsion to the perils of urban poverty and disease "Haussmann" (after the architect of bourgeois urban renewal in Paris, Georges-Eugène Haussmann). It was a prescient analysis with major relevance to the processes of gentrification in our own times. The enduring contribution of *The Housing Question* is that it shows us how capitalist urbanisation produces repeated crises of housing. This "secondary evil" would only be finally abolished with system's abolition as a whole.

The Commercial Core and the Classic Slum

At the city's core was its commercial district. Up until the 1830s it was also home to the grand houses of the bourgeoisie, following established space use laid down in older cities such as London. The first burst of Manchester's industrialisation followed this traditional pattern, with worker districts and factory zones jammed together on the peripheries of the town.

Until the 1830s the core was surrounded by a pestiferous

ring of worker barracks and factory zones. The archetypal example of this new proletarian slum was Ancoats. The cutting of the Rochdale Canal in the 1790s transformed it from rural to urban. Street patterns were laid out, awaiting the construction of terraced housing. Speculative private builders threw up jerry-built housing for the new workers, 800 of them between 1790 and 1830, housing between 5,000 and 7,000 people. Engels describes houses with walls a half brick thin, the builders doing so partly to save on costs, but also because the land upon which they were built was only leased from the original owner for a period of no more than 99 years. The landlords also spent as little as possible on repairs, "partly to avoid diminishing their rent receipts, and partly in view of the approaching surrender of the improvement to the landowner".[33] Rentierism, the speculation on housing and land, necessitated poorly-built homes for the working class, designed to last no more than 40 years.

These were some of the worst conditions of urban life hitherto experienced. There was no planning or control over the standard of the housing; the speculative builders were free to put up any sort of house they liked. They could, and did, crowd as many houses into an acre as the space could be made to hold. They built houses back-to-back, "blind", with no doors or windows at the rear. They were under no necessity to provide yards or airspace round the houses, or to put in a dampproof course. Stone floors were frequently laid directly onto the bare earth. Windows could be the smallest size possible, often not made to open at all. Sanitary accommodation would consist of one privy-midden, at a considerable distance away and serving several houses; water supply was a pump in the street or a single tap for several homes.[34]

The life expectancy statistics from this time tell their own story — the average age of death for a labourer, mechanic or family member in Manchester in 1842 was only 17.[35] Disease was rife, the cramped conditions and poor sanitation the ideal circulation for typhus, tuberculosis and influenza. These conditions were meticulously measured by J.P. Kay, a liberal, nonconformist doctor, in his 1832 pamphlet, *The Physical and Moral Conditions of the Working Classes Employed in the Cotton Manufacture in Manchester*. Kay, a doctor working at the newly-opened Ancoats Dispensary, was an outstanding example of the liberal impulse to measure, document and record would be institutionalised by organisations such as the Manchester Statistical Society, founded in 1833. Kay's work preceded Edwin Chadwick's more famous investigations into London by some ten years.

Of the major diseases that affected Mancunians in the nineteenth century, the most prominent was pulmonary tuberculosis, accounting for 10% of all deaths.[36] Cholera too was extensive, with outbreaks occurring in 1832, 1849, 1854 and 1866. Contaminated water was the source, with little or no separation between water for drinking and water for waste, particularly for the working classes. Angus Reach, a journalist who reported on the living and working conditions of the working classes, described the situation:

Manchester... is scantily supplied with water, and that which is to be procured is not by any means universally transparent or tasteless. The streams which traverse the town are incarnations of watery filth. A more forbidding looking flood than the Medlock, as it may be seen where it flows beneath the Oxford Road, would be difficult to conceive. The black foetid water often glistens with oily impurities which float upon its surface, and the wreaths and patches of green froth which tessellate it prove the effervescence produced by impute gases. For any household purposes whatsoever the water of this uncovered sewer is quite out of the question… Manchester therefore obtains its water partially by means of pipes, partially by means of wells and pumps.[37]

Kay's writings were hugely influential and had the effect of establishing the notorious reputation of "Little Ireland", a small district at a bend in the Medlock, jammed between canals and factories, where a majority of Irish immigrants lived. Its sunken position made it prone to flooding, and its dense housing was among many of the shocks that visitors noted. The problem was that this image wasn't strictly true. The conditions were bad, but not notably worse than those in other working-class areas of the city — for example, there were only a few cases of cholera recorded in the district in 1832 and 1849, despite an epidemic in the city.[38] But Kay's writings and their subsequent recycling (his pamphlet sold multiple editions) were able to establish in the liberal imagination the idea that Irish immigrants lived in the worst districts in a squalor that was the product of their own fecklessness and improvidence, that their presence lowered the wages of the native working class and that their drunkenness was a threat to the whole body politic. This image was used as an instrument of social control, a warning to the working class who did not exercise restraint, economy and self-improvement.[39] Even Engels, who at points praised the positive, galvanising Irish influence on the politics of the English working class, wasn't immune from this anti-Irish prejudice, repeating from Kay's works his descriptions of Little Ireland ("a most horrible spot") and peppering his writings with essentializing caricatures.[40]

Popular Culture in the Industrial City

Among this turmoil and degradation was an astonishing resilience and a thriving popular culture. Reach captures this, characterising Manchester as "a decidedly musical place", describing in vivid detail times spent wandering between its famous "music saloons", places for "lovers of harmony and beer". One such saloon is described as being tightly packed with artisans and millhands, with a proscenium at one end on which performers sing the songs of the day and below which a small orchestra of "fiddles and a pianoforte" are assembled. Another is dimly lit by "faintly burning candles, enclosed in greasy paper lanterns" which cast their "tallowy influence over tables slimy with cheap fish". Barrel organs play, "itinerant bands blow and bang their loudest", crooners sing out over pianos and seraphines. Somewhere else a "lout of a boy in shoes, with wooden soles an inch thick" dances a Lancashire clog hornpipe — a dance innovated by weavers and spinners, tapping their feet in time to the rhythm of the machines. On the corner of Oldham Road, one pub had the proprietor proudly show the organ and the removable hole in the floor that allowed performers to be seen from two levels. Even on Sundays it didn't stop, Oldham Road "rung with shouting, screaming and sweating, mingled with the jarring music of half-a-dozen bands".[41]

The pub lay at the heart of popular resistance throughout the whole period. It was the bedrock of working-class associational life, their public sphere, a wellspring of self-help and auto-didacticism.[42] Samuel Bamford, the great Middleton radical, refers to a "Jacobin library" held in the backroom of a pub just outside Oldham. There would have been many more such spaces. Cultures of resistance were shrouded by ritual and secrecy; informed by a keen sense of moral justice — the workshop acting in concert with the pub, creating a mutually reinforcing underground world of working-class solidarity.[43]

Life was bound by the rhythms of production and the fluctuations of trade. Workers were fully proletarianised, and frequent economic slumps — in 1819, 1826, 1837 and 1842 — threw thousands into unemployment. Technical advances in the textile industry, particularly the introduction of powerlooms, would have devastating effects on handweavers. Between 1835 and 1860 their number fell from 250,000 to 10,000 across the region.[44] In *Mary Barton*, Elizabeth Gaskell vividly describes the effects of unemployment on the working class, "the homes of those to whom leisure was a curse", contrasting it starkly with the opportunities trade slumps provided the bourgeoisie for time with family or hobbies. For the unemployed worker and their family,

the family music was hungry wails, when week after week passed by, and there was no work to be had, and consequently no wages to pay for the bread the children cried aloud for in their young impotence of suffering. There was no breakfast to lounge over; their lounge was taken in bed, to try and keep warmth in them that bitter March weather, and, by being quiet, to deaden the gnawing wolf within. Many a penny that would have gone little way enough in oatmeal or potatoes bought opium to still the hungry little ones and made them forget their uneasiness in heavy troubled sleep. It was mothers' mercy.[45]

Beyond these slums, at least until the 1830s, were open fields. A worker in the late 1820s noted how it was still possible to walk a circuit of the city in open countryside, no more than two miles in diameter from the Exchange. These fields, and moors beyond, were important meeting places for radical currents in the city up to 1830, close to the city but outside its administrative limits and beyond the reach of its authorities. However, the decade to come would lead to the most radical upending of this spatial logic, creating the class-segregated city that Engels would visit a mere 14 years later.

So Many Edens

Across the first three decades of the nineteenth century, the contradictions of Manchester's industrial urbanism grew. Steam-powered agglomeration simultaneously created the conditions required for exponential growth, while making the city unliveable for the bourgeoisie, who feared disease, noise, pollution and social unrest. This led to a startling resolution — the invention of the modern suburb. In *Bourgeois Utopias*, Robert Fishman makes a compelling case for nineteenth-century Manchester "establishing the pattern" for suburbanisation that in the following century would become standard in Anglo-American cities. In this process, the decade between 1835-45 was crucial, during which Manchester "achieved a higher degree of suburbanisation than London did between 1770-1870".[46]

The first suburb, setting the pattern for the rest, was built as a speculative enterprise by a merchant and factory owner, Samuel Brooks. In 1834, sick of the conditions in the centre and with an eye on profits, he purchased a large tract of farmland from the Egertons a few miles south of the city core. He called it Whalley Range, built himself a villa on it and subdivided the remaining land into parcels for sale, so other merchants could do the same. Once he moved, his Moseley Street townhouse became a warehouse.

Suburbanisation took advantage of rising land values in the city centre as owners sold up and invested in cheaper farmland at the peripheries. They took advantage of what land reformer Henry George called the "unearned increment" of rising land values. After purchasing the land, the developer would invest in laying out a street and sewer pattern, then sell individual plots to different builders, ideally a wealthy cash buyer who could finance the building of a house. But as the supply of these wealthy individuals was limited, speculative builders would take the land, deferring payment to the developer until the house upon it was sold. They borrowed heavily, 15-20 times their capital, to build the houses. A common source of funding was the private wealth of solicitors, lending out capital at 5% interest.

The aim was to build a few homes rapidly, sell them profitably enough to pay off the mortgage, and begin the process again. Often, though, builders went bankrupt, at which point the incomplete home would return to the lender, who would find another builder to finish the job. This could happen up to three times, with the house being built in a new style each time. This pattern of piecemeal development, and the tapping up of various sources of capital, meant that the building of the suburbs was irregular and patchwork; an anarchic mixture of crescents, circles and grid plans; an "archaeology of speculation" that amounted to an overarching "suburban style".[47]

The second, even grander, suburban development in Manchester was Victoria Park. In 1837 a group of local businessmen set up the Victoria Park Company, buying 140 acres to the south of the city. Here we encounter Richard Cobden, factory owner, calico printer and liberal agitator, the dynamic force behind Manchester Liberalism and perhaps one of the most gifted political campaigners of his age. He took on the role of secretary of the Victoria Park Company. Cobden converted his city centre townhouse into a warehouse, reinvesting his recently maturing factory investments into the suburban building spree.

For owners of capital, suburbanisation was a countercyclical investment. As profitability in the cotton industry waned at the onset of the economic slump of the "hungry Forties", factory owners like Cobden moved from the production of commodities to the production of space.[48] Later analysis of the urban process under capitalism would describe this as "capital switching", its true significance not becoming apparent until our own times. In the 1830s, Cobden and his fellow Anti-Corn Law League peers were deeply involved in the Victoria Park Company and can be counted among the city's first property speculators.

The bourgeoisie's move out of the centre had several consequences. The core became uninhabited, instead given over almost entirely to commercial use. Consequently, the dense proletarian belt that had hitherto marked the edge of the city was enclosed by suburbia, confining the working class to their districts. Between the inner city and the countryside lay the privatised, luxified space of the suburbs; villas enclosed by high walls, access to the the tree-lined avenues in which they stood forbidden except for residents and their guests. One group of workers, attempting to keep open an old right of way that once ran through fields and now crossed the grounds of a factory owner's villa, found themselves blocked, the new landowner having erected iron gates and ditches to keep them out.[49]

One contemporary guidebook described the new suburbs as "so many Edens", yet this utopian luxury was predicated on the poverty and slums of Ancoats and the rest. Victoria Park found its mirror in Little Ireland. This was the city Engels encountered, with its sharp class divides and its "hypocritical plan",

> built so that a person might live in it for years and go in and out daily without ever encountering working people's quarters, or even with workers; that is, so long as he confines himself to business or pleasure walks. This arises chiefly from the fact that by unconscious tacit agreement, as well as by outspoken conscious delimitation, the working people's quarters are sharply separated from the sections of the city reserved for the middle classes.[50]

Class Struggle

Across these decades, an unbroken working-class tradition of resistance emerged in the shadow of the cotton factories. In the face of repressive state legislation — from Pitt's Combination Act of 1799 that outlawed trade unionism and free association, to outright political violence, workers organised and fought for suffrage, dignity at work and political reform. The spirit of Jacobinism animated these years and the propertied classes fought back. Included among their number were the city's publicans, 186 of which signed a declaration in 1792 refusing the use of their rooms "to any clubs or societies that have a tendency to put in force what those infernals so ardently and devoutly wish for, namely, the destruction of this country". Gilt signs hung above pub doors: "No Jacobins Admitted Here!"[51]

Manchester was a notable stronghold for these movements. Mass rallies, open-air meetings and organised political clubs formed the dense bedrock of working-class agitation. The "Blanketeers", as we already have seen, originated in the city. The massacre at St Peter's Field, forever remembered as Peterloo, entered its folklore, an extraordinarily brutal episode of class struggle played out in the streets. The panic of the yeomanry — "the Manchester manufacturers, merchants, publicans and shopkeepers on horseback" — was not, E.P. Thompson wrote, "the panic of bad horsemen hemmed in by a crowd. It was the panic of class hatred."[52]

Undeniably, the Irish presence had a powerful impact on the growing movements for working-class emancipation — widening and strengthening their base.[53] On the day of Peterloo, a large contingent of demonstrators from the town of Middleton travelled down the Rochdale Road on their way to St Peter's Field. Samuel Bamford describes the scene as they passed through Angel Meadows, then an Irish district:

> We were welcomed with open arms by the poor Irish weavers who came out in their best drapery, and uttered blessings and words of endearment, many of whom were not understood by our rural patriots... we thanked them with the band striking up "Saint Patrick's Day in the Morning"; they were electrified; and we passed on, leaving these warm hearted suburbans capering and whooping like mad.[54]

These interlinkings and networks of mutual political reinforcement would continue for decades, up to the Chartist moment in the 1840s. The integration of English and Irish working-class movements was of particular worry to the establishment throughout the first half of the nineteenth century.

The disappointment in the years that followed the 1832 Reform Act saw several interlinked concerns raised: expanding labour rights; enacting factory reforms, in particular the ten-hour day; expanding suffrage; the repeal of the hated Poor Law; and the fight against the Irish Coercion Act of 1830. These struggles came together in the general political movement of Chartism, with its organised literary political machinery. Spurred on by a series of devastating economic downturns in the 1830s and early 1840s, we can date Chartism to the formation of the *Northern Star*, the movement's mouthpiece, in November 1837 and publication of the Charter in May 1838. Its demands were political, including for universal (male) suffrage, secret ballots, annual elections and the abolition of the property qualification to stand for Parliament. Women's political agitation flourished within the movement, particularly during its later period (1842-8). This was taken up by a raft of pre-existing working-class organisations; their agitators already well-versed in their craft from earlier anti-Poor Law and other radical movements.

Yet it was not alone in offering a solution to the crisis. In September 1839 the Anti-Corn Law League was founded in Manchester under the leadership of Richard Cobden and John Bright, a Quaker cotton manufacturer from Rochdale. It sought the repeal of protectionist Corn Laws, allowing the free import of cereals. Its leaders, all industrialists, couched the campaign in terms of an assault on the entrenched privileges of Britain's ruling class. Its critics were less sure — cheaper corn meant cheaper wages and higher profits for the mill owners. Marx would call the League the "party of the self-conscious bourgeoisie". It was brilliantly organised, Cobden, who had already honed his campaigning skills in the fight for municipal incorporation (to which we will come later) was the supreme political agitator of his day. The League positioned itself as the inheritor of the fight for reform and built a temporary wooden meeting hall on the site of Peterloo to this effect, which would become known as the "Free Trade Hall". Its strength lay in the institutions of the city's bourgeoisie, their Lit & Phil society, the Manchester Statistical Society, Cross Street Chapel and the Atheneum. Its influence was such that an entire school of liberalism would be named after Manchester.

The League was hostile to the demands of the Chartists; the Chartists mistrusted the League. Dorothy Thompson tracked this friction, arguing that the Chartists' continual emphasis on the need for independent working-class organisation, and their hostility to all exploiting classes, provoked hostility above all in those middle-class radicals who saw themselves as the natural leaders of society.[55] While most Chartists accepted the idea of the removal of restrictions of trade and the removal of taxation on basic foodstuffs, they knew that the existing protections did not benefit the farm labourer — nor would their abolition benefit the urban worker. As far as they were concerned, the repeal of the Corn Laws would simply lead to a decrease in wages, as food became cheaper. The same employers who used the rhetoric of "freedom" to defend the abolition of the Corn Laws used that same rhetoric to attack trade unions and oppose factory reform. Trade was not an absolute end in itself, but an aspect of economic policy that for the Chartists must always be submitted to political control.

Competing loyalties even broke out on the streets on occasion, as with a series of clashes between the League and the Chartists in the early 1840s. One of these took place in Stevenson Square, where a large open-air anti-Corn Law rally was planned for 2nd June 1841.[56] On the platform was Cobden and the Mayor of Manchester, Sir Thomas Potter. For days beforehand, placards had been put up across the city urging Chartists to demonstrate against the event. Cobden had even taken the precaution of hiring "League Police" armed with blackthorn sticks in case of trouble. The day came and 20,000 people had assembled in the square. As the first League speaker took the platform, the Chartists rose banners and flags, obscuring the speakers. The League Police moved in, the Chartists produced staves and a violent clash ensued.

In 1842 under the aegis of the Operatives Anti-Corn Law Association, the League sponsored a joint conference in Manchester of delegates from trade unions, workshops and other working-class organisations. Here, the delegates turned their back on the League, as the resolution was passed that the Charter "alone" was worth fighting for. In the argument over free trade and the Corn Laws, the Chartists came closest to articulating an alternative doctrine to that of the liberal political economists. But this hostility between the Chartists and the League was not merely at the level of doctrine; it existed in the very real conflicting interests of the employers and the employees. It was the political expression of a class-based society.[57] The dance of these two movements across the middle decade of the century, in Manchester and the country at large, represents the two competing political traditions of the city that would play out again and again across its history — between working-class radicalism and liberalism.

After backing away from a general strike in the summer of 1839, the *denouement* of Chartism came in the hot summer of 1842. In the face of the pains of the "hungry Forties", depression and unemployment, industrial unrest proliferated. Organised labour set the agenda and the Chartists followed. In Lancashire, the strike was spearheaded by the powerloom weavers, who had been at the forefront of wage struggles over the previous decade. Thomas Carlyle, in his 1843 book *Past and Present*, called this upsurge the "Manchester insurrection", as the rolling strikes and stoppages crystallised as a demand for a general strike. In early August that year, a powerloom weaver, Richard Pilling, moved a resolution in Dukinfield, to the city's east, that "people should turn out and stop out till they get a fair day's wage for a fair day's work; and until the charter becomes the law of the land".[58] For a brief moment, the twin struggles of political reform and industrial justice intermingled and the call to "strike for the Charter" was heard.[59] A conference of delegates at the Carpenters Hall in Manchester in August made this the movement's official position.

Strikes started in the coalfields and moved into the production districts. Workers marched in procession, factory to factory, calling their hands out. They strategically took the plugs from the boilers that powered the machines, the movement earning its name "the Plug Plot" as a result. Sometimes pitched battles took place outside the mill walls, as at Kennedy's in Ancoats, where on the morning of the 10th August, 40 to 50 police surrounded the mill, holding back the strike. By the end of that day only the three mills guarded by police and military were at work in Manchester. One eyewitness, Thomas Cooper, observed the halted production from his train carriage window: "the city of Long Chimneys where every chimney beheld smokeless".[60] State repression would be harsh. On 13th August, four workers were shot and killed in Preston as the military fired upon the crowd; at least five more died in Halifax on the 16th.[61] Hunger and ongoing repression forced the defeat of the strike. By 26th September, all Manchester weavers were back at work. Bury hung on a little longer, but the strike had been defeated. Chartism limped on, enjoying a brief revival in the years around 1848, until it was finally scattered. Its members would continue to exert an influence upon working-class political life, through cooperativism, local government and women's organisation, but the great challenge of 1842 would not be seen again.[62]

Incorporation and Reform

From the beginnings of industrialisation through to the defeat of the great strike in 1842, the working masses struggled to force their way into political life. This played out in the simmering cauldron of Manchester, as the urban working class made themselves a presence in the political landscape of the city, triggering crises of legitimacy for the ruling elites. Happening concurrently with this fight for reform and the Charter was a struggle over the governance of the city itself.

For the opening decades of the nineteenth century, Manchester's administration was a complex patchwork of overlapping institutions and jurisdictions. Some were ancient, tied to the medieval structures of manor and church, power concentrated in a closed circle of high church Tories. Some were more recent, such as the semi-democratic Police and Improvements Commission, established by Act of Parliament in 1792 to provide more coherent government and, crucially, *policing*, to the growing city. The bourgeoisie's fear of the restive masses was the principal spur for innovations in local government. Strikes, demonstrations, uprisings and political mobilizations on the part of the working class created a counter movement among the manufacturers towards the reform of municipal government. The second impetus for reform were the consistent health crises in the city, particularly the cholera epidemic of 1832. They created a crisis of legitimacy for the ruling elites, their archaic structures unable to cope with the changes wrought by industrialisation and mass urbanism.

It was Cobden who, in the wake of the 1835 Municipal Reform Act, spearheaded the campaign for municipal incorporation, the creation of a single governing body (the "Corporation" or "Council") for the town, with elected councillors and aldermen. In a prefiguration of his role in the Anti-Corn Law League, he acted as principal organiser and agitator. His 1837 pamphlet, *Incorporate Your Borough!*, ridiculed the archaic practices of the Manorial court as a closed circle round the absentee lord of the manor, Sir Oswald Mosely. He argued instead for a new reformed administration.[63] The pamphlet sold 5,000 copies. Opposed to Cobden and the Liberal plutocrats of the Cross Street Chapel were both the traditional powerbase of the Tories and the radicals and labour leaders, who, as well as regarding the Liberals with contempt for their failure to deliver universal suffrage in 1832 and introducing the Poor Law in 1834, viewed the creation of a municipal corporation — with its own police force — as merely a new device to oppress the working class. On 9th February 1838, at a public meeting of 2,000 people, Edward Nightingale, a prominent radical, accused Cobden of trying to "cast the rising liberties of Manchester, to commit robbery by taxation and to coerce and keep down the people".[64]

The matter was settled by referendum later that year. Cobden presented 11,780 signatures, while the Tory/Radical opposition presented 32,000. Yet, after investigation into "fraudulent" petitioners, the administrator of the vote whittled the numbers down to 7,984 in favour and 8,694 against. Further whittling occurred with the expunging of the signatories from women and small ratepayers, and a small majority of 752 in favour of incorporation was presented. The ratepayer assessment of the two sides showed a clear majority of the propertied in favour of incorporation; with £188,076 the value of the petitioners for incorporation, compared to a value of £165,841 against. The Liberals had won, overturning Tory rule, outmanoeuvring the radicals and laying the ground for 50 years of unbroken hegemony. For the urban workers, positioned beyond the ramparts of the city's political system, their only resort was mass protest. Over 30,000 of them would gather on Kersal Moor later that year, the opening to the campaign that would culminate in the Great Strike four years later.

The formation of the municipal authority is not just concurrent with, but also intimately bound to the wider class struggle that was unfolding at the time. The middle decades saw two forces competing for political power: one radical, one liberal. By 1848 the contest was determined decisively in favour of the latter. The struggle that defined the middle decade of the century had been won, decisively, by the League.

Cobden marked this moment by overseeing the reconstruction of the Free Trade Hall in stone, built between 1853-6 as a monument to the central idea of the Manchester bourgeoisie. He claimed that its location would honour and uphold the memory of Peterloo, folding the radical tradition into his own. The municipal reforms that followed — in housing, such as the banning of cellar dwellings in 1853 and back-to-backs in 1867, the mandating of back yards and dampproof courses in 1865 and 1890 respectively and the laying out of water and gas, sanitation and bathhouses; and cultural advances such as the formation of the Hallé orchestra in 1858 — were all products of the long liberal hegemony, cast in the shadow of the defeat of working-class radicalism in the 1840s.

The Two Traditions

By 1864 Manchester's leaders had decided to build a new Town Hall. Outgrowing the King Street site, the Corporation wanted to build a signal of intent for the city, a "worthy monument of the industrial greatness of Manchester", in the words of its mayor, Abel Heywood. A competition was held to find the best design, and Alfred Waterhouse won. Across the 1860s and early 1870s, Waterhouse was the favoured architect for a series of major Manchester institutions, including the Assize Courts (opened 1864), the panopticon of Strangeways Prison (1868) and the new university (1873) — pillars of the bourgeois order, set in Gothic stone. These decades were a time of much improvement in the city centre, as the bourgeoisie built Italianate warehouses, fancying themselves as heirs to the mercantile leaders of Renaissance Italy.

Waterhouse's Town Hall was a brooding creation, brilliantly contorted into a triangle due to the restrictions of the plot. Much of the building was devoted to the administrative functions of managing the Corporation's hugely profitable gas and water utilities, its "municipal capitalism". Town clerks and registrars took another side. A suite of ceremonial and reception rooms filled the front; the council chamber was relegated to a small room on the first floor. The whole construction was a kind of "gothic machine", its staircases and columns reminiscent of the cogs and crankshafts of the factories.[65] It was perfect for the breed of "hard-nosed shopkeepers" who ruled the city.[66] It opened in 1877 with a great ceremony. Abel Heywood, once Chartist publisher and now reforming mayor, ascended to the platform; a long procession of workers grouped into their unions marched past. The glasscutters carried a huge glass sword. The bakers a loaf of bread weighing 164 pounds. The umbrella-makers a banner with their motto, "self-protection".[67] Inside the Town Hall, Ford Madox Brown had been commissioned to paint a set of (largely fictional) episodes in Manchester's history — with one notable omission, Peterloo.

At the heart of this liberal hegemony was a core of shopkeepers, merchants and manufacturers who came to be known as the "Manchester Men". As Asa Briggs explains:

Part of the excitement of Manchester was that behind its smoke and its squalor it seemed to be creating a "new order" of businessmen, energetic, tough, proud, contemptuous of the old aristocracy and yet in some ways constituting an aristocracy themselves — an urban aristocracy — men who were beginning to seek political as well as economic power, power not only in Manchester but in the country as a whole.[68]

The image they had of themselves foregrounded their self-made quality, their worthy striving. The archetype was fictionalised by novelist Isabel Banks in Jabez Clegg, the protagonist of her novel, *The Manchester Man*, an original "rags-to-riches" story set in nineteenth-century Manchester. Their philosophy of rugged and ruthless economic individualism soon inspired international admirers and imitators.

But there was, as our history so far has shown, another tradition in Manchester — a working-class tradition of dissent. And it is at this time of the great bourgeois beautification of the second half of the century that we see it erupt again. 1864 was the final year of the "cotton famine" — the crunch in raw cotton supply caused by the blockade of the US South in the American Civil War, which had caused great misery among the factory workers of Manchester and revealed to many the source of their essential raw material in chattel slavery. This inspired one of the greatest instances of transnational solidarity in the nineteenth century, as Lancashire workers organised for abolition, refusing to break the blockade on the South. This flew in the face of British establishment and liberal opinion, which tended to favour the Confederacy.[69] The *Manchester Guardian* supported the Confederacy, declaring in October 1862 that it had been "an evil day" when Lincoln had won the presidency. Two months later, a meeting of Manchester workers passed a motion (with cheers) condemning the paper for having "pro-slavery proclivities and desiring of the maintenance of the institution of slavery".[70]

These plebeian circuits of abolitionism had been in place for some time, however. Frederick Douglass had visited the city on a speaking tour in 1846 and 1853, the Manchester leg organised by an ex-Chartist.[71] In 1859, while on a speaking tour of Britain and Ireland, the American abolitionist Sarah Parker Remond said to her audience:

> When I walk through the streets of Manchester and meet load after load of cotton, I think of those eighty thousand cotton plantations on which was grown the one hundred and twenty-five millions of dollars' worth of cotton which supply your market, and I remember that not one cent of that money ever reached the hands of the labourers.[72]

Drawing their attention to the global networks of coercion, which Manchester and the wider region's economy was tied to, she unveiled the hypocrisies of Manchester Liberalism, its racialised workforces and global nexus of exploitation.

As we have seen, Manchester in the second half of the

nineteenth century was the original liberal city. Run by the bourgeoisie, its wealth rested upon global chains of exploitation and domination. Its working class faced two fronts of exploitation — in the primary sphere of the workplace and the secondary sphere of the home. Their housing, and the city's entire built environment was dictated by the needs of the rentier, fused with the demands of the wider economy. From the end of the nineteenth century onward, the long fight against these rentiers would culminate in the struggle for public housing, one of the great symbols of urban modernity.

Chapter 2
Modernity and Apocalypse

These crowded cities have done their work; they were the best which society largely built on selfishness and rapacity could construct, but they are in the nature of things entirely unadapted for a society in which the social side of our nature is demanding a larger share of recognition.

Ebenezer Howard, *The Garden Cities of To-morrow*

We were operating in the midst of a radicalism unmatched in Europe, but it was a gay period, a period of purposefulness. You had the feeling that the truth was being told once and for all. Britain was really in a ferment — seething, in fact, like an African pot. And people wanted to know if the things which we spoke about were really true. So, the opportunity which that historic period provided us was rather valuable in the cause to which we were committed.

T. Ras Makonnen, *Pan-Africanism from Within*

This fella on the next bench said to me he'd taken out a 25 year mortgage. I laughed at him and said, "What a waste of time, there'll be a revolution before then!"

Eric Jessop, shop steward and Communist Party member,
Fairey Aviation, Stockport

At the height of the Depression, Harry Hardcastle, the central character in Walter Greenwood's novel *Love on the Dole*, is out of work, recently laid off once his "apprenticeship" (a ploy to keep wages down) at Marlowe's, an engineering firm, is over. Too poor to buy two seats at the cinema, he's in a deep despair. So, he heads to Trafford Park, an industrial estate, in search of a new job. For Greenwood, the estate exemplified the revolutionary powers of the bourgeoisie better than almost anything else:

Trafford Park is a modern miracle. Thirty years ago, it was the country seat of a family whose line goes back to the ancient British kings, and whose name the area retains. Thirty years ago, its woodlands were chopped down to clear the way for commerce, and to provide soles for Lancashire clogs; thirty years ago, the park-roving deer were rounded up and removed; thirty years ago the lawns, lately gay with marquees, awnings and fashionably dressed ladies and gentlemen, were obliterated. The Hall still stands. Though it now houses only dust and memories and echoes. And the twin lions surmounting either side the wide flight of steps now survey, instead of lawns alive with guests, a double railways track only six yards away, and, where the curves once wound their serpentine paths through the woods, the fungus of modern industry, huge engineering shops, flour mills, timber yards, oil refineries, automobile works, repositories for bonded merchandise, choke and foul the prospect. The river that flows at the foot of the adjourning paddocks is changed also: it now gives hospitality to ocean going shipping from the seven seas, shipping whose siren echo mournfully in the night: a river no longer in name even, but the Manchester Ship Canal. A five year plan, thirty years ahead of the Russian. Yesterday the country seat of an aristocrat, today the rowdy seat of commerce. Revolution! And not a drop of blood split or shot fired.[1]

What was it about Trafford Park that so thrilled Greenwood? Plainly, it was its modernity. It represented the triumph of modern industrial power, a pinnacle of technological sophistication and skill. But more than this, was its *revolutionary* aspect — in this case, the revolution of the bourgeoisie against the ancient rule of aristocrats. The culling of the deer, the obliteration of the garden parties, the Hall swept up with decay, all represented progress. Its construction alongside the artifice of the Ship Canal and inland port was a central symbol of Manchester's modernity.

The other pillar of modernity in Manchester was its public housing programme. Built as the result of a long war against the speculative landlord, council housing came to replace the slums as the key way the city's working class were housed. The practical result of this reform we might understand as the *euthanasia of the rentier* — their squeezing out by rent controls, public housing and direct demolition, the frenzy of private speculation tamed by rational public planning.

In his great work *All That is Solid Melts into Air,* Marshall Berman identifies the dialectical movement of modernity. Using Saint Petersburg as his archetype, he traces the movements of modernisation "from above" and "from below" — the forced construction of the city and the modern cultural political movements which emerged from it. The revolutionary productive forces unleashed by capitalism transform our landscapes, our cities, our work. The old ways are torn asunder. In response we are forced to live *as moderns* and a new way of living is born.[2]

Let's take Berman's concept and use it as a lens through which to look at Manchester and its two great modernisation programmes: its port and its public housing. This modernisation *from above* found its apotheosis in the 1945 Manchester Plan. The modernisation *from below* can be found in the modernity of Manchester's people — their political movements, culture and radicalism.

The Port of Manchester

Opened in 1893, the Ship Canal transformed Manchester into an inland port, consistently in the top four for import and export trade between 1904-1964. *Punch* dubbed the city *Manchester sur Mer*. Originating in the depression of the 1870s, the Ship Canal was an audacious attempt by the city's bourgeoisie to regain momentum in the face of competition from newer industrialising powers. In 1882, 70 members of this class gathered at the suburban Didsbury home of boiler manufacturer Daniel Adamson to plot the development of the Canal and how they would wrest the land required out of the hands of the ageing aristocrat Sir Humphrey de Trafford. Through a public shareholding model, they also attempted to build a form of popular capitalism, to yoke sections of the labour aristocracy into their scheme.[3] Their rhetoric echoed that of the Anti-Corn Law League of the previous generation. An intense lobbying campaign to obtain approval from Parliament followed and in 1885 the Ship Canal Bill was passed.[4]

Groundbreaking took place two years later "on a cheerless November day", according to one journalist. "There was no ceremonial, no spectators and no speeches. Even the spade which was used was an ordinary spade, which had seen some service and was to see more".[5] Dug to the same depth as the

Suez Canal and influenced by the same ideals of imperialism, an army of continually reinforced Irish navvies moved some 60 million cubic metres of earth and cut a channel to the sea. Then they built the colossal locks which made it possible to lift ocean-going steamers six metres up, out of the Mersey and into the Canal. Many died in the process from landslides, accidents or brute exhaustion.

As costs mounted, the Canal's original investors realised they would be unable to finance its completion. So the Corporation of Manchester stepped in, providing £5m, 32.5% of the total cost of the project, in exchange for the right to appoint a majority on the Canal's board. This was the latest in a line of experiments in "municipal capitalism", an early form of the entrepreneurial local state.

Since Manchester lacked the required land, the deep water terminal docks were built in Salford, whose population grew markedly as a result. In the 1890s it was growing at almost double the rate of Manchester's, peaking at 234,000 in 1921.[6] This created further pressure on a city already suffering as one of the unhealthiest places in Britain. Driven by the new wave of industrialisation and its incorporation of its surrounding townships, the population soared in Manchester too during this period, from 341,000 in 1881 to 730,00 in 1921, with the most rapid decade of growth between 1901 and 1911.

Working conditions in the port were harsh, with gruelling physical labour, long shifts and unscrupulous bosses. The work was precarious, allocated on a whim by foremen. Dockers would assemble at what was known as the "Old Control" and fight (sometimes physically) to get picked, hoping to meet eyes with a foreman they knew. They would largely work in gangs, normally composed of families and extended families who all worked at the docks together. From these conditions an incredible sense of camaraderie and community emerged amongst dockworkers, which translated into industrial organising. Strikes, official or unofficial, were commonplace throughout the docks' history.

The port also led to the first settled groups of Black people in Manchester, as African sailors settled in small numbers in the early twentieth century. Greengate, a district of Salford, had 60 Black people living in it by 1919. While some remained in the merchant navy, others moved into local chemical and munitions factories. In the aftermath of the war, racism and the competition for jobs and housing saw anti-Black riots take place in the port of Salford, as part of a wider wave of disturbances that swept Britain's port cities.[7] The neighbourhood would remain a centre for the Black community until slum clearance in the 1930s saw a migration to other parts of Manchester, notably Moss Side.

This period also marks the beginning of sustained attempts by the ruling class to racialise housing, particularly sparked by the growth of Jewish immigration from Eastern Europe. Housing was used as a pretext for the first immigration controls, and the "aliens crisis" a deliberate distraction from the root cause of poor housing, which was the speculative landlord.[8] A 1902 debate in Parliament argued over the negative impact of immigration on housing, with an amendment proposed by Major Evans-Gordon, MP for Stepney, that recognised "the urgent necessity of introducing legislation to regulate and restrict the immigration of destitute aliens into London and other cities in the United Kingdom". In seconding the motion, Forde Ridley, MP for Bethnal Green, said:

The British workman is thus squeezed out of his home and what happens? The house is immediately taken by five, six, eight, or ten of these aliens, who herd together under conditions which are at once degrading and insanitary. I know it has been said by some people that this is a racial question... this is not a question of Jew or Gentile. We are speaking of foreign paupers and aliens as a whole.[9]

The integration of racism and the housing question led to the introduction of the Aliens Act in 1905, limiting immigration from countries outside the empire.

Fordist Modernity in Trafford Park

The Canal transformed the city's industrial base. Cotton was already in decline in Manchester, with new centres of production emerging in the towns across the region, as Bolton, Oldham, Burnley and Blackburn became almost entirely dependent upon cotton cloth production. Production peaked across the entire region in 1913, with a total production of 6.4 billion metres of cloth. After that the collapse was rapid — two thirds of it was gone in 25 years. But Manchester itself, no longer so reliant on this commodity, was insulated from cotton's collapse. By the early twentieth century the city had become a hub of engineering, logistics, distribution and metallurgy. This had been apparent across the last decades of the nineteenth century. The Beyer-Peacock locomotive works in Gorton, East Manchester, which employed over 1000 in 1875, was typical of this new economic base. But it was the Canal, the docks at Salford and the industrial park which followed which were to be the basis of Manchester's engineering powerhouse.

The roughly diamond-shaped Trafford Park lies directly to the south-west of Manchester's centre. It's enormous, as cursory glance at any map will show, larger than the city's centre itself at around five square miles. When built, it was the largest industrial estate in the world, and today remains the biggest in Europe. It was also a private enterprise. In June 1893 Ernest Terah Hooley, later convicted financial fraudster, bought the site from Sir Humphrey Francis de Trafford for £360,000, transferring it to the new Trafford Park Estates Ltd, of which he was chairman and significant shareholder. Its manager, T.H. Stevens, summed up the unique offer of the Park for relocating production: "Lancashire people are brought up to work on a machine".[10]

"Trafford Park for Greater Manchester" ran an 1894 headline in the *Manchester Guardian*, demonstrating the central role envisioned for the Park in reshaping the region's economic geography.[11] By the early twentieth century, Trafford Park was an established landing strip for American capital. Easy access to labour, the railway network and the nearby docks made it an attractive prospect. In 1899 the American engineering giant Westinghouse purchased 11% of the park's area, transforming it into the largest engineering works in Europe, modelled on their original factories in Pittsburgh. By 1903 the company employed 6,000 hands, over half of the total employment on the Park.

In 1911 Ford Motors arrived. Propelled by the popularity of the Model-T, it became Britain's largest car manufacturer within two years. In 1914 the company installed the quintessential Fordist technology — the "conveyor system". At its peak, in 1920, it churned out 46,000 cars in one year, or 125 per day. Visiting the factory to view the assembly line was a popular activity. During Manchester Civic Week in 1926 more than 7,000 people visited the plant to view the production of the Model-T.[12] In 1931 it would shift production to Dagenham, along with 1,000 of its employees on specially chartered trains, but would return to Trafford Park during World War II, employing 17,000 workers in 1944. Over 200 American companies had their base at Trafford Park by the mid-1930s.[13] It became Britain's most concentrated seat of capital-intensive industry.

In the assessment of one of Ford's employees, the plant was "worse than Alcatraz".[14] As well as importing American-style production lines, the company brought American technologies of labour discipline. Hire and fire, a focus on efficiency and union crackdowns were pioneered at Trafford Park, first at Ford and then Westinghouse. One former worker, John Reid, described his time in vivid terms:

> You could not speak, you could not turn around, you could not even go to the toilet. It was ridiculous. Every minute was accounted for. I have been in there at eight in the morning crying because I could not get my quota done. We were all fighting with one another to keep a job. One gaffer used to come around with snuff at three in the afternoon when you were on your last legs, and offer it to you, just to wake you up and keep you going... It was his method of getting the most out of his men.[15]

During the 1930s, these conditions were responded to by robust organising by the Communist Party, which by World War II had powerful factory branches operating in each of the plants.

The Park's industrial peak came with World War II. Westinghouse, spun off in 1919 and renamed as Metropolitan Vickers (MetroVicks — the real life version of Greenwood's Marlowe's), became the central arsenal of the war effort, while the docks' westward orientation meant it became Britain's second oil port. In 1945 employment peaked at over 75,000 workers, a quarter of that employed by MetroVicks.

Trafford Park was one of the principal seats of Fordist industrial modernity in Britain. The role of the Corporation of Manchester in the creation of this industrial behemoth, through the financing and ownership of the Ship Canal, was significant. We might see it as the pinnacle of the "municipal capitalism" that was pioneered by the gas, water and electric companies of the mid-nineteenth century. From the Port of Manchester, we can look back to the industrialists of the mid-nineteenth century who founded the Corporation and see something of their vision fulfilled. But it also presaged a different future for the Corporation, a state body that would in the twentieth century play a dominant role in the restructuring of the city. From the port we can also see that other milestone of modern Manchester — its public housing programme.

The Idea of Wythenshawe

Directly south of Manchester lay the aristocratic landholdings of the Tatton family, a branch of the Egertons, who we have already encountered. Their lineage could be traced back centuries, deep into the medieval past. Their lands were, in the decades around the turn of the century, a popular site for working-class day-trippers escaping the smokestacks of the city. To get there, a rambler might walk, catch a tram or bus from the city, disembark at the southern limits and cross the floodplains of the Mersey. These excursions provided a real expansion of the spatiality of life for the workers, who had been cut off from the countryside by the expansion of the suburbs 80 years prior. For a long time, the Mersey acted as a physical barrier, passable only by fords or toll bridges. At the turn of the century, however, Henry Simon, a wealthy German emigré, Hallé sponsor and flour-mill industrialist, financed the building of a bridge across the waters, providing easy access to the "Poors Field" beyond. His Rugby- then Cambridge-educated son Ernest Simon, a noted radical liberal, city Alderman and later MP, would later be key to the expansion of Manchester across the Mersey, through the fight to build the "garden suburb" of Wythenshawe.

Just before Christmas in 1925, in the pages of the *Manchester Guardian*, Ernest Simon made the case for the Council to purchase the Tatton estates south of his father's bridge. It had been trying to buy the land for some time, as, just as in the days of Samuel Brooks (who had bought land off the same family), agricultural land near the city fringes was substantially cheaper to develop. Expansion was deemed a radical solution to the city's population growth and its inner-city slums. They had been stymied, however, by the old head of the Tatton family who had refused to sell. But in 1924 he died, and a significant obstacle in the path of those who dreamed of Manchester's southwards expansion was removed — his heir was more amenable to the sale. Early the following year the Council was set to make their decision. Simon argued that this would be the most important decision it would make for the next twenty years, equal in prominence to the commitment to build the Ship Canal 30 years prior. Not willing to take any chances, Simon and his wife, Sheena, would personally expedite the move southwards by buying from the Tattons their ancestral seat, Wythenshawe Hall, and its lands, and donating them to the City of Manchester early in 1926 to be held in trust as open land. Ultimately, the Council would heed their call, buying the remainder of the Tatton estate that same year, paving the way for incorporation in 1931 and the construction of Wythenshawe, the world's largest garden suburb.

The Fight Against the Speculative Builder

Wythenshawe was just one episode in the longer history of the fight to abolish the slums (and speculative rentier landlords) from the late nineteenth century, occurring at different scales and paces across the country. A consequence of industrialisation was the appalling living conditions for the working class. Left to the tyranny of private landlords, the working class remained housed in dense back-to-backs. As we have seen, the ruling elite's fear of insurrection during the 1840s, as well as the impact of repeated cholera epidemics, spurred on a long campaign to address these conditions. The first intervention was the 1848 Public Health Act, which gave authorities the power to supply water and drainage. Following it, in 1853, a local Act was passed prohibiting new cellar dwellings. Yet these were isolated reforms. In the minds of the city's leadership, the right to private property remained absolute — and so the council focussed on improving conditions *around* the houses, not tackling the conditions of the houses themselves.

However, over the following decades, this common sense would crumble. In 1867 a local Act was passed permitting the Council to close homes "unfit for human habitation"; another the same year banned back-to-backs. These powers paved the way for "reconditioning" — the forcible improvement of homes deemed unfit. Between 1885-1906, 500 houses would be reconditioned in Manchester every year, growing to 2000 per year between 1906-1914 once T.D. Marr, councillor for New Cross, Ancoats and campaigner for housing reform, became chairman of the Housing Committee.[16] One policy he was extremely insistent upon was cottages for workers — not tenements. This would have a powerful effect on Manchester's housing policy for the next 100 years.

A tranche of national Acts accelerated the growing power of local government over housing conditions. The Housing of the Working Classes Act 1885 empowered the condemnation of slum housing. A follow-up act in 1890 gave local government the power to buy land and construct tenements and housing estates, though it gave them no specific finance to do so. This marked the birth of public housing, and Manchester was a pioneer. In 1891 it started work on Victoria Square, an apartment block of 522 bedrooms in New Cross, Ancoats, which opened in 1894. This was followed in 1897 by nearby "Sanitation Street", a neat terrace of houses which contained the first example of individual toilets per house in the district. Then, in 1904, the Council purchased 28 acres in Blackley for municipal housing. These tentative and experimental forays into the direct provision of municipal housing, as well as the programme of reconditioning of slum clearance, began to set a consensus that only decisive municipal action could adequately address the city's long-term housing problems.

Consensus that this was the correct course of action was consistently built by a voluntarist, civic-minded movement outside the Council. In the spirit of their forebearers J.P. Kay and Edwin Chadwick, reports were produced detailing the conditions of the slums. The founding of the University Settlement in Ancoats in 1895 to engage residents through leisure, advice, cultural and welfare activities, while allowing liberal reformers to study the lives of the urban poor, was a key milestone in this movement to document.[17]

The key turning point came in the aftermath of World War I, when the national government made a series of historic interventions in housing, spurred by a desire to provide "homes fit for heroes" and the very real threat of a nationwide rebellion (the Glasgow Rent Strike of 1915 and copycat actions across the country in particular focussed attention on the housing question and the "tyranny of landlords").[18] Rent controls were introduced in the private sector. The 1918 Tudor-Walters Report laid out minimum space standards for future public housing. The Addison Act one year later accepted the principle that the private sector would never be able to produce the homes needed for the working class, providing instead grants to councils to build public housing.

In Manchester, in 1917, the Council established the Housing Special Committee to design a postwar rebuilding programme of 4,000 homes. By 1919 this target had expanded to 17,000 homes across four years. Shortage of materials, labour and capacity in the Council meant that this target was never reached, with only 4,000 built by 1923. The passing of the Wheatley Act by the first Labour government in 1924 provided further financial aid to Councils to build housing, and Manchester set a new target of 10,000. *Laissez faire* was gone, the speculative builder no longer able to build whatever they liked, and the development of the city was controlled by the Town Planning Act.[19]

The Battle for Wythenshawe

This departure from the commercially-driven free-trade era of *Manchestertum* would be the key political shift in the twentieth century. No longer would development and working-class housing be left to market forces alone. Instead, rational planning would create the society of the future. This came about through a cross-class alliance of reforming liberals and the growing political muscle of organised labour. The defence of *laissez faire* was left to the Conservatives, who opposed across this era the growing ambitions for local government, such as municipal housing and the Council's direct works board. Progress on the Blackley municipal housing was stymied by Conservative opposition, such that by 1914 only 203 houses had been built. Through clever manoeuvrings — controlling key committees, building political pressure outside the council and forging alliances — the reformers gradually gained the upper hand. Their task was made easier in 1919 when the Conservatives lost their overall majority on the Council due to Labour gains in the industrial wards.

To find the greatest example of these political manoeuvrings, we can look again at the battle for Wythenshawe — the apotheosis of interwar rational planning. Following Simon's call in the letter of 1925, the Council held a vote on 3rd February 1926 over the purchase of the estate. It passed, via a quirk of the proceedings — after a three-hour debate, the Conservatives proposed a wrecking amendment to the proposal, which passed, with Conservative and some Liberal support. Upon its passing, the majority of the Conservative bloc left the council chamber. But, noting that only an *amendment* had passed, not the final bill, Alderman Jackson, a hugely influential Labour figure in the interwar years, proposed a further amendment — this time to reverse the Conservative amendment and order the purchase. Ruled in order, the amendment, and then the bill, passed, with Labour, Liberal and some dissenting Tories voting for it. Through the thickets of bureaucratic procedure, the purchase was authorised and made good in May that year.

However, the purchase of the land was only half the battle. Now, the reformers faced a new adversary in the Cheshire parish authorities in the areas that had been bought. The Council only owned the land — its location in the jurisdiction of another authority meant they didn't control planning powers. It also faced the dilemma that, were it to move its ratepayers from the inner city to the new suburb, it would lose the revenue to another authority. An Act of Incorporation from Parliament was required, but in 1927, Parliament, with a large Conservative majority, rejected incorporation, sensitive to Cheshire's plea for its ancient rights, "Cheshire should be kept as Cheshire" was their battle cry.

In response, the reformers established the Wythenshawe Estates Special Committee. Chaired by Alderman Jackson and including both of the Simons, the eight-person committee was tasked with guiding and controlling the development of the Council's new lands. Described as a "Council within a Council", it led a four-year fight to overturn Parliament's rejection of incorporation. The Committee appointed Barry Parker — the socialist disciple of Ebenezer Howard, who had previously worked on Letchworth and was a key figure within the Garden City movement — as lead architect and tasked him with drawing up a plan on the same principles. Simon had long been an advocate of the Garden City movement, arguing in 1922 at a conference for the suburbanisation of the working class, that they too should benefit from the hallmark of bourgeois civility, and its light and air. Workers living in the new estates would travel, by new public transport lines, to Trafford Park.

Jackson, Parker and the Simons were ideologically in lockstep and together formed the core of the Committee. They worked to change the facts on the ground — in 1928 submitting a plan to Bucklow Council for 1500 houses for the working class in Northenden, calling the bluff of the antediluvian Cheshire authorities.[20] Bucklow dragged the approval — by 1929 only 142 houses had been built. But the election of a minority Labour administration in 1929 changed the balance of forces. All parties had stood on a platform of abolishing the slums — the 1930 Greenwood Act which compelled councils to produce slum-clearance plans a product of this moment. Simon had been elected as Liberal MP for Withington, and in summer 1930 Parliament approved the incorporation of Wythenshawe into the City of Manchester.

The date for transfer from Cheshire was set for 31st March, 1931. Come the day, the Parish held a funeral feast. Residents fired their chimneys to clean them one last time — a practice illegal in Manchester. The Lord Mayor of Manchester, addressing the feast, marked the historic occasion by noting that the residents would go to bed in Cheshire and wake in Manchester. Dryly, he said how unusual it was that the Parish had invited the undertaker to its own deathbed feast. Midnight struck, the parishes were dissolved; newspapers announced: "Lancashire Bigger Tonight!" The building of the garden suburb began in earnest.

Little Red Viennas

Despite the desires of the prominent reformers within the Council, it wasn't just cottages that were built by the Corporation during the interwar period. In north Manchester, on either side of the Irk Valley, striking complexes of brick flats were built in the modern, Art Deco style.

In Collyhurst, the Collyhurst Flats were built between 1936-9, a complex of five-storey apartment blocks. Most were laid out in rows, one section set out in a graceful curve. Two of the blocks had a large arch or portal in the centre of them, reminiscent of the design used for public housing in Vienna (for example, "Karl Marx Hof ") only years previous. Aerial photographs which show them under construction give us a real sense of how dramatic a departure they were from the terraces: set back from the road, surrounded by open space, a breezy and bright vision of modernity.

More unusual still was Kennet House, an oval sweep of flats rising to five storeys. They were designed by Bolton architect Leonard Heywood, who also worked on Wythenshawe at the same time. Set alongside the mines and soot-blackened terraces of Smedley, its brickwork alternated in strips of black and white. Its futuristic clean lines earned it the name the "Queen Mary", owing to its ship-like appearance. Within the complex were greengrocers, a hardware shop, butchers, a communal washroom, a youth club and even its own church. Its 181 flats, with their light and airy rooms, inside bathrooms and modern plumbing, were highly sought after. Public housing was in tune with the mood of the times, Manchester's projects northern variants of the push for decent housing then being put forward by the London County Council under Herbert Morrison.[21]

Alongside housing, from Wythenshawe to the Collyhurst Flats, was the commissioning of major civic buildings in the city core, such as the Town Hall extension and the magnificent circular Central Library (and its Library Theatre company in the basement). Taken together, they represent the emergence of an interwar modernity in the city. Much of this effort was driven by the Council, but private commissions also served to change the character of the built environment — the new Kendal Milne department store on Deansgate and Edward Lutyens' Midland Bank both exemplars of the new style. Clad in white Portland stone, these landmark buildings were representative of the wider efforts of the city planners to throw off the Victorian past, reject the association of interwar depression, boost employment and project an image of progressive civic modernism to the world.[22]

Modern Manchester's civic core

Responses to the Slum Clearances

The 1930 Greenwood Act set ambitious targets for slum clearance and provided councils with the finance to do so. Manchester set about the process with alacrity. Plans were drawn up to demolish swaths of the inner city, with Collyhurst, Ancoats and Hulme identified as having the worst conditions. Extensive surveys were conducted, coordinated by the University Settlement, which emphasised the poor conditions in the slumbelt. In Chorlton-on-Medlock (once "Little Ireland") it was found that of all the houses built between 1794 and 1820, most were without water supply, drainage or sanitation. Some had been reconditioned, but most were in poor condition — doorways without steps, stone-flagged rooms, bedrooms without doors, no washrooms or spaces for food.[23] Although much reduced, cellar dwellings still existed.[24] In many ways, the city that Engels observed 80 years previously still remained.

This extensive surveying in the early 1930s provides us with a valuable insight into the response of communities to clearance and displacement. We also get an accurate picture of *who* lived in the slums. Dispelling the stereotypes of the itinerant, dangerous and outcast slum-dweller — a legacy of *Mary Barton* — "Some Housing Conditions in Chorlton-on-Medlock" depicted a community of artisanal workers: printers, wholesale clothiers, finishers, pattern card makers, yarn merchants, rubber stamp makers, shippers, joiners, engineers, box makers and motor mechanics.[25] Pieceworkers predominated over fixed employees in the big factories and firms. A report into Ancoats demonstrated their longevity — nearly half of those surveyed had lived in the area over 20 years, while 259 of the 476 interviewed had local relatives. These were settled working communities.

These reports dispelled the view that the poverty of the slum-dwellers was the result of poor habits, drinking, hygiene and large families. Rather, they demonstrated the structural impact of capitalist urbanisation on the lives of the working class — their disposability resulting in low pay, compounding the challenge of supporting children, and resulting in ill-health.[26] Identified too was the tyranny of landlords in a climate of intimidation. Fear of reprisals meant tenants were reluctant to complain, raise repairs or press for redress. In one case, a tenant was banned from bringing furniture into his home because the landlord felt it would make him more difficult to evict. Structurally powerless, the tenants of the slums lived under the shadow of the eviction notice, with its one-week notice to quit. On multiple occasions, the researchers conducting the survey were pursued by landlords, who monitored their tenants' responses.[27]

Because of this complex picture, tenant responses to slum clearances were mixed. While overall they preferred the prospect of Council homes to the slum landlord, they did not universally welcome displacement. In Ancoats, 60% welcomed the prospect of a better house and amenities, and a fifth the prospect of better health for them and their children. In Angel Meadows, only 60% were willing to leave the area, the rest wanted to stay. The distance of the new estates was also an issue, only one in ten wanted to go as far as Wythenshawe.[28]

Many wanted to stay in the area closest to where their families and community networks were. The loss of these networks had multiple effects: women no longer able to rely on nearby childcare or the local shop where food was cheap and credit available to trusted customers. In Ancoats, 94% of people were concerned about the risk of higher rents and travel fares to get to work, which could be disastrous on tight budgets.[29] One man, indignant, said he "would not move for the Town Hall clock!", another that he "wanted to be buried where they all are buried".[30]

A final concern of those in the clearance zone was particularly illustrative of the limits of the paternalist mindset that ran through the whole clearance programme: the lack of pubs on the new estates. Since the late nineteenth century, a seam of moralism had run through the efforts of the housing reformers, and the new estates were seen as an opportunity to rid the working class of the perceived vice of drink. This tendency had its origins in the voluntarist, charitable nature of the reform movement. Surveillance and social engineering were often baked into the new plans. In Chorltonville, a new estate built in the late nineteenth century, the "right sort of tenants" was wanted. In Victoria Square, rooms were built without wooden skirting boards, on the assumption that the tenants would rip them out and use them as firewood. The principles of the housing reformers from Octavia Hill onwards had a conservative strain to them. The continuing poverty of the poor was assumed, the challenge was merely to house them cleanly and keep a close eye on them.

In this vein, the University Settlement developed plans to establish new research centres in the estates built in the 1930s. Not everyone was in favour of this, and in 1935 Alderman Titt, a Labour councillor, launched an attack on plans to set up a University Settlement in the new estates — "For God's sake!" he pleaded "do not give room to these self-appointed social investigators who went about dissecting and investigating the life of the working classes!" His motion failed, with the Liberals and Tories blocking the Labour councillors.[31] Of course, this tendency was not the sole motivation of the interwar housing programmes — a more utopian desire to provide good housing for the working classes was a greater motivation — but it nonetheless remained a component of it throughout.

As the scope of the clearances grew, so too did the ambiguous views held by tenants. At times, they tipped into outright resistance, as the Council's plans increasingly felt like something done *to* tenants rather than *for* them, without consultation and consent. In the 1930s, these contradictions came to a head in Hulme, the district that would for the remainder of the century come to epitomise the triumphs and failures of the Council's housing policy.

Built as an improvement upon the old core of Chorlton-on-Medlock, Hulme was by 1900 in a parlous state. In 1914 the tenants presented a petition to the Council calling for sanitary improvement. This verdict was echoed by the city medical officers' report in 1920. By the summer of 1933 the plans for wholesale demolition were unveiled, with the Council determined to push forward. This was not wholly welcomed — resistance was organised by an alliance of organisations, including the local rectors. The campaign was women-led, and on the night before the inquiry it held a 1000-strong public rally. Rev Chevassut, one of the local rectors, addressed the crowds. People deserved to have a say on where they lived, he exclaimed. The crowd was, he felt, "fighting for something more than housing, they were fighting for liberty".[32] It was in vain. By 1934 clearance began and tenants were decanted to the newly-built Wythenshawe.

Indeed, across the city clearance continued apace. Red Bank, Collyhurst, St Clements and West Gorton were all slated for demolition. Tenants in Collyhurst panicked at the sight of Council inspectors. In the elections of 1933, the Conservatives ran on the platform of rehousing on the same site, while Labour and the Liberals stuck fast to the policy of clearance. Rent strikes erupted in Blackley. The *Manchester Evening News* ran the headline "DICTATORS WANTED", calling on the leadership to "GET IT DONE". By 1937, 12,136 houses had been cleared: a displacement of around 50,000 people. Only 9,435 houses had been built to replace them. Chevassut condemned the failure of the Council to consult with tenants as the "upper limit of cynical brutality".[33]

Modernism from Below

Attempts by the local state to build new housing for the working classes and the restructuring of local industry into the engineering plants of Trafford Park and East Manchester represent the powerful ways that modernity was imposed from above. In a counter movement, people of the city were becoming modern too. We see this in the struggle for women's suffrage — the heirs to democratic movements of the century before. Manchester was a nodal centre for the fight for true universal suffrage; the Pankhursts originating from Moss Side, and the city host to the spaces where that movement interacted with and drew support from the wider labour movement.

By considering two further "modern" movements, we will attempt to grasp at the totality of Manchester's modernity. These are Manchester's communists and its Black radicals. These currents sought to upend the most fundamental structures; to end capitalism and overthrow empire; to grasp the very foundations of the world and, through organised human effort, abolish them. The width of their vision and height of their ambitions made them heirs of the city's seditious traditions of 100 years prior; updated for a world ruled by electricity, the combustion engine and aerial bombardment.

Recall Harry Hardcastle looking for a job on Trafford Park at the height of the Depression. While he was fictional, his story was not. Though Trafford Park provided some resilience in the regional economy during the depression, tens of thousands were thrown out of work. In response to unemployment, and the introduction of measures like the hated "means test" by the national government, the mood of desperation was met by the resurgent National Unemployed Workers Movement (NUWM), which had been founded in 1921 with the support of the Communist Party of Great Britain (CPGB).[34]

Holding meetings at the Salford Workers Arts Club, based in Hyndman Hall, a cultural and political centre founded by the Social Democratic Federation, the NUWM quickly began to amass 100 regular attendees at its weekly meetings. Its chair was a young unemployed toolmaker and committed communist,

Eddie Frow.[35] The branch resolved to call a demonstration, set for 1st October. The plan was to assemble on the croft next to Hyndman Hall and march to Salford Town Hall. The day arrived, and numbers were greater than expected. Speeches were made. Ewan MacColl and Alec Armstrong arrived as the "Red Megaphones", an agit-prop theatre group inspired by Soviet dramaturgy, adding to the atmosphere by the ringing of bells. This day, significant as it was due to the violence of the police, was just one of many across the autumn of 1931 as the NUWM led the battle against the cuts, yet the Battle of Bexley Square passed into legend due to the eyewitness of Walter Greenwood, who immortalised it in *Love on the Dole*.

The Communist Party was not the only force mobilising in Depression-stricken Manchester. Oswald Moseley, who formed the British Union of Fascists (BUF) in 1932, was particularly keen to establish a base in Manchester, as his ancestors were the old lords of the manor. He organised a series of rallies across 1933-4 in Hulme and Cheetham Town Halls, in the open-air Albert Croft in Miles Platting, at venues including the 7,000 capacity Kings Hall in Belle Vue and the Free Trade Hall. By 1934 the BUF had 18 branches in the city and satellite towns. Virulently antisemitic, they established their headquarters on Northumberland Street, just to the north of Cheetham Hill, a neighbourhood that in 1933 was home to 35,000 Jews. Chanting antisemitic slogans, the BUF organised marches through the district and would sell their paper outside the cinema.[36] In other districts like Hulme they targeted the local Irish population.

At every turn they were met by organised resistance by the Cheetham Young Communist League, one of the largest branches in the city. It was led by an extraordinary set of second-generation Jewish immigrants whose parents had fled the pogroms in the Russian Empire. People like Benny Rothman, a car mechanic, leader of the 1932 Kinder Scout Mass Trespass and later MetroVicks engineer and shop steward; Maurice Levine, a tailor who would fight in Spain; Frank Allaun, who would go onto be Labour MP for Salford; and Issy Luft, who would go on to be principal organiser for the Aid to Spain movement and secretary of Crumpsall CPGB. Forming the "Jewish Lads Brigade", they confronted Moseley's Blackshirts, disrupting meetings, blocking marches and fighting them in the streets. Establishing the Challenge Club in 1935, hosting dances, cultural events, left-wing book clubs, political meetings and classes, they were able to draw in an estimated 400-500 people in its membership and wider periphery.[37] The efforts were mirrored elsewhere in the city — Bessie Wild, a member of the Hulme branch of the CPGB, recalls heckling of Moseley at Hulme Town Hall that went on until 1:30 in the morning.[38] Their collective efforts at confronting the fascists were so successful that by October 1936 Manchester Council became the first nationwide to ban the wearing of political uniforms at rallies.

The struggle against fascism soon acquired international dimensions. Hitler's rise to power in 1933, Mussolini's invasion of Ethiopia in 1935 and Franco's nationalist uprising in 1936 structured the decade. These crises were responded to by mass meetings. In August 1935 C.L.R. James and George Padmore's International African Friends of Ethiopia organised a rally at Manchester's Milton Hall on Ethiopia, unanimously adopting a resolution recalling the various pronouncements of British, French and Italian governments guaranteeing Ethiopian independence and protesting the embargo upon the export of arms to the Ethiopian people. It was one of a series of rallies that summer on the issue.[39]

The call from the Spanish Republic for volunteers was also heard. 28-year-old Sam Wild from Ardwick, working then as a boilermaker, left for Spain at the end of 1936, being promoted to commander of the British Battalion by 1938. "I felt strongly about fascism", he said,

What I'd heard about in Abyssinia, saw what Hitler was doing in Germany to the Jews and the Communists, the Japanese in the Far East. I concluded that fascism was about to conquer the world, and it was about time somebody started to do something about it. I had no sense of adventure; it was a profound political feeling.[40]

He was not alone. Joining him were people like Joe Norman, a boxer and engineer from Hulme, who had been politicised earlier in the decade at Hyndman Hall and through the NUWM; Clem Beckett, a daredevil speedway racer in Belle Vue and YCL member; Ralph Cantor, a musician and Challenge Club member; Red Megaphones member, roof slater and actor Alec Armstrong; and the aforementioned Maurice Levine. Around 130 men volunteered from the Manchester region, with some, including Armstrong, Beckett and Cantor, dying for the Republic.

The Aid for Spain movement and the Medical Aid Committee coordinated the provision of medical and food supplies, the raising of funds and awareness. Issy Luft established the North Manchester branch, supporting the work of Madge Addy, a hairdresser-turned-nurse from Rusholme who left for Spain in 1937 to become head nurse for the International Brigades. That same year, 30 women in Moss Side were engaged in making bandages for the Republican Army.[41] Theatre of Action, the company formed by Joan Littlewood and MacColl, put on Living Newspapers and works by Spanish playwrights at the Free Trade Hall, while between 1st and 15th February 1939, Picasso's *Guernica* made an extraordinary appearance at a car dealership near the cathedral as part of a fundraiser for a food ship campaign. Entrance was 6p, and £3000 was cabled to Spain shortly after the exhibition closed.[42]

Despite the effervescent nature of the work or the Communists during the interwar years, the bedrock of the CPGB's strength across the decades remained its industrial base. Operating a network of factory branches, it had a dense presence in places like Fairey Aviation in Stockport and the vast MetroVicks plant in Trafford Park. This was all completely clandestine — known Communists would be expelled in those years. It ran sector-based newspapers, like *The New Propeller* for engineers and *The Salford Docker*. Its cadres — people like Frances Dean, secretary of the Fairey branch, and Hugh Scanlon, at MetroVicks, later General Secretary of the Amalgamated Engineering Union — were shop stewards and union representatives leading disputes and strikes for pay and conditions, including equal pay for women. In March 1941 the CPGB coordinated a strike of 9,000 apprentice engineers, winning a rise in the national rate of pay as a result.[43] But, it was in the critical war years of 1941-5, once the Soviet Union had entered the war, that the factory branches reached their peak — working in tandem with management to optimise production of the war effort; a common front against fascism producing rare years of industrial peace. The wartime cooperation between the CPGB and Ernest Bevin, the wartime Minister of Labour, was part of the backdrop that propelled Labour to their landslide victory in 1945, with Hugh Scanlon standing down as the CPGB candidate in Stretford, and Benny

Rothman running an extensive ground operation in Hulme to get the Labour candidate, Fred Lee, elected.[44]

In his memoir, Ewan MacColl captures in rich detail those years — the political and agitational activity, getting up at the crack of dawn to sell copies of the *Salford Docker* at the port gates. He also gives us something of the inner world of Communism: the utopian old-timers on Sunday afternoons at the Workers Arts Club discussing science, religion and the works of mid-nineteenth century philosophers; the excursions with the Red Megaphones to the cotton towns in the height of the Depression, performing agit-prop on platforms that explored the impact of automation on cotton production; the fight for access to the countryside. He writes too of his work with Joan Littlewood, writing and producing plays about colonialism, fascism, peace; building links with the German and Russian workers theatre movement, and of how Tuesday evenings were kept free for Hallé concerts, where he and his friends would absorb the moderns — Schoenberg, Bartok, Stravinsky — eagerly discussing them into the night afterwards at the Imperial Cafe. The febrile atmosphere made for intoxicating engagements with history.[45]

Len Johnson

One arena of struggle that is conspicuous for the lack of sustained organising by the Communist Party during this period is housing. Unlike in London, where the CPGB created the Stepney Tenants' Defence League, which was the bedrock of their fight against fascism and racism and the organised base of one of the Party's four MPs, Phil Piratin, or the "Red Clydeside" era in Glasgow which was a high point of the rent strike, in Manchester the Communists appear distant from the tenant struggles that were happening at the same time.[46]

There is, however, one notable exception from after the war — a CPGB pamphlet from 1957 entitled *Fight the Landlords' Rent Increase*.[47] Its author was the remarkable figure of Len Johnson.

Born in Clayton in 1902, Johnson's father was a seaman from Sierra Leone, his mother Irish. Throughout the 1920s he was a champion middleweight boxer, but his career was limited by the colour bar that operated in the sport at the time. In 1930 he met the great Communist and Civil Rights hero, Paul Robeson, which he said "put new life" into him. This marked the start of his politicisation throughout the 1930s, shaped by his experience of racism, and during the war he joined the Communist Party. In 1945, along with his white friend Wilf Charles, secretary of the Party's Moss Side branch, he was part of the Party's delegation to the fifth Pan African Congress happening in the city at that time. Charles in fact put Kwame Nkrumah up for the duration of the conference.

One year later he founded the New International Club, a Party-affiliated social club in the mould of its interwar predecessors in Moss Side. Its aims were "free internationalism, colonial liberation, peace and the ending of race discrimination". In 1949 it hosted Paul Robeson at the Kings Hall in Belle Vue, where thousands turned out to hear him sing — much to the consternation of the Pan Africanists, some of whom opposed Communism. It proved to be a high-point. The club sat uneasily with the postwar Communist Party, which was turning away from what it termed the "narrow limits" of anti-racism, and it never received the financial support from the Party it needed. It closed in 1950. Nevertheless, Johnson continued to be politically active — overturning the colour bar at the Abbey Taphouse pub in Hulme in 1953 with mass pickets after he and Charles were refused service and standing as

Communist Party candidate for Moss Side on six occasions between 1947 and 1962.[48]

Black Radicalism in the City of Cotton

Following Len Johnson's trajectory brings us to Pan Africanism, then at work in the city as well. Johnson's contact with the Pan Africanists — at the Congress, through his community organising in Moss Side and over the dispute regarding Robeson's visit in 1949 — offers us a fascinating way to explore the complex and sometimes fractious relationship between Communism and Black radicalism in the interwar years. These traditions, operating in Manchester simultaneously, collided at the New International Club and in the wider work of Johnson. To grasp this, we must trace the origins of the Congress, a key episode in the city's radical politics and its "modernity from below".

With the onset of the war in 1939, the network of Pan Africanists that had emerged in London in the interwar years spread out to avoid conscription and retaliation by the state. One of them, T. Ras Makonnen, came to Manchester on the invitation of Peter Milliard, who was already based at the city's university. He enrolled on a course there to study history, hoping to specialise in the struggle against Roman rule, believing "there would be important parallels for the process of colonial freedom".[49] In the late 1930s he had been instrumental in establishing the London-based International African Service Bureau, alongside George Padmore, C.L.R. James, Jomo Kenyatta and George Wallace-Johnson, acting as treasurer to the organisation (a financial "magician", according to James). He, along with Milliard, brought these networks to Manchester.

At the same time, African and Caribbean sailors and a growing local population of Black people made Manchester an increasingly important hub of Black networks. This was bolstered by the arrival of American soldiers in the region, as Black GIs served in the American military during the war in two major air bases in Lancashire, Burtonwood and Bamber Bridge. Segregation in the US army was upheld by the British military and extended to some of the towns across the region, which operated colour bars. So, Manchester became a hub where African Americans would spend time on their days of leave. These transnational encounters between African and Caribbean seamen and African American soldiers created a ferment which would have a significant impact on the city's culture for the rest of the century.

The lack of Black establishments in the area, and the colour bars that operated in many white businesses, meant that Makonnen took matters into his own hands. He opened a chain of cafés, restaurants and clubs down the Oxford Road, as well as a bookshop called The Economist, from which he published the journal *Pan-Africa*. Starting with the Ethiopia Teashop, he soon expanded, opening the Cosmopolitan, a curry-house called the Orient, a club called the Forum where the great Calypsonian Lord Kitchener performed, and a place called Belle Étoile. One of these, the Cosmopolitan, was a considerable success. At its peak of operations, he had 62 workers on the payroll, including Jomo Kenyatta during his wartime stay in Manchester, who worked for Makonnen variously as manager, bouncer and sometime potato-peeler, and Kath Locke, a Moss Side community activist who would act as Secretary to the Moss Side Housing Action Group and found the women's Abasindi Co-operative.[50]

His businesses' profits would fund the Congress in 1945. Makonnen remarked that he felt, in a "mimicking" of history, "like Engels", whose wealth had "supported Marx in his great undertaking".[51] His business acumen was therefore one reason for that astonishing gathering in Manchester in 1945 — Padmore, Du Bois, Kenyatta, Nkrumah, along with around 90 delegates from trade unions and liberation movements from across the colonised world. With notably more representation from the mass organisations of liberation than earlier congresses, the Manchester Congress made 1945, as Du Bois insisted, "a decisive year in determining the freedom of Africa".[52] Manchester had also by this point, in Makonnen's estimation, become "quite a point of contact" with the Black proletariat in Britain.[53] Overthrow of colonial rule internationally came into dialogue with combatting racism in the metropole. The final reason for it happening in the city was put clearly by Makonnen:

Looking at our conference and residence in Manchester you could say that we coloured people had a right there, because of the age-old connections between cotton, slavery and the building up of cities in England. We also felt that in a way we were remaking history by coming to stir up that other side of Manchester, its fierce anti-slavery streak... So, Manchester gave us an important opportunity to express and oppose the contradictions, the fallacies and the pretensions that were at the very centre of the empire.[54]

These connections and contradictions emerged in a series of murals Makonnen commissioned for the walls of the Cosmopolitan, painted over four months by his friend Jean, a Jewish Austrian he had met in London.[55] These "murals of humanity" depicted the contribution of all peoples "whether African, Scots, Welsh or Austrian" to the fund of "common humanity", but also displayed the contradictions of colonial oppression and resistance in these decades. One wall showed "the death of Poland in Europe with the cannons and the invasions, and then in the New World we could see the Pole reappearing, but this time what was portrayed was the typical immigrant Pole, leading the charge against the Blacks. I had [Jean] write above this 'Whither Mankind'".

Here, under Jean's murals in the Cosmopolitan, we end our exploration of "modernism from below". What affiliations and frictions characterised a night at the Cosmopolitan, as Black Americans shared tables with Jamaicans, and Nigerians negotiated the stairs with Guyanese. What was made of the murals? What was made of the food supplied by Cypriots and cooked by two Chinese chefs from Cardiff? ("it really was cosmopolitan", remarked Makonnen).[56]

The Cosmopolitan, like the Challenge Club and Hyndman Hall before it, and like the New International Club after, were fundamentally modern places. Under their rafters, transnational movements for emancipation gathered, rising out of a dialectical opposition to capitalist modernisation. A modernisation that had turned Manchester into a port, cleared whole swaths of the inner city and built new garden suburbs in its place. In the slums created by speculators for the working class, currents had grown that faced fascism, out-organised the bosses and plotted the downfall of empires. In the ports and on the seas, threads of rebellion had been spun. In the factories, in the shadow of the Blitz, men and women dreamed of new horizons.

New Jerusalem

In the winter of 1940, Manchester was heavily bombed. Buildings were destroyed, the Victorian warehouses up in flames — eyewitnesses spoke of cotton bales hurled through the night with the force of the explosions. The Cathedral, the Royal Exchange, the Free Trade Hall and the Assize Courts all sustained damage, with Waterhouse's courts condemned to demolition shortly after. In the years after, under wartime stars, the city leaders devised a radical reinvention: the 1945 City of Manchester Plan.

The plan was published in a large, cloth-bound book, running to nearly 300 pages and covering every aspect of the city, from its transport infrastructure to housing, from industry to its public services and parks. Complete with detailed maps, photographs and coloured plates, it is an object of profound ambition for the city and its peoples. The aim of the plan, set out clearly on the first page, was "to enable every inhabitant of this city to enjoy real health of body and health of mind", its need "dictated by our pressing and unavoidable obligation to provide anew for the tens of thousands of our citizens who are living and working in unsafe, unhealthy, outworn and overcrowded buildings".[57]

It was one of the most radical reimagining of a British city ever conceived. In the aftermath of the war, the planners saw their chance to rid the city of bomb-ruin, Victorian decay and speculative landlords. Wide, tree-lined boulevards would be cut through the city centre. Warehouses, mills, terraced housing and even the city's "Gothic machine" would be cleared. A new station was planned at Piccadilly; new civic buildings dedicated to the arts, education and the sciences were to be built. Smoke itself would be abolished. Lead planner, Rowland Nicholas, asked,

Is Manchester prepared once again to give the country a bold lead by adopting a standard of reconstruction that will secure to every citizen the enjoyment of fresh air, of a reasonable ration of daylight, and of some relief from the barren bleakness of bricks and mortar?[58]

The vision of the interwar reformers, the builders of Wythenshawe, Kennet House and Central Library, lived within the pages of the plan. In his preface, Alderman Jackson, now Lord Mayor, wrote:

> Today our country is at the beginning of the great transition from war to peace, and all thinking people will wish to inquire about the sort of work to be built for posterity... The extent to which the Civic Authorities will be able to remodel Manchester as a fairer city with greatly improved living and working conditions will depend ultimately upon the interest, determination and wishes of the citizens, to whom I commend this book for careful study.[59]

What is of course striking about this Plan is its public spirit and ethos. Public good was placed above private gain, rational planning above the chaos of the speculator and rentier.

Accompanying the publication of the plan was a documentary film, *City Speaks*, commissioned by the Council and directed by Paul Rotha, a key figure within the British documentary films movement. The film shows an urban utopia in the making, using montage, aerial footage and a symphonic soundtrack. It opens with a prayer, narrated over sweeping vistas of the city:

> Oh God, grant us a vision of our city, fair as she might be. A city of justice, where none shall prey on others, a city of plenty where vice and poverty shall cease to exist. A city of brotherhood, where all success shall be founded on service. Honour shall be given to nobleness alone. A city of peace,

where order shall not rest on force but on the love of all for the city, the great mother of the common life and weal.

It's a stirring vision. We might see secular prefiguring of it in the night walks of Ewan MacColl throughout the city in the 1930s. Skint and hungry, he watched the moonlight reflect off the wet roofs of the factories and houses and was filled with a potent vision of hope. "One day", he thought, "when I grow up I'm going to tear all this down, I'm going to make something so beautiful and so unobtrusive that men can become human".[60]

One thing essential to grasp is that the planners imagined the future city as retaining its industrial character. While the production of the original commodity, cotton, had long been in decline, the manufacturing base had, across the modern era, been supplanted by engineering. Indeed, in the immediate decade of the postwar era, this industrial society remained intact. Peak tonnage at the Port of Manchester was in 1959. That same year over half of the entire working population of Greater Manchester still worked in manufacturing. The 1945 City of Manchester Plan was drawn up in the light of the modernised and industrialised society that David Egerton painstakingly reveals as the middle century.[61] But postwar austerity delayed the implementation of the plan; the city remained decaying, sooty and largely Victorian. As the tectonic plates of the economy began to shift by the end of the 1950s, the vision of the plan seemed more and more unachievable in the face of precipitous decline.

In an eerie premonition, MacColl in his memoir recalls walking through Ancoats in the 1930s, in awe at the ruined McConnell and Kennedy mills, "where broken windows revealed shattered weaving-frames and rusted overhead drive-shafts", a pocketbook Engels as his guide.[62] The general crisis, the *apocalypse*, of the industrial city would come 30 years later. One by one the city's engine rooms shut up shop. Of course, over the 200 years of its existence, the original capitalist city had been no stranger to crises of employment. Gaskell and Greenwood have provided us with vivid descriptions of its effects; the "Hungry Forties" and the Great Depression had both scarred the lives of the city's workers. But this time it was different. The changing global economy meant that Manchester's days as an industrial powerhouse were numbered. Productive capital was withdrawing from the original industrial city. Into the vacuum came crisis — of industrial society and the postwar settlement. This was the backdrop to political battles of the 1970s and 80s, which is where our narrative will take us next.

Bleston

Accounts that come down to us of Manchester in the 1950s invariably emphasise the grimy, decrepit, almost haunted nature of the city. One of the most poetic is Michel Butor's nouveau roman *L'emploi de temps*, published in French in 1956 and in its English translation as *Passing Time* four years later. The story concerns a Frenchman, Jacques Revel, who comes to "Bleston" — a fictional Manchester — for one year to work as a temporary clerk for a shipping company. Over the course of its fugue-like structure, the narrator is beset by loneliness, an interminable mystery surrounding the near-death of a detective novelist, failed love interests and the ever-present sense of being an outsider. If there's one persistent theme, however, it is the weather: "It rained almost the whole day yesterday, one downpour after another, thunderclaps and brief bright intervals close on one another heels". Wraith-like, a choking smog besets the whole town; mysterious fires glow in the industrial suburbs, "rainy darkness thickened outside my window, on which the drops, like thousands of transient, tremulous mirrors clung for an instant before running down". Under its pall our narrator's sanity disintegrates.

The author of *L'emploi de temps* spent two years in Manchester from 1951-3, teaching in the French department at the University of Manchester. We can assume that many of the details in the novel are autobiographical. Critic Sophie Atkinson has written of how the abiding impression of the work is its capturing of the immigrant experience.[63] Through this lens, its fleeting impressions of Black Manchester are of great interest: the narrator's first acquaintance, an African restaurateur, and his memories of a New Year's Eve spent in a Black tavern, drinking "as I had never drunk before in Bleston nor since".

These may well have been one of Makonnen's establishments, who remained in the city until 1957 when he emigrated to newly independent Ghana. But not necessarily, as by the late 1940s there was a very well established infrastructure of Black leisure venues, including restaurants, boarding houses, licensed clubs and social centres. By the mid-1950s they would be joined by the proliferation of unlicensed shebeens or blues.[64] These were most concentrated in the district south of where Makonnen had operated — in the streets around Denmark Road, eastern Moss Side, an area where Black sailors had congregated since the 1930s. The practice of "house farming", where wealthy landlords subdivided older three-storey houses into bedsits, meant cheap accommodation was always available, and racial exclusions from council housing forced Black tenants into the private sector. Kwame Nkrumah had held open-air rallies in the 1940s on Denmark Road, such was the presence of peoples from Africa and the Caribbean.

These infrastructures would have a huge cultural impact on the city. The Black clubs and especially the shebeens were at the centre of a growing all-night Black dance culture, as people danced to imported American jazz and soul records that found their way to Manchester through Burtonwood. By the 1950s this had triggered a wave of interest in jazz across the city. There's a clear lineage from here through to the famous music of the city in the 1970s via venues like the Reno. Persian, who would later be the principal DJ at the Reno, arrived in Manchester in 1943 from Jamaica, and by the early 1960s, aged 18, he and his friends opened a shebeen in the cellar of Denmark Cafe on Denmark Road in Moss Side. Undoubtedly this culture was at the cutting edge of musical modernity in Manchester, and as our account has shown, has its origins within the transformations across the first half of the twentieth century.

A final musical modernity to briefly consider is that which emerged among an extraordinary collective of students at the Royal College of Music in the first half of the 1950s. Our way into this is through the figure of Alexander Goehr, a conscientious objector who came to Manchester in 1952 to work as a ward orderly in Crumpsall General Hospital in lieu of national service. The son of noted German Jewish conductor and student of Schoenberg Walter Goehr, who had fled Berlin in 1933, Alexander Goehr was drawn to Manchester for political reasons — his hope of finding a Marxist Zionism in Cheetham Hill. By day he swept the wards; by night he debated at the political school and read his Marxist pamphlets. He lodged "in a fairly grim part of Manchester with a landlady who allowed me to use her parlour piano for an hour after tea, in exchange for singalong renderings from *In the Persian Garden* and such like".[65]

He took classes from Richard Hall, an iconoclastic figure in Manchester's music world, first as a private teacher, then enrolled at the Royal College of Music, which he described as looking terrible, but in comparison to the London establishment retaining "a certain Central European feeling about it". There he met Harrison Birtwistle through the Hall class and Peter Maxwell Davies after a concert of Berg clarinet pieces. Goehr sussed him out over coffee at the Kardomah Cafe, opposite the Free Trade Hall. Alongside fellow students John Ogdon and Elgar Howarth, they formed "New Music Manchester", and would go onto pioneer a serious engagement with serialism in postwar British art music. Their concerts, happening in the ragged city described by Butor, speak powerfully to the bright dialectic of modernity in postwar Manchester. In those postwar years, it was cities in the industrial north which made the best claim to represent modernity in Britain.[66]

These modern cultures (and there are more: consider Granada TV, founded in 1956 by Sidney Bernstein, who hung Chagall in his offices; or Shelagh Delaney, the working-class, autodidact playwright whose *A Taste of Honey* would become a national sensation) were the great inheritance for the Manchester of the 1970s and 1980s, a message in a bottle passed over and out of the death of the industrial city.

Anthracite City

We end our investigations through the eyes of our last visitor, another German. In 1966 W.G. Sebald moved to the city, to take up a teaching job at the University of Manchester. He was 22, Engels' age, on his arrival 124 years later. There he found (with Butor as his guide) "a soot blackened city, drifting steadily towards ruin". 44 years later these experiences resurfaced, disguised as fiction, told by the narrator of the fourth story in Sebald's novel *The Emigrants*. After landing at Manchester's Ringway Airport, Terminal One, our narrator rides a taxi to the city centre:

> We drove swiftly through the not unhandsome suburbs of Gatley, Northenden and Didsbury to Manchester itself. Day was just breaking, and I looked out in amazement at the rows of uniform houses, which seemed the more run down the closer we got to the city centre. In Moss Side and Hulme there were whole blocks where the doors and windows were boarded up, and whole districts where everything had been demolished... One might have supposed that the city had long since been deserted and was left now as a necropolis or mausoleum.[67]

Once settled into his new lodgings, put up by the doughty Gracie Irlam, he starts to spend his Sundays walking the city, "among the one-time Jewish quarter around the star-shaped complex of Strangeways prison, behind Victoria Station... All I found still standing was one single row of empty houses, the wind blowing through the smashed windows and doors".[68]

One day he walks further, in a south-westerly direction, along the network of fouled up canal, passing "long-disused gasworks, a coal depot, a bonemill, and what seemed the unending cast-iron palisade fence of the Ordsall slaughterhouse, a Gothic castle in liver-coloured brick". Then he reaches the port of Manchester, "where docks kilometres in length branched off the Ship Canal as it entered the city in a broad arc". Dereliction abounds, "one could see nothing had moved for years. The few barges and freighters that lay apart at the docksides, making an oddly broken impression, put me in mind of some massive shipping disaster".[69]

Here he meets the painter Max Ferber, a solitary German Jew who fled the Nazis and came to England in 1939, winding up in Manchester in 1942. His parents had been killed in the Holocaust. The narrative weighs the horrors of the twentieth century — modernity's horrors. But after every flight into memory, it returns to anthracite-coloured Manchester:

> In Ardwick, Brunswick, All Saints, Hulme, and Angel Fields too, districts adjoining the centre to the south, whole square kilometres of working-class homes had been pulled down by the authorities, so that, once the rubble had been removed, all that was left to recall the lives of thousands of people was the grid-like layout of the streets. When night fell upon those vast spaces, which I came to think of as the Elysian Fields, fires would begin to flicker here and there and children could stand around them or skip about, restless shadowy figures. On that bare terrain it was in fact always and only children that one encountered. They strayed in small groups, in gangs, or quite alone, as if they had nowhere that they could call home.[70]

This apocalyptic vision is the final chapter of Manchester's industrial modernity. From its shock beginnings to its dramatic death, Manchester had been at the forefront of innovations in productive capitalism in Britain. Its collapse and deindustrialisation would shake the city to its foundations, as global capital circulation retreated from the city. Amidst the ruins, two possible futures would contend with one another across the 1970s and 1980s, during the fight to determine in which direction the crisis of the postwar consensus would be resolved.

Part 2

The Interregnum

Chapter 3
The Rise and Crisis of the New Urban Left

Dem a sus dem a sus, right here in the Moss
Dem a sus dem a sus, don't let them pressure us.

Harlem Spirit

We are a socialist council elected on a clear mandate to stop the Thatcher administration from destroying jobs and services for Manchester residents.

Graham Stringer

On the 8th October 1974, two days before the second general election of that year, the Moss Side Neighbourhood Council squatted a newly completed council house on Quinney Crescent.[1] Over 80 people, including parents and children, took part. It was part of a series of actions that week to force attention on the conditions Moss Side's tenants were enduring in the flats at the neighbourhood's District Centre, where mice and cockroaches ran free (some of which had been collected and thrown into the Council chamber in an earlier action). The Council had tried to blame the tenants — saying that they had brought in the vermin themselves with their second-hand furniture. But in truth the issues were due to design faults. Built to a low-spec prefab design only years previous, they had become riddled with damp; the flimsy internal walls built from "stramit", a type of compressed straw, a breeding ground for every kind of vermin and bug. The service ducts became a highway for infestation, the building materials a major fire risk.

One District Centre resident said:

This is ten times worse than the old Moss Side. Then, you knew who was who, you could go out and leave the door open at 12 o clock at night and walk the streets at two in the morning — here you daren't go out after eight. I wouldn't take one rent free. This is a bigger slum than whatever Moss Side was... In the old terraces you grew up with most of them and you knew whether you could trust them or not. But here, you just don't know.[2]

Another tenant, who complained of experiencing an electric shock each time she went to the toilet, recalled being asked by a man in the Town Hall whether she had considered wearing Wellington boots.[3]

Timing their occupation around the election, they extracted a promise from Labour MP Frank Hatton — who was defending only a 2,000-vote majority — to meet with the Council's housing chiefs to press their case. On 15th October, the Council promised a comprehensive fumigation and disinfection of the District Centre and neighbouring homes. Two days later, the squatters withdrew, and a crowd of 60 blocked the traffic on Moss Lane East. The police responded heavy-handedly, tipping over a pram with a baby still inside and pinning the father down so hard his arm broke. Speaking to *Red Weekly*, John Miller, press spokesperson for the Moss Side Neighbourhood Council, branded the police attack "entirely unprovoked", while Tom McClure, a committee member, added, "we are more determined than ever to step up the fight. Moss Side is just the tip of the iceberg. If they defeat us it will close the door on future tenants' struggles in Manchester."[4]

The following year McClure would run as candidate for the Council ward of Moss Side, standing for the Moss Side Neighbourhood Council as an independent tenant representative. He lost narrowly, with the campaign group Manchester and Salford Housing Action (MASHA) claiming that the rain had suppressed the tenant vote, electors in the District Centre opting to stay home.[5] This occupation of the council house in 1974 and subsequent fielding of a candidate was the crescendo of a wave of tenant and resident action in Moss Side that had been building since the late 1960s. The predecessor organisation to the Neighbourhood Council, the Housing Action Group, had led the opposition to the Council's programme of slum clearance in the neighbourhood. Woven through the housing agenda of these organisations was a wider politics of anti-racism and combating police abuses. Gus John, later the chair of the Moss Side Defence Committee during the 1981 uprising, reflected on the situation he encountered in Moss Side in 1971, the year he arrived:

The local authority was doing compulsory purchases and knocking down houses which were actually rather sturdy — some of them had fallen into disrepair but structurally they were pretty fine. There were campaigns to save these houses because people were not enamoured with what they had seen in Hulme — these deck access crescent buildings, which were not just an eyesore, became very dangerous after a while. But the two things that stuck out for me were, first, a lot of young people coming out of school and being unemployed for a long time. The second thing that was obvious was the way in which the police operated within the community — they tended to see Black people as exotic.[6]

Slum Clearance Since the War

Tenant reactions to slum clearance swung back and forth over the middle decades of the twentieth century. During the 1950s the Council demolished an estimated 46,000 homes. To rehouse the inner-city working class it had pursued a policy of overspill estates outside the city limits, built along the principles of Wythenshawe. At this point, many tenants were in favour of clearance. Wartime damage plus lack of repairs meant the old terraces were in a parlous state. In part, this was the self-fulfilling result of the clearance zones — what landlord would pay for repairs in a house that was due to be demolished at some point anyway? In 1956, tenants in Harpurhey, dreading another winter in their leaking homes, presented a 112-signature petition to Council planners calling for their demolition. A further 800 names were tallied in Miles Platting, while 30 mothers from Collyhurst led a protest march to the Town Hall. In Greenheys, Hulme, tenants gathered a petition of 2,000 signatures and held a rally demanding that their area be declared a slum-clearance zone. An estimated 1,000 people attended.[7]

The pressure for clearance was building. But by 1960 the rate of rebuilding was nowhere near the amount still to be demolished. Cheetham MP Harold Lever pointed out that there were still 60,000 homes to be cleared, but the Council was only building 1,500 per year. At that rate it would take 40 years to complete the process — condemning tenants to a lifetime in conditions that would have seemed bad in the nineteenth century. New directives were issued in 1961 to force the pace and expand the clearance zones. Vast holes opened up in the inner city.

The problem of where to rehouse the tenants remained, and, with the Council's efforts to build overspill estates stymied by the lack of available land, it began to embrace system-built high-rises in the inner city. Volume builders provided contracts to the Council to create the components for modular housing at scale. It appeared to be the solution to the problem and was heavily supported in the local press. This style of housing emerged all over the city, but the flagship development was in Hulme. Here, architects Wilson and Womersley, who had previously worked on Sheffield's Park Hill Estate, were contracted to produce a masterplan for the district. Its centrepiece would be Hulme 5, the Crescents. Designed to hark back to the sweeping Georgian crescents of Bath, the four giant structures were capable of housing 13,000 people. Their ambition was laudable, but cost-cutting and corruption by the system-build companies saw corners cut and the quality suffer — something which soon became apparent to the new tenants, who moved in when they opened in 1971.

But by this point, opinion was moving against slum clearance too. There were two proximate causes for this. First, the clearance zones began to move out of the immediate inner city, where the oldest and worst stock was, to encompass neighbourhoods with a generally better condition of housing. Improvement seemed to some a more attractive alternative to demolition. Second, it became increasingly obvious that the alternative to the old "slums", which was beginning to emerge in Hulme and elsewhere, was no better, and in many cases worse. These trends emerged clearly in Moss Side.

In 1969 the houses around Denmark Road were declared a slum-clearance zone. This area was characterised by three-storey terraced houses, run-down, but not fundamentally unsound. It was home to a large element of Manchester's Black community and a wide network of their cultural and social institutions, including venues like the Reno, the importance of which throughout the 1930s to 1950s we have already seen. By the 1960s, *Windrush*-era migration had drastically increased the Black population, with 4,000 Caribbean-born people living in Manchester in 1961. Much of this population was concentrated in the area around Moss Side, a place that was safe for Black people, in contrast to areas of the city marked by racist hostility.[8] Its proximity to Trafford Park and the expanding hospital also made many jobs easily accessible. Finally, exclusions of people born outside the country from Council housing also was a significant "push" factor, forcing recent migrants into private lets.

In Joe Pemberton's novel *Forever and Ever Amen*, he tells the story of James, a nine-year-old living in Moss Side in the late 1960s, a fictionalised version of himself. The narrative switches between memories of James' life in St Kitts and in Moss Side, prior to the clearances and the family's move to the overspill in Ashton in 1970. Through a child's-eye view it captures something of the world-shaking effects of the clearances:

Only last week it had been a row of houses. Fairlaw Street, next to St Bees Street next to another road James couldn't remember the name of. Each house had three floors and a million stairs to the top. Only last week the streets were full of kids playing catch and cars driving past the women gossiping on the corner. But not any more, all that was gone and all that was left was a pool the size of a school yard and a reflection of the church spire.[9]

In many cases Black people had bought their homes through syndicate savings schemes, and homeownership was higher among Black residents than white ones.[10] This means that the the Council's compulsory purchase orders, aside from breaking up the community, also had a disproportionate impact on the asset wealth of Black migrants. As they watched the future emerge in neighbouring Hulme, realising that this was the life planned after the clearances in Moss Side, residents were determined to hold onto their homes and communities.

The Moss Side Housing Action Group (later Neighbourhood Council) — branded "Black power boys, parasites and stirrers" by the Tory councillor for Moss Side (a comment widely condemned, including by his Labour ward colleagues) — agitated for greater community consultation on the programme of slum clearances.[11] They refused to meet Council chiefs in the Town Hall, instead demanding that they came to Moss Side to meet with the community. Their newspaper, *Moss Side News,* had a circulation of 1,500, sold through the network of local newsagents, providing comprehensive information to residents on the progress of slum clearance. In its editorial for its March 1970 edition, commenting on plans for the rehousing of 2,650 families, it asked, "Is the Town Hall purposely destroying a multi-racial community or is it bureaucratic bungling of the worst kind?"[12]

The Moss Side Housing Action Group was just one of many tenants groups that had sprung up across the city in the 1970s to demand improved conditions. In some cases, particularly in the high-rises affected by budget cuts and a lack of maintenance, they demanded rehousing. In Hulme, after a child fell from the top floor of the Crescents in 1974, the tenants formed a campaign to have families moved out of the new buildings. In Cheetham Hill's Kennet House in 1977, a survey of tenants revealed that 87% wanted to leave, the once-futurist block ground down by lack of investment and repair.[13] In other cases, tenant groups sought to resist slum clearance.

Manchester and Salford Housing Action was formed in March 1973 to provide resources and support to the different tenant groups across the city. Its composition was largely middle-class activists, academics and professionals — though it worked in partnership with a range of tenant groups across the city of a more proletarian character. Its central demand, echoed in the Housing Action Group and others, for greater public participation in planning was in tune with the mood of the times — Arthur Skeffington's 1969 national report *People and Planning* made similar arguments. In its newsletter of June 1975, it celebrated the abandonment of the slum clearance programme in favour of the introduction of General Improvement Areas — funds to repair and maintain older housing stock. "Even the most dogmatic of the old 'I can spot a slum at 200 yards brigade' are now talking about flexibility, the virtues of Area Improvement, and the need to involve residents in decision making."[14] Although, it added, community action was unlikely to be the primary cause for the about-face — far more significant was the question of money and the expense involved in demolition and rebuild.

The politics of slum clearance and the problems that began to emerge in the system-build housing from the mid-1970s tell us much about the fate of the Modernist vision for the city at the dawn of the postwar period. Accelerating deindustrialisation was rapidly destroying the ground on which the modern city was supposed to be built. The net figures for job decline in Manchester between 1971-1997 are 90,000, or a 26.2% decline. More than half (48,000) of these were in the 1970s alone, two-thirds of the region.[15] These figures hid a more dramatic picture sector by sector — service jobs increased but the overall picture is of decline, because the loss of industrial jobs was so extreme. Manufacturing, textiles, engineering and distribution were typically concentrated in larger firms, and were vulnerable to restructurings in the economy. Between 1962 and 1972 the inner core of Manchester lost 30,000 manufacturing jobs — a fall of over a third.[16] In the 1970s this collapse accelerated, with 40,000 jobs lost. By 1997 a further 39,000 had gone. Across these three decades, then, over 100,000 jobs disappeared. The remaining jobs that were available were increasingly part-time — the loss was of full-time employment, and the bulk of people losing their jobs were men — 81,000 between 1971-1997, again with almost half lost in the 1970s alone. Across the same period, only 5,000 part-time roles were created and taken by men. In all, there was a 38.1% decline in male employment, as compared to 9.5% in female employment.

The collapse of industry in Manchester ended a city whose economy was based on the productivist primary circuit of capital. This of course was happening across the industrialised Global North. What followed was an interregnum as two political visions for the future developed in tandem. On the one hand were the politics of the neoliberals and New Right, who sought to cut back the social democratic state and reorientate state power towards the promotion of market forces. On the other was a socialist-inspired approach that sought greater democracy in the economy, extended state spending and investment, and control on capital implemented. As we know today, this contest over the new settlement after the collapse of social democracy would ultimately be won by the neoliberals. In the next two chapters we will trace the political battles of this interregnum, first showing the defeats inflicted by Thatcher on the left, then the roll-out of neoliberalism at an urban scale — where Manchester was the model city. This, we will go on to argue, paved the way for the return of the rentier.

The Rise of the New Urban Left

This account of the contradictory politics of the slum clearances and inner-city policy by Manchester City Council in the aftermath of World War II helps us to understand the context for the rise of what John Gyford termed the "New Urban Left".[17] The New Urban Left arose, he argued, in part as a reaction to the postwar traditions of "municipal Labourism" — the political machines that had emerged to manage the social democratic consensus, with local authorities set up as key pillars of the wider welfare state. But as that consensus broke down, cracks began to show in the edifice of municipal Labourism. Assessing its legacy, Gyford wrote: "usually it did the right things *for* people; but sometimes it could do the wrong things *to* people; and only rarely had it previously discussed either of those things *with* people".[18]

This complex relationship between sometimes high-handed and closed Labour Town Hall administrations and the residents of the cities they governed contributed to the widespread unpopularity of the Labour Party at the end of the 1960s. Councils also became embroiled in scandals surrounding planning and housing, particularly around the often too cosy relationships with system-build companies; while the disappointments of the first Wilson administration compounded Labour's unpopularity at a national level. "If any single set of events can be said to have eased the way for the eventual emergence of local socialism", he writes, "it was, paradoxically enough, the massive anti-government swings from Labour to the Conservatives in the local elections of 1967 and 1968."[19] This had the effect of knocking out the powerbases of the entrenched municipal old right. The groups that took over once Labour regained power in local authorities (in Manchester, the brief period of Tory rule was 1967-1970), while not being drawn from the left themselves, permitted a certain flexibility and openness which offered space over the following decade for the left to assert itself.

Gyford also traced the impact of deindustrialisation on the ability of the traditional base of the Labour Party to replicate itself. This effect was particularly felt in highly unionised workplaces — engineering, transport and logistics, and industrial production. The shifting of employment into white-collar sectors, spurred by the dramatic expansion in clerical and public-sector jobs since the war, particularly in health, education and local government, and the fact that these workplaces — particularly in the public sector — tended to be highly unionised, was influencing the composition of the Labour Party. It was less proletarian, more middle-class; a class character compounded in Manchester which had always had a larger middle class presence than comparable northern cities.

At the same time, views on the left towards local government was changing. Here, the long effect of the community action movement — which the previously examined tenant and resident groups can be seen as an expression of — played a role, leading to a more sophisticated engagement with the Labour Party by sections of the left which in the 1960s had turned away from the party. Furthermore, new theorizations of the local state, influenced partly by the thought of Ralph

Miliband, meant that the left began to see an opportunity within the democratic aspects of the local state to use it as a counter-weight to corporatist tendencies and a platform for the advance of open government and democracy. This theoretical framework provided a justification for the left to be involved in local government — something of a shift from the middle decades of the twentieth century, where national government had been the major focus of the Labour left.

The fizzling out of both the first (post-1956) and second (post-1968) New Lefts in Britain, and their failure to form mass parties or organisations of their own, also acted as a spur to those who sought a re-engagement with the Labour Party.[20] There was therefore a degree of pragmatism to the move, and it represented in its way a rejection of ultra-left sectarianism and an attempt to influence the mainstream. With this came the influence and concerns of new social forces which had emerged after the moments of the New Left. The New Urban Left was anti-racist, feminist, anti-homophobic; it was liberatory in multiple senses and drew much of its strength from the "new social movements". It drew little distinction between parliamentary and extra-parliamentary politics and saw itself as an expression of wider political movements and trends in society. These politics drew the ire of the right, which was quick to brand this new variant of Labour the "loony left", but to the left themselves it was a badge of pride — Ken Livingstone, after taking the Greater London Council in 1981, described his cohort as "the post-1968 generation in politics".[21] We might here identify the women's movement as having among the greatest significance for wider New Urban Left municipal politics, due to its trenchant critiques of the male-dominated and hierarchical traditions of municipal labourism.

One of the paradoxes which emerged across the 1970s

for this new municipal left was that the things they regarded as their greatest successes — such as public ownership, the welfare state and municipal housing — were often considered by the working class themselves as part of a general force that was oppressing them. Relatedly, there was growing concern over centralising and unaccountable bureaucracies that managed these public services. A current of thinking on the left that grew throughout the decade posed greater participation, decentralisation and democracy as a route out of the impasse — a way to discover a "socialism of a different kind".[22]

If all these ideas and tendencies were in the mix post-1968, gradually making their way into the Labour Party and towards local government, there was one key impetus above all that cohered and shaped the agenda of the New Urban Left in this period. This was the resistance to the cuts which Labour began to bring in nationally after 1975. A large brunt of this fell on local government — Antony Crosland's famous speech outside Manchester Town Hall in May 1975 made clear that "the party's over" for Labour councils. The aftermath of the IMF bailout and the introduction of the programme of cuts, properly beginning the neoliberal period, sparked a wave of anti-cuts opposition which snowballed across the following decade. Local government became a target and the left moved to its defence.

Writing in 1984, Doreen Massey saw in the experimentations of the New Urban Left a potential socialist response to the crisis of social democracy — a rebuke to the "great moving right show" which could be fought on the left's terms. The political struggle was live, and the future was not predetermined. "Thatcher's attacks on local authorities were not simply because they are big spenders", she wrote, "but because *they have the potential to show that there is an alternative*. The basis for the defence of local authorities *must not* simply be 'defensive.'"[23]

The New Urban Left in Manchester

This picture provides us with the general outline and common trends of the New Urban Left during the 1970s and 1980s. In reality, each area which saw left administrations in the early 1980s had their own specificities. It may make more sense to speak of New Urban Lefts in the plural. Recent work has been done re-evaluating the experience of these lefts — with London's GLC, the "Socialist Republic of South Yorkshire" in Sheffield and Liverpool's left administration all having been the subjects of studies.[24] Manchester, by contrast, has received comparatively less attention.

The trajectory and timeline of Manchester's New Urban Left is slightly different. While in London and Sheffield the left had taken power by the early 1980s, in Manchester it took five years of internecine conflict as the left inched towards a majority position within the ruling Labour group, winning selection by selection and taking "unwinnable" seats, all while trying to shape the agenda and policy within the party and the city more broadly towards a "no cuts, no redundancies" position. Then, as we shall see, a section of the New Urban Left *remained in power* throughout the 1980s. While the GLC was abolished, giving it a sort of heroic aura, Liverpool and Lambeth went down in dramatic defeat, with coucillors surchanged, and many of Sheffield's key figures became MPs, in Manchester the key leadership remained *in situ* well into the 1990s, steering the city's journey towards the embrace of the Thatcher consensus.

In 1970, though, Labour was out of power in the city, the

Council was facing increasingly strident opposition to its housing agenda and the left was reconstituting itself within the Constituency Labour Parties (CLPs). Among the earliest in Manchester was a cohort of key women in the CLPs: Kath Robinson, Val Stevens, Frances Done and Kath Fry. Stevens would chair the Equal Opportunities Committee and become deputy leader in the left administration of the 1980s; Done would be the influential Chair of Finance; Robinson the deputy leader in the 1990s; and Fry would provide a detailed account of the left takeover in her unpublished book *Manchester 1984*.[25] By 1971 Labour were back in control of the Council, led by elements of the traditional municipal Labourist right. The party fared poorly in the 1975 local elections, losing seats to the Tories. The cuts agenda from 1976 onwards cohered the city's left into a general anti-cuts position. This included elements of the community action movement, with Manchester and Salford Housing Action joining the broad anti-cuts campaign at the end of 1976.[26] It was through this broad anti-cuts movement of the late 1970s and early 1980s that one Richard Leese, a youth worker and mathematics teacher who would later become the Labour leader of Manchester City Council, got involved in politics.

Another critical figure in the rise of Manchester's New Urban Left was Graham Stringer from Beswick, who in the summer of 1974 returned to the city after studying chemistry at Sheffield University. Alongside him was another recent graduate, of the London School of Economics, Pat Karney, who was from Collyhurst. Both threw themselves into the growing political contestation. Karney would later reflect on their return to the city, saying "the young Turks were back on the scene... we were a new phenomenon in the Labour Party and the old stagers didn't really know where we were coming from or how to handle us".[27] By 1977 they had enough support to become chair (Stringer) and secretary (Karney) of Manchester Central CLP. In 1979 they were both elected as ward Councillors in Harpurhey, north Manchester. In time, they would take major roles in the left administration that took over in 1984, with Stringer becoming Council leader.

Trench Warfare

When Thatcher took power in 1979, urban electorates swung to Labour. In Manchester, Labour gained ten council seats over the Tories, bringing their total to 63 seats, 13 of which were a bloc of left-wingers, including Stringer and Karney. Despite having a small bloc with the Council, however, which was controlled by the right, the left had control of the District Labour Party. The two groups were headed for a collision course. At the time, Thatcher was determined to cut back the powers of local government through the reduction of their direct grants from national government. In 1980, the District Party proposed a clear "no cuts, no rent rises, no rate rises" line. Come budget day, however, the right-controlled Council leadership moved for £13.7m worth of cuts. After the left bloc of 13 councillor refused to vote with the leadership, they were expelled from the Labour group. At the time this was completely unprecedented. What followed was a four-year campaign by the left to fight the cuts and organise a takeover of the Council.

Here it is important to be specific about the dividing line between the right and left. Often this was not entirely clear-cut — both sides had a broad commitment to the social democratic programme of delivering services, and the old "right" council was behind policies like the city's status as the world's first Nuclear Free Zone in 1980 (a policy pushed by those Communist Party-aligned elements of Labour which were concentrated in the engineering districts and who also folded under the leadership of the right). What set the two sides apart were principally three things. The first, and most significant, was the question of whether councillors would be prepared to take action that was potentially illegal to protect and extend services. Setting a no-cuts budget was out of the question for the right for this very reason. The left were more open to attempting to bend and if necessary break the law. Second, was the centrality of the equal opportunities agenda to the programme of the left. On gay rights and women's liberation, the left were a sharp contrast to the traditional social attitudes of the old right. Finally, the left's commitment to open government marked it out from the previous administration. Rolled into this was the desire to democratise services and do away with some of the old traditions, like the practice of wearing evening suits in full council and the trappings of the Lord Mayor. Beneath these three core principles, varying hues of left were held in a single bloc.

So, the battle lines were drawn. The fight took the form of a grinding numbers game. Each cycle of elections offered an opportunity for the left to win selections and expand their number in the Council chamber. Gradually, the left bloc increased over the next four years. At the same time, the left group of councillors and party activists began to caucus in secret, away from the structures of the Council, in local pubs such as the Rising Sun. Meeting on a Sunday afternoon, this allowed the left to maintain strategic independence, plotting selection battles, shadowing all committees of the Council and beginning to outline their programme for running the city.

In 1984 the Labour Party fought the local elections on the left's manifesto and returned to power with ten new left-wing councillors, including Richard Leese and John Clegg, a council tenant and party activist who would go on to play a major role in the Council's equal opportunities agenda. The left now had a slight numerical majority within the Labour group, with 42 councillors out of 78. Further negotiations brough four more on side, bringing the broad left bloc to 47, a clear majority within the group but agonisingly short of a full majority within the full Council with its 99 seats. A last-ditch attempt by the leadership to expel the left councillors was quashed by the Merseyside MP Eric Heffer, then national party chair and in the party's Bennite faction, who overturned the expulsions and ordered a new AGM date to be set.[28] On the 15th May 1984, Graham Stringer and John Nicholson were elected leader and deputy leader of the group respectively, and the left took control.

The First Confrontation with Thatcher

Across the 1980s there were three major confrontations with the Thatcher government, the outcomes of which profoundly shaped the trajectory of the decade. The first was the inner-city uprisings that took place across Black neighbourhoods in English cities in 1981. The second was the miners' strike in 1984. The third and final confrontation was the 1985 rebellion by a range of Labour-held municipalities against Thatcher's proposals to bring in "rate-capping" — the imposition of restrictions on the spending powers of local government. The systematic defeat and decomposition of these oppositional social forces by the Thatcher government allowed her to secure key strategic goals: the releasing of controls on finance via the 1986 "Big Bang", the resuscitation of the private landlord through the 1988 Housing Act, and the extension of the neoliberal agenda into the heart of urban Britain.

The first of these confrontations came barely a year after her election, beginning in St Pauls, Bristol in April 1980. The wider wave would come the year after, in Brixton the following April, and then Toxteth in Liverpool and Moss Side in July 1981. The wider backdrop to the uprising was the particularly concentrated way in which unemployment fell on inner-city Black communities. In Manchester, job losses had not fallen evenly across the city, and were most dramatic in the inner core, where unemployment was between 26-32%.[29] Race was a further structuring factor — most Black people were employed in skilled work, in Trafford Park and in the hospitals.[30] Deindustrialisation and cuts in public expenditure caused Black unemployment most acutely. By the 1980s much of the Black working-age population were unable to find work after their traditional industries had collapsed.[31] Added to this was a steady rise in racist sentiment among the political mainstream since the late 1960s, and outright street fascism throughout the 1970s with the growth of the National Front, who had staged provocative marches through Black neighbourhoods in Manchester in 1977.

The proximate cause, though, was police provocation and abuse. Here the role of Chief Constable James Anderton of the Greater Manchester Police is central. Described by anti-racist campaigner Gus John as a "foul human being", Anderton was the city's deeply reactionary and religiously motivated police chief.[32] By 1981 he had been in the role for five years, restructuring the Greater Manchester Police along the lines of the Met and the Royal Ulster Constabulary by introducing the mobile "Tactical Aid Unit" (TAU). A moralist and homophobe, he was noted for his frequent raids on Canal Street, the centre of the city's gay community. He didn't believe in "policing by consent" and instead opted for "hard" tactics. Throughout the 1980s he enjoyed the full support of Thatcher and was in many ways the polar opposite of the New Urban Left — much of their activity across the 1980s, right down to the Council's attempts to extend licensing, was a generalised push against Anderton and everything he represented.

Anderton's policing strategies were the source of serious friction in Moss Side, where tensions between the police and community rose across 1980. On 16th August a march protesting the police harassment of Black residents took place, and community representatives warned of the likelihood of unrest. In September that year Anderton made a speech where he denounced "race relations" as being "infiltrated by anti-establishment factions, one of whose aims is to continuously impede the police".[33] The following year, it was discovered that the police were holding a cache of illegal weapons in Moss Side police station. The tension ratcheted across 1981, with events like the New Cross Fire, which killed 13 Black people in London in January, standing seemingly as proof of the police and authorities' indifference to Black lives. On 2nd March, 20,000 people marched through London carrying placards that read: "Thirteen Dead, Nothing Said" and "No Police Coverup". In July a "violent eruption of protest", in Gus John's words, took place across five days. There were reports of police provocation, in reference to the events in Toxteth the weekend before, taunting local youths that they were "too soft to riot".[34] On 8th July around 300-1000 people picketed Moss Side police station.[35] Anderton responded with force, disavowing community relations and dispatching the TAU in a way reminiscent of police tactics in Northern Ireland.

The uprising, not spontaneous or irrational, was a legitimate expression of grievances against the police and wider racism in British society. In Defence Committee member Eloise

Edwards' words, they "were an attempt from people in the area to put a lot of the wrongs to right".[36] The antipathy towards the police was deep-seated — even a 61-year-old Conservative-leaning white man from the neighbourhood described the attack on the police station as the best thing to have happened in years.[37]

It left an enduring mark on the urban politics of the 1980s across both left and right. On the right, as we shall see later, the uprising was used by Michael Heseltine, Minister for the Environment throughout the first part of the Thatcher government, as the pretext to expand property-led regeneration into the heart of Britain's inner cities, via the instrument of the Urban Development Corporation. Restriction on the licences of venues such as the Reno in Moss Side was an immediate follow on from the uprising, an attack on associational life in the neighbourhood, but the full "retaking" of the inner city was to come. On the left, in Manchester and elsewhere, the outcome of the uprising was two-fold. First was an emphasis on police monitoring. Second was a wider anti-racist politics, bound intimately within the broader political project of the New Urban Left.

The Left in Power

"Manchester is being destroyed before our eyes." So opened the 1984 Manchester Labour manifesto:

> The re-election of the Conservative Government means yet more misery, neglect and high unemployment for the people of this city. Unemployment now hits one in every four households in Manchester. We need a massive injection of resources into our services, the creation of new worthwhile jobs, a challenge to urban decay and positive

action to end all discrimination based on sex and race. Otherwise the people of Manchester will continue to be the victims of a Government that no longer cares about the quality of life for working women and men.[38]

30,000 copies were printed and distributed to all Council employees, as well as put on general sale for 20p a copy — it was a sell-out publication.

The manifesto provides us with the clear sweep of the left's agenda on taking control. Its core priorities were to defend jobs, improve housing standards, promote peace and equal opportunities, promise open government and ensure economic development. We see within its pages the fruit of the previous decade's struggles. The commitments to open government, making the workings of the Council accessible, promoting channels for the public to input into decision-making and devolving services to the neighbourhood level appear a rebuke to the high-handed municipal Labourism of the 1970s. On planning, it boldly stated: "We must avoid repeating the planning mistakes of the past… We must involve local residents and community groups much more closely in decisions on planning and land use." Public land would be held by the city for economic development, cooperative enterprise would be promoted, contracts given only to companies with good labour conditions and which complied with the city's Nuclear Free Zone policy. On housing, it stated "We are against the privatisation of public assets", and pledged to stop the sale of Council houses to private developers and campaign against Right to Buy, initiate Council house-building programmes and ensure the end of system-build. Tenants associations would be supported and promoted by the Council and given representation on housing committees and a role in estate management.

The equal opportunities agenda also assumed a central place in the Manifesto's priorities. It stated:

We are totally opposed to sexism and racism in all their forms and to discrimination against lesbians and gay men and disabled people. We are committed to ensuring that the Council adopts policies to combat all direct and indirect forms of discrimination based on sex, race, sexual orientation or disability.

Here, it pledged to establish an equal opportunities structure within the Council, to fight discrimination, improve child care, continue to fund and expand the Gay Information Centre (which was the first such publicly funded organisation in Britain) and make Manchester "a city at the centre of opposition to racism". It cited immigration law, employment, education, housing and policing practices as areas where discrimination was "particularly severe" and pledged to establish a Police Monitoring Group to campaign for "real accountability" over the police.

The incoming administration formed a range of Council committees to drive forward the work outlined in the manifesto. The bulk of the new structures fell under the equalities agenda, but the first to be established was the Campaign and Public Information Subcommittee. Its chair was Pat Karney, secretary of the Labour Group. Its first task was the relaunch of the Council's magazine, *The Mancunian Way*, as *The Manchester Magazine*. Published every two months between July 1985 and May 1986, and thereafter monthly until the early 90s, it offers a fascinating insight into the priorities of the Council across these years. In its inaugural edition it laid out the priorities of the new administration.[39]

The local Tories hated the magazine, dubbing it "socialist propaganda on the rates", but for the insurgent Council it was an essential tool to defend its agenda in the face of massive assault. The equalities agenda in particular attracted the criticism of the *Manchester Evening News*, which used every opportunity to castigate the left administration. "It was incessant", said Clegg, who became vice-chair of the Equal Opportunities Committee in 1986 and was a major force behind anti-deportations work and in getting the Gay Information Centre funded:

> They would come to meetings and they would take notes of what people said in meetings and then you would be quoted in the paper. But they would only use half of what they said, it was the usual sort of story, you got misquoted. It was sensationalised.[40]

One particularly egregious example he recalled was when the Council gave a £250 grant to a gay men's group to plant flowers in Piccadilly Gardens in commemoration of gay men killed in Nazi concentration camps. "That was on the front page of the *Evening News*. 'City council give grants to gays to plant flowers in Piccadilly.' It didn't say anything about the politics of it, it just said that's what we gave them."

Great strides were made in equal opportunities in the first year of the administration, and a great deal of effort was put into the work. Manchester was one of the first councils in the country to establish a paid officer for each minority, and can justifiably be regarded as at the cutting-edge of this agenda. Combatting the misogyny of traditional Labour politics was high on the agenda, particularly for the new women councillors. As just one example, at the first Labour Group meeting in 1979, one old right-winger said to Kath Robinson, "You should be at home making your husband's tea". He was stunned by her reply — "He's at home making mine".[41] A key issue taken up immediately under this agenda was childcare provision. A set of "under fives" centres were established across the city, with the Town Hall itself being turned into a creche.

The struggle against deportations became more prominent as time went on. A series of increasingly high-profile deportation attempts were made, and the Councils' equalities unit was a key part in resisting the Home Office's efforts to deport. In March 1985, Val Stevens, chair of the Equalities Committee, said:

> For people to be deported because their marriage has broken down cannot be fair or just. These racist immigration laws bring racism in their wake and individual cases of injustice are bound to follow. We will continue to fight until families and individuals are allowed to stay and are reunited.[42]

The Second and Third Confrontations with Thatcher

Thatcher knew that to implement her programme — to break the bonds on finance and landlords that had been in place in Britain since the start of the postwar era, and to "change the soul" of the country — she would be forced to confront and defeat the social forces that stood in her way. We have seen how the first confrontation was with Britain's inner-city Black communities. The second was with the most powerful of her opponents, the trade unions. The strategy for confrontation was laid out in a report 1977 by Nicholas Ridley, a key ideological ally of Thatcher. In the report, he proposed how the government could fight, and defeat, a major trade union in a nationalised industry. The third, following on from the defeat of the miners, was local government.

The left took power in Manchester two months into the 1984-5 miners' strike. Around the strike an astonishing solidarity movement emerged, drawing in support from across the country. The struggle of the miners was integrated with the wider confrontations with Thatcher, particularly in the cities, where left-led councils coordinated support for the strike. Links were forged between the women's movement, the peace movement, the gay liberation movement and the strikes. Other trade unions made donations to the National Union of Mineworkers (NUM). Toxteth, one of the epicentres of the 1981 uprising, was the first area in Merseyside to set up a support group, being set up "overnight" at the end of April. Doreen Massey, in her 1984 essay "Beyond the Coalfields", gives us a sense of that time. "There was a feeling that at last a trade union battalion, the most militant, had gone into action. As the strike developed, the significance of the support groups became clearer. It seemed increasingly that their work was crucial to the miners' power and their chances of success. A new do it yourself politics flourished out of necessity." That year, Women Against Pit Closures handled nearly £2m in solidarity donations.[43]

In Manchester, the Council and Labour Party immediately moved to support the strike. Clegg recalled the huge levels of support. "There were collections going on all over the place." For solidarity parties, "councillors were dishing out street licences like toffees... we would hold regular events and parties for the miners' children, collections of food, all sorts of things like that." The hire fee was waived for the Free Trade Hall for a major rally, where NUM leader Arthur Scargill spoke after a march of 10,000 through the city centre, something the Tory councillors tried to block and get charged to Stringer personally, to no avail. Everything was considered, up to the Council chopping up old furniture from its housing stock and sending them to the pit villages as firewood. "People were looking at every way they could to support the miners," said Clegg. "Right across the board."

At the same time, Labour local authorities were gearing up for their own fight with Thatcher. A sense that a dramatic confrontation was coming had pervaded the February 1984 Labour local government conference held in Nottingham. Eric Heffer, speaking from the platform, reminded assembled delegates that it was the fiftieth anniversary of the destruction of Red Vienna by the guns of the right-wing Dollfuß government.[44] Some months later, at the follow-up conference in Sheffield, a position was adopted to not comply with the government's rate-capping. This was a deliberate attack on the financial capacities of local government, and in turn, its ability to deliver and maintain services. The strategy adopted was to run down the clock beyond budget day without setting a rate. It was hoped that if enough councils took this route, the government would be forced into concessions. This had been inspired by Liverpool Council, which in the first half of 1984 had adopted this strategy, forcing the government to back down in July in exchange for limited concessions.

On the 19th July 1984, Thatcher addressed a meeting of the backbench 1922 Committee in Parliament. In it, she remarked on the defeat of Galtieri's forces in the Falklands War two years previous. The "enemy without" was vanquished — now the country faced an "enemy within, just as dangerous and in a way more difficult to fight". These forces, the "Miners' leaders, Liverpool and some local authorities" were, she said, "dangerous to liberty and a scar across the face of our country".[45]

The position to not set a rate was made official in full Council in September, where a motion was carried, opposing Thatcher's rate cap, expressing support to those councils opposing it and setting up a campaign to force the government to change course. By that time, the miners were seven months into their strike. Across the next eight months a "Petition for Manchester" garnered 100,000 signatures and coordination with the other councils opposing the cap continued. In February 1985 Stringer and Nicholson led a delegation to Downing Street to lobby the government to change course — but the Secretary of State refused to meet them. In March that year Stringer outlined the goal to get through the "April 1st barrier" without fixing a rate. A rally was organised in Albert Square to bolster support for the position and 10,000 turned out.[46] By this point, the miners had been defeated.

By now, the deadline to set a rate was bearing down on the Council. It would come down to arithmetic. A careful balancing act was required between the left and what Stringer termed the "three opposition groupings" — the 14 Tories, six Liberals and 28 councillors of the Labour right. The broad left had a majority of one, but eight of these couldn't be relied upon, putting the left in a minority. Three full council meetings took place between 22nd and 31st March, where voting came down to the wire. The no cuts position was defeated by the Labour right voting with the opposition Tories and Liberals. But they refused to back a Tory budget, so a backbench Labour budget was passed. The attempt to get past the April 1st barrier without setting a rate had failed. On 10th April, Stringer addressed the District Party: "Our withdrawal from the national campaign is a real disgrace".[47] But without the numbers in the council chamber, there was nothing to be done. Across the country, councils withdrew from the rate-capping rebellion, until only Liverpool and Lambeth remained — with councillors later surcharged. The third confrontation, like the second, had ended in defeat.

The "Lingering Death"

The front page of the May 1985 *Manchester Magazine* depicted two doors, side by side. One was 10 Downing Street with protestors standing outside. The other was of a council house, daubed in racist graffiti. The double issue highlighted the twin concerns of the day. On one hand, the door was "closed to democracy" — highlighting the recent defeat of the rate-capping rebellion. The other, was a focus on the anti-racist and wider equalities agenda of the Council.

John Nicholson has characterised this period, between the defeat over the rate-capping in 1985 and Thatcher's election victory in 1987, as one of "lingering death" as the left tried to hold on to and extend some of the gains that had been made in the first year of the administration.[48] This particularly included fighting to hold onto the restorations in the housing budget so that adequate improvements could be made, and around the consolidation of the equal opportunities agenda. The cover of the *Manchester Magazine* in May was instructive — with a focus on combatting racist abuse that was being directed towards Black tenants. "This is a very serious problem", said Nicholson, then chair of the Housing Committee:

> It is not just a dispute between neighbours of people who don't get on with each other. It's persistent harassment of people because of their colour. It interferes with the quality

of their lives on council estates. The Council has to look at a way of dealing with it and put it at the forefront of tenancy arrangements.[49]

The highest-profile aspect of the anti-racist struggle during this time that the Council actively supported was anti-deportation. This issue had been growing throughout the years of left administration — the *Manchester Magazine* in November 1984 details the first campaigns against deportation of Manchester citizens. One name among the four mentioned is Viraj Mendis. Mendis, a Sri Lankan student and political activist, had lived in the UK for 13 years. At that time, there was a ruling that anyone who had stayed for ten years would become a citizen — but the Tories had extended this to 14, making Mendis illegal. In 1985 Mendis was visited by plainclothes policemen at his home in Hulme, taken to the airport — in the shadow of the planes — and questioned about his political affiliations. He had his passport confiscated. In response, the Viraj Mendis Defence Committee was established, run by the Revolutionary Communist Group, of which Mendis was a member. It was given offices by the Council in the top rooms of the Town Hall, with Clegg instrumental in arranging this. By May that year, 15,000 signatures were handed to Thatcher against his deportation, as Mendis feared for his life on returning due to his support for the Tamils. In March 1987 he was given sanctuary in the Church of Ascension in Hulme, where the rector, Father John Methuen, housed him for over two years.

The opposition to the campaign — from the *Manchester Evening News* in particular — was frenzied. The final confrontation revolved around Mendis' application to a job within the Race Unit, which despite being approved through a legitimate interview procedure, was widely condemned both by Labour councillors and the paper. They pilloried the post and the appointee, just as they had responded to the overall campaign with a mixture of ignorance, disdain and overt racism. The funding ended up being blocked by the leadership. In 1987 the party lost seats, and the "Viraj Mendis factor" was blamed. At dawn on 18th January 1989, 100 police officers smashed their way into the church and took Mendis, ending his 671 days of sanctuary. Within 55 hours he was on a flight to Sri Lanka.

New Economic Strategies

In this same period, the Council began tentative forays into alternative economic strategies. Following the lead set by Sheffield and the GLC, the Council established the Centre for Local Economic Strategies (CLES). A strong showing for Labour nationwide in the local elections of 1986 raised hopes that Thatcher could be defeated in the looming general election. In November that year, Council leader Graham Stringer pronounced that "Manchester Council rejects defeatist Keynesian and monetarist policies that would consign the cuts to the economic scrap heap. That is why we are developing a radical strategy for employment".[50]

CLES's launch featured David Blunkett and John Prescott, both of whom would go on to be prominent ministers in the Blair government, who spoke in front of a hand-made cloth banner. A flurry of reports and briefings followed, on worker cooperatives, municipal energy policy and planning, solutions to Black unemployment and on food sovereignty and production.[51] Many of these were grounded in histories of worker control and socialism. The most interesting of the early outputs was a report by Robin Murray, former chair of the GLC Enterprise Board, commissioned in late 1986 and called *Breaking with Bureaucracy: Ownership, Control and Nationalisation*. It advanced a critique of top-down "Morrisonian" nationalisation (so-called after Herbert Morrison, the influential interwar leader of London County Council who pioneered municipal ownership along corporatist lines), but affirmed the centrality of public ownership in socialist economics, the aim of which was "to change the social relations in production". Murray reflected on his experiences at the GLC and how they had been stymied by bureaucrats within the state who had been unwilling to work with the left's agenda. In a rhetorical flourish, he compared the fight for socialist economics to a "guerrilla movement" and stressed the need to build

> liberated zones within which an alternative administration is established. To maintain popular support, the new order must be a palpable improvement on the old, for on that popular support will depend the very lives of the guerrillas, as well as the progress of the movement. This is the daily democracy that characterises guerrilla struggle. At first these zones are established where the old regime is weakest, but as popular support is established and experience grows, the heartlands of the old regime are surrounded.[52]

By the time *Breaking with Bureaucracy* came out, in July 1987, it already felt like a relic. Labour's failure in the elections that year to gain national office, with Thatcher elected for a third term, dealt the final hammer-blow to aspirations of the New Urban Left. Reflecting later on the efforts of 1986, one Manchester City Council employee said the vision was for the restructuring of the economic department along the lines of Sheffield, with a whole load of teams... in the expectation of a Labour government. They imagined 60-70 people coming into the department, which would have been a massive transformation of the political considerations of the city. But all this was jettisoned when the Tories won the election.[53]

The Final Defeat
Surveying the aftermath of Thatcher's third election victory in 1987, Massey wrote:

The election of 1983 was not an aberration. The patterns that were evident then are stronger now. What happened in this election, fundamentally, was that Labour strengthened its position in its traditional bases, but failed to break out of them. The Conservatives also consolidated their hold where they were already strong. The difference is that they have power, and they have a strategy for attacking Labour's citadels, especially in the inner cities."[54]

The bitter irony of Murray's arguments about the "liberated zones" was that this was precisely the strategy the New Right were to pursue, only in reverse — building zones liberated not from capital, but from democracy.

Thatcher's third victory prompted a major debate within Manchester's Labour movement. The strategy of opposition appeared at an end. Stringer moved quickly; as soon as the election results came in he embarked on a six-week tour of every constituency party and trade union branch in the city. This great debate, which included a packed public event at the Free Trade Hall with the massed ranks of council workers, culminated in a vote of the District Party. Stringer made the case that the no cuts position that had been adhered to since 1984 would have to give way. Cuts would have to be made, with private capital, European funding and central government bid money making up the rest. There would have to be an expanded role for the private sector. At the packed meeting of delegates, 185 in attendance, the motion passed overwhelmingly with only 20 or so voting against. The cuts would happen. The die was cast and Stringer wrote a letter to Nicholas Ridley, the Conservative Minister for the Environment, that said very simply, "Okay you win, we'd like to work together with you".[55] There was a note of exhausted resignation to his missive. Reflecting on this process later to the *Manchester Evening News* political editor Ray King, Stringer described it as among the hardest things he had ever done.

The remainder of the 1980s saw further assaults on local government. At Conservative Party Conference in 1987 Thatcher made a speech that put local government firmly in the spotlight. She was determined to finish these redoubts of "municipal socialism" once and for all. The 1988 Local Government Act, the Poll Tax, and the privatisation agenda were all part of an attack on local democracy and the capacities of councils. A whole range of functions that had for generations felt like the natural patrimony of local government came under attack — planning, housing, local government finance, policing, education and urban renewal. The Housing Act also paved the way for the creation of a private rented sector that would, in time, replace council housing as the main rental tenure. In Manchester the composition of the Council was changing. Some key left figures, like John Nicholson, had already stood down. A new wave of councillors, with no hinterland in the struggles of the early 1980s, were joining the Labour Group. Neoliberalism was at the start of its long hegemony, and the entrepreneurial turn was to be its local manifestation.

Left Disintegration

As the bulk of the Labour group, and the leadership, moved towards a position of cuts and, as we shall see, an embrace of urban entrepreneurialism, a small left opposition to the Stringer leadership fought on into the early 1990s, unwilling to back down over the cuts. Over time this tendency weakened, as the leadership sidelined critics, key figures stood down and exhaustion set in after a near-decade of struggle. There was an unsuccessful attempt to challenge Stringer for the leadership, based on an unsteady alliance of the anti-Stringer left and the old Labour right. Stringer maintained his position. But the general picture of these years post-1987 is one of disintegration and defeat. A new direction had been set, and the wind had turned rapidly against the left.

If there was one final effervescent moment for the progressive spirit that had initially served to cohere the New Urban Left, it was perhaps the stance that the Council took in 1988 in the face of Thatcher's Section 28. The Council had always had a strong position against homophobia. The fight to build the Gay Information Centre, in the teeth of opposition from the *Manchester Evening News*, which sought to rubbish the project and financial objections from the officers, was hard fought. "Every other week there was something about the Gay Centre, the Gay Centre is this, the Gay Centre is that", said Clegg, who was instrumental in steering the project through the objections of the officers. At the height of the HIV/AIDS crisis the Council had been firm in pushing a clear anti-discriminatory and pro-public health line. In the pages of the *Manchester Magazine* in 1985, Paul Fairweather, the Gay Men's Officer at the Council, wrote, "Aids is not a GAY disease. Neither is it a PLAGUE".[56] In 1986 Manchester became the first council in the country to develop an AIDS policy that ensured that staff or members of the public with AIDS were not discriminated against. Their opponent was James Anderton, who attracted national condemnation when he described HIV/AIDS victims as "swirling in a human cesspit of their own making".[57] So when Section 28 was being introduced, Manchester hosted a national rally on 20th February 1988, "Never Going Underground." An estimated 20,000 people attended, with trains put on from London to bring people up. Stringer addressed the crowd, drawing the links between the assault on public services and local democracy with the attack on gay people. A concert was held in the Free Trade Hall, with performances from Jimmy Somerville, Tom Robinson and Ian McKellan.

This example helps us to nuance the argument about the so-called "u-turn". In both academic and popular literature, the idea of the 1987 u-turn in the Council's policy from an approach of "municipal socialism" to "urban entrepreneurialism" has been persistent.[58] The reality is more complicated. We can — as the next chapter will demonstrate — recognise a very real transition in policy from 1987 onwards. Cuts were made, partnership with the private sector was embraced and the Stringer leadership abandoned what had previously been its core principles. However, this discontinuity masks continuities. The Council's protest against Section 28 shows an ongoing commitment to aspects of the equal opportunities agenda (even if, as we have noted, the anti-deportation and anti-racist struggle would be sidelined). The Council's firm commitment to gay rights was made in the face of a virulently hostile media and police chief. Anderton, who left his post in 1991, also acted as a brake on the Council's attempts to create a leisure economy in the city centre, as he was decidedly against relaxation of licensing. Once he had gone, the opportunities to expand this leisure economy were widened.

Equally, the economic agenda of council intervention into the local economy, pioneered by the New Urban Left nationwide in the early 1980s (with Sheffield perhaps as the pre-eminent example) was a distinct break from the older traditions of the provision of services. It also has a clear continuity with the entrepreneurialism of the Council from the late 1980s onwards. This is a question we will explore in more detail in the next chapter — but the essential point to conclude this part with is that we might see the tendencies towards "urban entrepreneurialism" present within the Council's agenda from early on in the period of the left's control. It didn't suddenly arrive in 1987, but rather the direction chosen was a natural outgrowth of processes already in train.

One place we can see this clearly is in the pages of *The Manchester Magazine*. If we read its contents from the summer of 1984 up to 1987's u-turn and into the early 1990s, the gradual arrival of the policies that Manchester would explore with gusto after Thatcher's third victory is obvious. One example should suffice to explain this point. In November 1985 a new campaign was launched by Pat Karney called "Manchester: It's Beginning to Buzz". Two themes condensed into this campaign. First, in the vein of the commitment to open government was a desire to create a more accessible Council — the bee chosen as "an attractive and trendy way of advertising the Council's services".[59] Second, and pointing towards the wave of the future, was a look at the leisure economy of the city centre — its nightlife, its bars and its Christmas lights shows.

Councillor Jack Flanagan, chair of the Economic Development Committee, explained the significance of the campaign:

> Behind the spectacle is a serious purpose. The Council is committed to the campaign because of the place it occupies in our economic strategy — namely, the cushioning of the effects of deindustrialisation on unemployment by the creation of service jobs in the city centre.[60]

If urban entrepreneurialism emerged out of aspects of the programme of the New Urban Left, then this occurred under the conditions of defeat for the wider political left. This chapter has traced the closure of a left route out of the crises of the 1970s — the comprehensive defeat by Thatcher of her opponents across the 1980s. These political defeats had a profound impact on what was possible for left councils to achieve. Reframed in this way, it appears that the crucial threshold were those first months of 1985. The defeat of the miners, closely followed by the inability to hold the line in the rate-capping rebellion, seems to be the moment that another future of economic democracy and the expansion of public services became impossible. Under these conditions of defeat, a new order emerged. How this new order came about, and who its drivers were, is the story to which we now turn.

Chapter 4
The Manchester Model

Although the words partnership and confidence are synonymous with Manchester today, it was not always thus. The ideological tripe which was peddled by those on the far left, may, for a time, have convinced a few zealots who were against us being a democratic nation with a mixed economy. For that same length of time, however, nothing — but nothing — positive happened.

David Trippier, Minister for Housing, Inner Cities and Construction, 1987-1989

Olympic bid? What d'you fucking think this is? Summer fair on the green and whatever? This is Manchester! Are you fucking joking?

Roy Oldham, Leader of Tameside Council (apocryphal)

One story goes that as Manchester embraced an entrepreneurial agenda, clever branding and the ability to compete in a global contest of cities, one man above all was the inspiration. He was a peculiar mix of impresario, entrepreneur and blagger. He seemed so right for the city that he was dubbed "Mr Manchester" — a sort of new Manchester Man for the postmodern age. He's presented as an animating spirit through which you can trace a straight line from his enterprises of the 1980s to the gleaming towers of today.

Of course, in many accounts, "Mr Manchester" is Tony Wilson.[1] Wilson, the charismatic Granada TV presenter who moved into music, founded Factory Records and the Haçienda, which defined a sort of "Manchester sound" from this era, is a well-worn figure. Of course, this is a partial reading of what was a far larger music scene, the accumulative effect of commentators back-projecting the sound of this one label — or even one band, Joy Division — as encapsulating an entire "feel" of the era. At times it feels as though these tales have curdled into a rigid dogma. The Haçienda's haze seems to obscure more than it reveals. Perhaps there is a personal motive in play too by those who have ended up shaping the narrative — whether there is not too much at stake for these cultural commentators not to put their own youthful pill-popping at the heart of the story.

However, we are not talking about Wilson, but another "Mr Manchester". Bestowed this name by the press, he won many plaudits, dubbed by *Business Life* as "the man who gave Manchester a vision of gold". His background was in the city's theatres, and in 1985 he opened the Cornerhouse Cinema, but for nearly a decade between 1984 and 1993 he was mainly focussed on another stage entirely — chairing the bid to host the Olympic Games. Manchester made three bids in total for the 1992, 1996 and 2000 Games. Aside from the first bid, Manchester was the UK's candidate city. At the heart of all this was a man who arguably was of far greater significance than Wilson — a man named Bob Scott.

The Olympic bid sheds light upon the constellation of private sector actors who came together to exert a profound influence upon the trajectory of the city from 1985 onwards. After 1987 and the third Thatcher victory, these networks grew in importance — well-integrated into government-funded programmes like the Central Manchester Development Corporation and Hulme Regeneration Ltd. Thatcher's third term was marked especially with a focus on the inner cities, as she sought to extinguish resistance among Labour councils, which she had come to see as the last bastions of hated socialism. These apolitical (i.e., Conservative) local businessmen were seen by central government as a counterweight, undermining democratic authorities and permitting a more entrepreneurial society. It also saw the introduction of the Housing Act 1988, which created the conditions for a profitable private rented sector with the abolition of rent controls and the introduction of the "no-fault" eviction and the assured shorthold tenancy.[2]

Buffeted by these political winds emanating from Whitehall, and lubricated by the growing partnership arrangements within the city over projects like the Olympics, the role of the private sector became increasingly central to Manchester's development agenda. Key rising figures like Howard Bernstein, future Chief Executive of the Council, acquired major responsibilities in the bidding process — particularly for the third and final bid. Looking back on the bidding years from the vantage point of 2002, it was observed that "the partnership process that the Olympics so clearly symbolised led to a major reimagining of local governance... this new approach to entrepreneurial urban governance was effectively normalised in Manchester".[3] It was during this period that "entrepreneurialism" became the standard formula for cities across the Global North.[4]

The Olympic bid efforts also began almost concurrently with the high-point of the rent-capping rebellion of 1984/5. Graham Stringer, on one hand leading the Council and the Labour movement's efforts to resist Thatcher, was on the other beginning to move in the charmed circles of Bob Scott's bid team, and the bizarre Byzantine world of the International Olympic Committee (IOC).

As Council leader, Stringer was increasingly in very different spaces to the committee rooms and meeting halls of the Labour movement which had characterised his experience of the early 1980s. At the airport he met Alan Cockshaw, Chief Executive of civil engineering firm AMEC, who would come to have a key role in the regeneration of Hulme in particular. At the Ship Canal he met John Whittaker of Peel Holdings, the reclusive yet influential property magnate who flew in from his home on the Isle of Man to do business in the north-west.

These networks created a familiarity and even a sense of camaraderie with the local business grandees of the city, the new "Manchester Men" who would come to sit at the heart of the emergent "Manchester Model". Therefore, with the collapse of resistance to rate capping in 1985 and final defeat by Thatcher in 1987, these relationships with the private sector offered an alternative. A new direction crystallised around public-private partnerships. To trace this trajectory we must return to "Mr Manchester" — Bob Scott — and the origins of the bid.

Bob Scott and the First Olympic Bid

Scott wasn't from Manchester. Rather, he hailed from a military and diplomatic background. His father had a long career after the war in the diplomatic service, across Britain's retreating empire. Because of this Scott grew up abroad, in apartheid South Africa and Southern Rhodesia, where he went to school in Salisbury (now Harare). Aged 18 he went to Oxford, where he studied dramatic arts and got involved in theatre.[5]

In 1968 he was sent to Manchester on an Arts Council training programme for theatre management. He became the administrator for 69 Theatre, a new company based at the university and headed by five artistic directors. In 1973, 69 Theatre moved to what would become its permanent home — the old shell of Manchester's Royal Exchange. Scott was instrumental in negotiating the deal with the Council and the owners of the Exchange, to open a temporary theatre in the building. Greater Manchester County Council funded a ten-month run of plays in the new space in a giant 430-seat tent. The textile giant Tootal donated the fabrics. Shortly thereafter a 25-year lease was negotiated and the theatre became permanent, opening in 1976 under the new name of The Royal Exchange. It is a very early example of culture-led regeneration in the city centre.

The following year Scott moved into commercial theatre, and alongside property magnate and Brahms aficionado Raymond Unwin, worked to reopen two of the old Victorian theatres in the city centre, the Palace and the Opera House. The Palace was redesigned to the specifications of the English National Opera, with an extended deep stage. It became hugely successful, cementing their position as the northern home of the touring West End shows. But by then, Scott was looking for a new challenge. It presented itself to him one day in the summer of 1984 while broken down in a lay-by on the road to Suffolk. Through the radio came Terry Wogan, introducing the Olympics, due to open in Los Angeles later that evening. As hours rolled by Scott got thinking — why shouldn't Britain host the games? And if Britain, why not Manchester? On his return to the city he began sounding out support for the idea. By October 1984 he had had his first meeting with Graham Stringer, who agreed to support it, provided that none of the ratepayers' money was put into the bid. Scott reassured him, "if this idea takes root, when we have meetings in the Town Hall, I will pay for the coffee and biscuits".[6]

At 8.10am on 21st February 1985, Scott heard on the radio again that, in light of the great success of the LA games, Thatcher had instructed her Sports Minister to prepare a British bid. Immediately, Scott called Mike Unger, the editor of the *Evening News*. He blagged: "a Manchester Olympic Committee in the process of formation, bidding to host the Olympics". Intrigued, Unger asked for the full story by the time they went to press at 11am. Scott called round the great and the good from his phonebook, assembling a committee with himself as chair. By 11am the list went to Unger and the evening papers splashed the news: "MANCHESTER GOES FOR GOLD".[7] Within a few months the committee was formalised, the Duke of Westminster agreed to become its president and Scott had raised £180,000 from local businesses to fund the bid. But by July it was all over. Birmingham was selected as Britain's candidate city, going on to lose to Barcelona the year later. Scott, undeterred, planned to try again.

This first surge of interest in Manchester in the Olympics happened almost concurrently with the climax of the rate rebellion. In February, the month of the Olympic Committee's formation, Graham Stringer had led the delegation to Downing Street. The rate paying rebellion collapsed at the start of April 1985, the first Olympic bid was four months later. From the Council, the main engagement came from Stringer, particularly among the elected councillors. He had invited John Nicholson to be involved, bringing him to a lunch with Scott early on, but he had quickly withdrawn, believing the bid to be "bread and circuses... a complete distortion", a world away from the delivery of local housing and local services.[8] Kath Fry also retrospectively expressed her dislike of the process, "I (and many others) had been disgusted at the hoops through which everyone had to jump in order to woo the

IOC officials... It made me sick to see Graham Stringer and senior council officers working so hard to persuade and cajole IOC officials into supporting Manchester's bid." She reflected on how the bidding process, happening concurrently with the fights over rate capping, highlighted the split nature of Stringer's position in these times: "it is difficult to understand how Graham could have been thinking about Olympic bids in the context of dissent and disunity in the Labour Group and the Party... it demonstrated his ability to detach himself from his colleagues and move in completely different circles".[9]

Manchester Plays Games

In 1986, Manchester began again to pull together another Olympic bid on an altogether more serious footing. Scott reassembled the bid committee, packing it with "players who feel easy with million dollar games, achievers not talkers".[10] A group of officers within the Council, including Bernstein, pushed for this bid to explicitly include the construction of new sporting facilities within Manchester to create a "legacy" for the Games. The plan was to use the Games to leverage private investment into the city — particularly in the derelict ex-industrial areas of East Manchester. In May 1988 Manchester wrested the position of bid city away from Birmingham, deeply impressing the British Olympic Association with its vision of an LA-style "private enterprise games".[11] By 1990 plans were developed for an 80,000-capacity stadium to host the Games in East Manchester on the site of a former coal mine. Despite all this, Manchester lost out to Atlanta at the IOC in 1990.

The defeat of the second bid takes us up to the end of the 1980s, almost to the end of the Thatcher government. We must at this point pause our narrative. We have posited Bob Scott as an alternative to Tony Wilson as "Mr Manchester", and his Olympic Bid the key vehicle through which the Council leadership came to embrace entrepreneurialism. But the problem with the "Mr Manchester" narrative is that the development of a city can't be told solely with reference to one theatre entrepreneur or music mogul. We need a more sophisticated understanding of the wider politics of neoliberalism at the end of the 1980s, and how these played out at the city scale.

The New Right, the Inner City and the Zone

The history of the New Right can be read through the urban lens.[12] Two policies were of crucial importance: the "enterprise zone" and the "Urban Development Corporation" (UDC). Both these policy ideas had at their heart a similar idea — the stripping back of the powers of the social democratic state and replacing it with a business-friendly, government-appointed authority outside of democratic control, responsive to market signals only. In their pure forms they were both efforts to achieve that core neoliberal goal: capitalism without democracy.[13]

Tory MP Geoffrey Howe, who would become Thatcher's first Chancellor of the Exchequer, first aired his ideas about "enterprise zones" at a speech to the Bow Group, a right-wing thinktank, in June 1978 at the Waterman's Arms in the heart of the decaying Docklands in East London. His speech was called "Liberating Free Enterprise: A New Experiment" and in it he said:

> The urban wilderness, which does so little credit to the effectiveness of well-intended political initiatives, has spread further. The London Dockland is far from being the only example of this… anything that can be seen beside

the Thames can be matched by examples of dereliction on almost as large a scale beside the Mersey and the Clyde. Manchester, Leeds, the West Midlands — in almost every city of the same size one can see similar devastation.[14]

What marked these policy instruments as distinct from earlier, Wilson-era state investment in areas to improve local economy and society was a stripping back of controls, taxation and planning regulations. The state would "pay" not through investment, but through lost future revenue. The inspiration came from, among other places, Hong Kong. As well as Howe, other key players within the upper echelons of the Conservative Party at the time were also discussing the potential of these zones, including the neoliberal ideologues Nicholas Ridley and Keith Joseph. In a memo to Thatcher from Joseph written a month after Howe's speech, he described the zones as "demonstration areas… where conditions more encouraging to enterprise might be established — to show what would then result". They were in a hurry — they could "move administratively more quickly than we could legislate, to pave the way for legislative change later".[15]

The first 11 of these zones were announced in the 1980 budget, as part of the opening salvo of the Thatcher administration. Sites included Salford Docks and the Trafford Park area, but nothing in Manchester. While couched in the language of urban regeneration, in reality these zones were the opening moves in a far more ambitious attempt by the New Right to reset the structures of local government. In the assessment of academic Sam Wetherell, these enterprise zones

were more than short-term policy tools to achieve urban regeneration. Instead they were intended to become laboratories for incubating a new kind of economics, an economics whose popularity would be spread by the success of the zones... The zones, which would be introduced as bi-partisan attempts to solve the growing urban crisis and garner the support of Labour local councils were intended to be perforations in the fabric of the welfare state, ruptures through which a national and even global new style of economics would leak.[16]

The concept of the UDC can be traced to Michael Heseltine's time as junior minister in the Department for the Environment in the Heath Government. Then, he asked his civil servants to explore the possibility of a development corporation to have responsibility over the development of London's South Bank.[17] This thread would be picked up again in 1979, transposed onto the far larger zone of the London Docklands. In the face of a well organised "People's Plan" for the area, Heseltine proposed a private-sector-led UDC to be granted planning and land assembly powers, stripping those powers from local government and creating a territorial suspension of democracy. Liverpool's docks was also selected as a test case. Initially, key figures in the government were opposed, with both Keith Joseph and Geoffrey Howe seeing UDCs as too interventionist. Heseltine was able to win Thatcher's support for the idea by insinuating that the local governments who were set to lose their authority were "almost certainly controlled by the communists".[18] UDCs would have the power to sidestep local authority and submit proposals directly to the Secretary of State. In the aftermath of the uprisings across 30 cities in the summer of 1981, Heseltine wrote a paper, "It Took a Riot", which proposed massive urban regeneration in response — all coordinated through the vehicle of the UDC.[19]

In concert with Right to Buy, also steered through by Heseltine's ministry, these policies were attempts by the New Right to strike at the heart of the citadels of their political opponents in local government. At the same time, they brought new social forces to their side, expanding their hegemonic bloc. Spurred on by the defeat of the rate-capping rebellion in 1985, the urban agenda of Thatcher's government would become one of the core animating principles of her third term of office. In her 1987 conference speech she set her sights on the problem of the "inner cities", beset by dying industries, soulless planning and municipal socialism. To tackle it she announced a raft of reforms — measures "to clear derelict land, renovate run-down council estates, to regenerate city centres and to turn dereliction into development".[20] Also included were reforms to local rates and the introduction of the Poll Tax, as was the extension of the UDC outside of the original two sites of Liverpool and the London Docklands to nine new sites, including central Manchester.

This agenda of liberated zones for capital, the suspension of democratic controls over planning and the proliferation of quangos had a clear purpose for the government — to form alternative structures of local governance, a "political power base for the right in the heart of enemy territory".[21] It also marked the start of a long assault on the independent powers of local administrations, and a powerful centralising impulse in Whitehall.

How the New Governance Arrangements Played out in Manchester

Dispatched to Manchester to lead the task of setting up the Central Manchester Development Corporation (CMDC) was David Trippier, the Tory MP for Rossendale and Darwen in

Lancashire and former leader of Rochdale Council. In 1987 he was given the brief of Minister for Housing, Inner Cities and Construction under Michael Heseltine. Trippier had had no time for Manchester's left-wing council, which he described as "like a banana republic".[22] Aghast at the selling off of the military silverware and short-lived abolition of the Lord Mayor role, he recalled a time when the Town Hall had been "extraordinarily scruffy and there seemed to be crèches all over the place".[23]

In July 1988 Manchester's District Labour Party passed a resolution condemning the "anti-democratic UDC in central Manchester", a "propaganda ploy" that the government was using to take credit for projects that in reality were "already underway". It called on the Labour Group to "Identify all means possible by which the Council can inject some local democracy into the UDC's decision-making processes".[24]

Around the same time, Graham Stringer had been meeting with Trippier in a series of private meetings in his capacity as Council leader. Trippier had apparently decided that Stringer was someone he could "do business with". He made it clear that the funding the Council required, the new all-encompassing "City Grant", would only be forthcoming if the private sector was in the lead on projects. The imposition of the UDC was presented as an inevitability. Privately, Stringer and Trippier struck a deal — Stringer would attack Trippier publicly, but in exchange would assent to the UDC and acquiesce to Trippier's request for Stringer, and another councillor, Jack Flanagan, to join the board. This suited Stringer, allowing him to protect the Council's position and assuage fears of a democratic deficit in the District Party.

The CMDC's boundaries formed an arc along the southern edge of the city centre — another redrawing of a boundary within the city, this time to facilitate capital circulation. Initially, they had been drawn in such a way as to exclude the Free Trade Hall, as Trippier felt that the building's iconic history and position on the site of Peterloo would cause friction with the Council. Instead, Stringer requested that it be included within the zone, as he was determined to secure government funding to build a new modern concert hall for the Hallé. It had been longstanding Council policy that the site where the Bridgewater Hall now stands was to be reserved for a major civic building, and accordingly the "Great Bridgewater Initiative" was to be the first major project of the CMDC. It was funded as a public-private partnership, opening in 1996 at the cost of £42m, the first new concert hall in Britain since 1951.

Alongside the Bridgewater Hall, the CMDC pioneered residential development in the city centre. It drove forward the Great Northern Warehouse Initiative, converting a former railway warehouse on Deansgate into an apartment complex and a convention centre. It converted warehouses along Whitworth Street and the decaying canal-dock complex at Castlefield into apartments and an urban heritage park. Reflecting on the CMDC to Ray King years later, Howard Bernstein picked out the Bridgewater Hall and surrounding Barbirolli Square ("shifting the city centre by 500m", as he put it) as the key achievements, setting the tone for the city's development for many years:

A small step for mankind, if you like, but a giant leap for Manchester. The effectiveness of partnership between the City Council and the private sector was demonstrated conclusively. At the end of the day, that's what developed the strategy we adopted, and the Council's approach to the massive development of the business district around Spinningfields more than fifteen years later and just about everything in between.[25]

The final public-private partnership of the Stringer era was the redevelopment of Hulme. This had been a policy goal of the Council for a long time. Earlier attempts to impose a "Housing Action Trust" (HAT) on the area, effectively mass privatisation, had been blocked by the residents, organised into the Hulme Tenants Alliance. They launched an anti-HAT campaign, determined to "hold onto what we have" and propelled by the fear that the HAT, dominated by private interests, would see working-class residents replaced by "yuppies".[26]

In place of this, a study was commissioned to investigate alternatives. Resident involvement was seen as central to the success of any redevelopment plan. Ultimately, £37.5m of funding was procured through Heseltine's 1991 City Challenge programme. At the heart of the plan was the Hulme Design Guide, inspired by modish architectural ideas of new urbanism, seeking a return to the pre-1960s Hulme street layout. The project was delivered by a partnership between private sector organisations, principally Alan Cockshaw's AMEC, central and local government, housing associations and organised tenants' representatives.

City Challenge and the regeneration of Hulme was deemed to be a success. The final report of the City Challenge project concluded that it had successfully delivered most of its intended outputs in the fields of economic development, employment, infrastructure, the environment, housing and services. Two surveys conducted of residents in 1996 and 1997 both showed that most felt Hulme had improved during the period of the

City Challenge programme, and 83% of residents surveyed in 1997 were happy with their new homes.[27] It is worth noting how social housing played a major role in the new tenure mix of the redevelopment — the secret to its success.

City Challenge and the CMDC were two key examples of the proliferating governance arrangements in the city which facilitated the greater influence of private actors. Of course, the Council was forced into these arrangements by central government policy and it maintained its influence throughout — it was able to shape or even determine the agenda. In a 1990 report to the Joint Policy Committee on the activities of the CMDC this is made clear: "Much of what the Development Corporation achieves are things that the Council had planned to do but were unable to begin because of central government policy". It recommended that the Council "should rightly take its share of the credit for any achievements within the DC area".[28] But over time these new arrangements changed the balance of forces within the city, weakening its democratic forces and the empowering its private ones.

The Gateway to the New Millennium

In 1990, the city bid again for the Olympics, Scott regarding all previous failures as a learning curve. After fending off a poorly organised rival bid from London, Manchester was again picked as the British candidate city. John Major, the new Prime Minister, was fully behind the bid. The city commissioned studies looking into creating sporting facilities, even if the bid was ultimately unsuccessful. To coordinate and deliver the project, executive power over the bid was delegated to Bernstein, by now a bright rising star. In March 1992, Stringer and Bernstein successfully convinced Heseltine to fund the bid, arguing for the merits of using sport as a tool to advance regeneration. The government agreed to provide £70m in support of the bidding process and the construction of core facilities: an indoor arena, a cycling velodrome, a swimming pool and the acquisition of a stadium site in East Manchester. By this point, discussions had already begun with Manchester City Football Club over possible future relocation.

Manchester never won the 2000 Olympics. Its dreams of being Britain's gateway to the new millennium were shattered in 1993 by Sydney, whose bid committee commissioned a propaganda video that contrasted Manchester's derelict and rainswept warehouses, wharves and factories with sunny Sydney, its downtown harbours and glinting skyscrapers.[29] One wonders how much this moment stung the leaders of the emergent new Manchester. Scott and Stringer held a press conference announcing a new tilt for the Commonwealth Games, which the city was eventually to win in 2002. The Velodrome opened in 1994, the Arena in 1995 and the swimming pool on Oxford Road in February 1997. The city eventually got its new stadium for the Commonwealth Games, with Sports England providing £77m and the central government £55m. Major signed it off and Blair laid the foundation stone.

By this time, Bob Scott had left the city — the 2000 Olympic Bid was to be his swansong. But old habits die hard, and he would later be found leading the efforts to build the Millennium Dome and then Liverpool's bid to be European City of Culture in 2008. Reflecting in 1994 on his time leading the Olympic bids in *Business Life*, he said:

One of the problems in British life is the bogus antagonism between the Labour Party in local government and the

Conservative Party in central government. Actually an effective leader can talk to either, and be an important conduit between people who otherwise can't engage in dialogue. The most important role is that of the person who leaves the trench first and goes over the top between these great battalions. If the leadership isn't talking to each other, you have to enable them to do so.[30]

Scott saw himself as someone who broke the political mould and bureaucratic rules. His rhetoric painted the image of newly freed private sector and entrepreneurial initiative cajoling the hidebound politics and bureaucracy of local government into a dynamism, stressing the right of the private sector to manage the city. Through the bid, public-private partnership networks came into being and the momentum behind the emergent "Manchester Model" grew. One bid committee member put it as follows:

You see the links between local business leaders. They're on Bob's Olympic Committee. Some of them are on the City of Drama committee. They're on the Hulme Regeneration committee… You don't really know about party politics, although you could have a good idea… There is a sort of collective ambition to do something for the area that is noticeable… and generally put your shoulders back a bit and stop walking around looking depressed. There's not much future in that. The Olympic bid was a deliberate attempt to develop a chauvinist attitude. To stand up and stick your chin out and say, "To hell with it. There is a problem, but there's no point in just going on being pessimistic about it, let's have a go".[31]

The New Manchester Men

The Manchester Model was devised and delivered by a network of businessmen and a few crucial figures in the Council. The public authorities held and facilitated these networks, but in many cases the private sector formed the leading edge. The most striking fact of all was how male these networks were. Particularly when considered against the previous era of left leadership, when feminism was at the core of political life in the city, the new era was a (re-)masculinisation of the politics of local government. One forum, the North West Business Leadership Team, chaired by the Duke of Westminster, was entirely composed of men.[32] Cutting across all these networks was a male-dominated elite network of power, the self-proclaimed "Manchester Mafia". As one male media executive put it:

> Who is the Godfather of the Manchester Mafia? Who is it? It is difficult to identify. There are six or seven people who make up the being. It's me, Bob, Alan Cockshaw, the Duke of Westminster (Gerald Grosvenor)... can't ignore Graham Stringer.[33]

Outside the reach of democratic control, business was re-emerging to make a new order, remaking local governance in the process. So striking was the pattern that one pair of analysts could only conclude that "the emergence of a new business politics in Manchester is characterised by a systematic and pervasive exclusion of women from the local structures of power".[34] The new business elite in Manchester were self-consciously presenting themselves as heirs to the "Manchester Men" — invoking parallels with their nineteenth-century predecessors. This reflected a new-found self-confidence in the business community, tied together by webs of male fraternity. "Much of what we've done", said one member of the Business Leadership Team,

> has been achieved by the very good fortune of the chemistry that developed between the individuals, which is extremely fortunate. We knock about a lot, because we can pull each other's legs in a way that never happens to us in our business because you are the chair or whatever. You walk in and people say "what the bloody hell have you been doing here?" because we are all friends you see. It is good. It has got a good atmosphere which is very important.[35]

Across the 1980s, a gradual eclipsing of the democratic structures of the local state took place and the local business elite took their positions as major stakeholders in the political process. Economic issues were privileged over social interests. Time and again the idea of the "real decision-makers" appears — not located within the state, but in the hard world of business. They were increasingly playing the tune that the whole city danced to. A 1993 editorial in the magazine *City Life* summed up the situation:

> Today the same names crop up on virtually every committee and board, the Plowrights, Gil Thompsons, Stringers, Glesters, Scotts, etc. These men — and they are all men — are highly successful; and very powerful. They know people in high places. They have clout. In the late 20th century that is how to get things done. The Manchester Labour Party swims with the tide, it is part of the "establishment". Local people don't have a say in Metrolink, the Olympics or Trafford Park Development Corporation — to name but a few — except through their (outvoted) councillors. [36]

ISAAC ROSE

Re-Reading Factory

These were the planks of the city's trajectory throughout the
late 1980s and early 1990s. It really wasn't much to do with
Factory or the Haçienda. If anything, by this time the chaos of
clubland, overrun by Salford gangs, was seen as a hindrance to
the developing image of global, business-friendly Manchester.
Indeed, when pressed, Leese himself confirmed as much,
describing the influence of Wilson et al as "a bit overstated".[37]
In so far as it was useful, it meant that foreign dignitaries
visiting the city or entertaining delegations from Manchester
on business trips or Olympic bid duties were often aware of
the city. It helped build its brand. But here it was just one
among many things (football and sport being predominant)
skilfully exploited.

The cult around "St Anthony", as Wilson was sometimes
known, his contradictory, complex personality, his ability to
draw on varied avant-garde, situationist socialist and esoteric
sources, conceal much more than they reveal. In some quarters
there's even a tendency to see Factory Records as some great
proto-revolutionary force. It provides a legitimising myth
to the Manchester story. Here we're looking to escape that,
focussing instead on the restructuring of power in the city
throughout the late Stringer period. But if we are to consider
Wilson for a moment, perhaps the entrepreneurialism of
1990s Manchester was always the trajectory his brand of
so-called "situationism" was headed to. In 1984, fresh from
his return from New York, he said "I'd like to build lofts
in Manchester".[38] By the 2000s, under the spell of Richard
Florida's ideas of the "creative city", he was heading up the
regeneration quango "Elevate East Lancashire". Whatever
countercultural modernist impulses he had once had were
gone, swept away in a froth of boosterism.

The conditions that birthed the effervescent music of 1980s Manchester were late products of its modern moment: cheap space, public arts and the long cultural and intellectual legacies of mid-century Modernism. Factory's output at its best owed their existence to this tradition. Black music, the undisputable wellspring of the "rave" moment of 1987, had had a presence in the city for decades. The first DJ at the Haçienda, Hewan Clarke, had previously played in the city's Black clubs, including the Reno. The centrality of Black culture, Black music and Black clubs to what is now looked back on as something emanating from the Haçienda is too often forgotten, whitewashed out of history.[39] Indeed, the Manchester music of the 1980s at its best was borne out of an anti-racist cultural and political movement. The impact of Rock Against Racism in launching the post-punk movement has been well-traced.[40] This culture had far more in common with the movements around the New Urban Left coming out of the 1970s than it did with the transition into entrepreneurialism a decade later. Perhaps the pinnacle of it all was Mancunian ex-jazz dancer A Guy Called Gerald's *Black Secret Technology*, a futurist masterpiece all stretched loops, breakbeats and polyrhythms; rooted in the echoes of soul, reggae and jazz, playing homage to the Reno and the Nile, resolutely looking forward. Coming out in 1995, it was a last brilliant beacon before Britpop, gentrification and urban entrepreneurialism rushed in like a cold tide.[41]

Continuity or Break?

Did the "Manchester Model" — the embrace of urban entrepreneurialism, the ever-thickening webs of influence and control with the private actors — emerge as a repudiation of the aims of the New Urban Left, or was it, somehow, a continuity of them? We have already questioned the received narrative of the 1987 "u-turn", suggesting that the reality was much more nuanced. One of the reasons this narrative has taken hold is because many who deploy it fundamentally regard the approach of the New Urban Left in the early to mid-1980s as a load of nonsense. It follows from this that the left "growing up" and embracing reality (i.e., neoliberalism) is a convenient narrative. Here we have tried to sympathetically reconstruct the broad context of the New Urban Left and excavate their attempt to deal with the crisis of social democracy from the left. Ultimately, this attempt was defeated by Thatcher.

The "u-turn" theory also obscures the interesting continuities in approach across the watershed of 1987. The transition in the late 1980s was in important respects a continuation of the assumptions that had underpinned the New Urban Left policy of the first part of the decade. We can look at the example of Sheffield, where, like Manchester (and unlike the GLC, which was abolished), the political leadership had to reckon with the conditions of the late 1980s. Here, as has been recently observed by Allan Cochrane and Ross Beveridge, the "fundamental aspect of the shift in focus" was to "reposition the Council as an active participant in shaping the local economy and creating worthwhile employment for its people".[42] An interventionist local government carried over into the entrepreneurial period.

Looking at it from the perspective of the late 1980s, we can see how there was a belief that the achievement of long-term policy goals could only be reached through some accommodation with the government. The note of resignation in the private letter to Nicholas Ridley from Graham Stringer rings of someone who feels all options are exhausted. In terms of specific things delivered in the years after, the major new concert hall and the Hulme regeneration had been long-term ambitions of the Council. Tactical partnerships saw these delivered.

But we also now see how through these processes the nature of the local state was remade. This was partly organic — the thickening of relationships between politicians and the private sector; key individuals like Bob Scott and Alan Cockshaw embedding themselves within circuits of power. It was also the product of a rising generation of new councillors and officers, who were more distant from the struggles of the early 1980s. Both Richard Leese and Howard Bernstein, who would go on to become the power-duo at the top of the local state as Leader and Chief Executive of Manchester City Council respectively, fit this mould.

The Entrepreneurial Turn

Across the period examined, from 1984 through to the end of the decade, two potential futures were developing in tandem. On the one side, the coming to power of the left, the equalities agenda and an attempt to implement some kind of alternative economic strategy on the local scale. Manchester came to this fight late — almost four years behind similar movements in Sheffield and London. At the same time, Stringer was increasingly drawn into the orbit of private business. The Olympic Bids were important for developing a shared sense of purpose between the Council and local elites. It seems that the twin defeats for the left, in 1985 over the rate-capping rebellion, and then in 1987 when Thatcher won again, meant that the trajectory of the city crystallised into one camp not the other.

The defeat opened the path to the neoliberalisation of local government, Thatcher's goal for her third term. What the urban electorates wanted was increasingly irrelevant as the leadership of the city was answering to the "partnerships" with stakeholders in business and in Conservative national government. In the eyes of business, these turns may have contributed to the rehabilitation of Labour as a party of government in the mid-1990s. This proto-Blairism on a local scale would be stepped up over the coming decade. The period of interregnum was coming to an end — the era characterised by the return of the rentier in the urban economy was dawning.

So, what was the Manchester Model? The word that comes through, time and again, is "partnership" — the linking of the aims and goals of the public and private sector. Contradictions that might exist were subsumed under an overriding desire to "do what's best for the city". This entailed an interventionist attitude on the part of the Council, which on top of this, exhibited a canny navigation of the grant landscape. It's been posited that what was put together was a "grant coalition" — partnerships adept at winning bids for funds, either central government or European funding. Through winning these grants major policy objectives were met.

This was accompanied by a sense of the dramatic — the legacy of Bob Scott, and the Olympic bid — a sense of "nothing ventured, nothing gained". It could equally apply to Tony Wilson or Howard Bernstein. The Manchester Model was about hype or it was nothing. Finally, there was a democratic deficit. The restructuring of the local state and growing role for a coalition of private actors meant, necessarily, a decline in power within the city's democratic forums — principally the structures of the Labour movement. In part this was the inevitable result of the collapse of the industrial unions, which had provided a democratic counterweight in the postwar era. But it also was the result of the empowering of the Council's executive, both elected and non-elected elements, the inevitable result of the managing of stakeholder relationships. In the late 1980s, faced with Thatcherite supremacy, perhaps there was little alternative. Whether that remains the case today is a matter entirely up for debate.

Part 3

The Secondary Circuit

Chapter 5
From the Bomb to the Crash

I love starting out with crappy sites or buildings, then working with great people to turn them into great places to live, work and play.

Tom Bloxham, CEO, Urban Splash

Urban Splash have got this vision and they think it will work, but it won't work because they are segregating the core of the community to outside areas. I have fought and fought damn hard for this community, and if Urban Splash or whoever think they can come in here and tell us what is best for us then they've got another thing coming... I think the only thing that Urban Splash and English Partnerships are interested in is money, and that's the truth.

Jean, resident of the Cardroom Estate, Ancoats

Middle aged arseholes in the press managed to turn Liverpool into a Beatles theme park for the past 40 years, they're doing the same thing again to Manchester. Unless you're in your 40s and writing for Q magazine you should be railing against all this shit, not shuffling your feet saying um its ok cos there's no good new bands, might as well just give up on the city and let the hookmobile raze it to the ground and rebuild it as Madchester pleasure beach.

FUC51

On a clear, blue morning on Saturday, 15th June 1996, the switchboard at Granada Studios received a phone call. "A bomb is going to go off within hours in Manchester city centre." As such calls often happened as hoaxes, the caller used a codeword known to the Special Branch, signalling that the tip-off was genuine. Minutes later the police noticed an unusual van parked outside the Royal Exchange, which on closer inspection revealed wires running from the dashboard and into a hole at the back. The threat was plain — the alert was raised and the police and fire brigade evacuated 80,000 people from the city centre. Bomb disposal teams dispatched a robot to try and defuse the primer, but they were too late. At 11.17am, one and a half tons of explosive went off, blasting debris half a mile into the sky. Miraculously, nobody was killed, but the scene on Cross Street was pure devastation. The frontages of Marks & Spencer and the Arndale Shopping Centre had been ripped clean off and lay in ruins. The glass dome of the Exchange had collapsed, the upper-level windows of St Ann's Church blown out. In all, more than a million square feet of retail and office space had been completely wrecked.

That day, Richard Leese was in the Town Hall, 500 yards away from the bomb site, poring over local election data. Six weeks earlier he had succeeded Graham Stringer as leader of Manchester City Council, after Stringer had secured nomination for the north Manchester parliamentary seat of Blackley. Though he had wanted to stay in role until the general election, Leese had insisted on an immediate handover. When the bomb went off, he felt Waterhouse's Gothic machine shake to its very foundations:

My first reaction was to get everyone out of the city centre completely. My second — like most people that day — was to make sure my family and friends were okay. Third was to set about checking what the hell the Council's role was supposed to be in circumstances like these.[1]

First he went down to the Town Hall's emergency bunker, a spartan committee room in the basement with direct phone lines to the police and other emergency services. Then, along with his deputy, he went out into Albert Square and began fielding questions from the press. Defiant, he declared, "Manchester will be back on its feet to fight another day". After that, he watched England beat Scotland in the Euros and headed up to the Irish World Heritage Centre in Cheetham Hill to have a pint of Guinness in a show of solidarity with the city's Irish community. The next day's headlines beat an optimistic tone: "The Miracle of Manchester".

On the Sunday, in the Town Hall, Pat Karney and Graham Stringer had deputy Chief Executive of the Council Howard Bernstein pinned up against the wall: "You've got to fucking sort this!" they said, in no uncertain terms. "You move into a different gear then", reflected Bernstein later.[2] Immediately he set about instituting some organisation. His first call was to the Bank of England's man in the North West, Tony Strachan, who he asked to get the heads of all the clearing banks in the city together in Strachan's office. To the assembled bankers Bernstein made the extraordinary request: that they would give him the absolute commitment that no businesses would be foreclosed without reference to him first. Incredibly, they agreed.

Reassuring business was the leadership's absolute priority. At the Town Hall Karney chaired mass meetings of representatives from some of the 670 affected businesses, assuring them they would get them back on their feet and that the Council would rebuild Manchester. Elsewhere Bernstein, Leese and David Trippier, now chairman of Marketing Manchester, received a standing ovation from assembled business leaders. Business helplines were established. By Wednesday the Lord Mayor had set up a recovery fund for small traders, with donations flooding in from the bigger businesses, individuals and, eventually, central government. On Saturday, a week after the blast, Karney, as chair of the City Centre Sub-Committee, organised a family fun day in Albert Square, painting a big "I Love Manchester" heart on his face. "I wanted to try and create a carnival atmosphere to show that Manchester was up and running... and that we weren't destroyed."[3]

On Wednesday 26th June, Michael Heseltine arrived in Manchester. By this time, the line from Leese and Bernstein had been agreed — the bomb was an opportunity "to rebuild the city for the 21st century".[4] Heseltine concurred and within a week had put together an initial aid package of £21m to support the city centre's recovery. To lead it, a public-private partnership was established, "Manchester Millennium Ltd". On Heseltine's suggestion, AMEC's Alan Cockshaw was made chair. Leese was his deputy. On the insistence of Cockshaw, Bernstein was made its chief executive. Completing the board were David Trippier, Marianne Neville-Rolfe, the most senior government civil servant in the region, Tony Strachan, Kath Robinson, the Council's Deputy Leader, and Pat Karney, dubbed by Ray King as "the councillor for fun".[5]

As with Hulme, Manchester Millennium Limited opened a design competition to come up with a masterplan for the city centre. 27 bids were submitted, and the winner, announced to much public interest, was a consortium of architects led by Ian Simpson, who would go on to have a massive impact on the built environment of the city which continues to this day. His practice, in partnership with Rachel Haugh, had already been responsible for the redevelopment of Knott Mill as part of the Central Manchester Development Corporation. Their masterplan for the city centre was ambitious, opening new sightlines between the Cathedral and St Ann's Church, moving the medieval "Shambles" — two timber-framed pubs — to a new location by the Cathedral and building new frontages for M&S and the Arndale in a Postmodern style. The tip of it all was a new glass museum, the ill-fated "Urbis", or Museum of Urban Life.

Part of the urgency underlying the response to the bomb was spurred on by what many in Manchester perceived at the time as an existential threat — the opening of the Trafford Centre, an out-of-town shopping centre built over the former hamlet of Dumplington on the edges of the Ship Canal on the fringe of the city. This gaudy palace of consumption had been the masterplan of John Whittaker, chief of Peel Holdings, ever since he had struck the deal with Stringer in the 1980s to buy the Council's seats on the board of the Ship Canal Company. His prize had been the land around the canal stretching from the heart of Manchester to the Irish Sea. The Council, along with eight other neighbouring authorities (all Greater Manchester Authorities, apart from Trafford), had tried to stop it, fighting a bitter court case to overturn planning permission that they eventually lost in the House of Lords. Construction had begun a mere two months before the bomb. The priority, then, was to get Manchester's central shopping district up and running as quickly as possible.

The reconstruction after the bomb would therefore have a profound impact on the city centre of Manchester. This impact wasn't only in the built environment, but also in its governance arrangements. The change was the arrival of the Manchester City Centre Management Company, renamed "CityCo" in 2000, to manage the "Business Improvement District' (BID) of the city centre. With CityCo, Manchester was a pioneer of this model. A BID is a company that imposes a levy on all local businesses.[6] In exchange, they work to improve what it terms the "trading environment", operating on the principle of a "hierarchy of business needs". First, "clean and safe" environment; second, "transport and access"; third, "marketing and branding for an area"; and finally, "memorable experiences for visitors". Accountable to the bottom-line of their members — local businesses — BIDs treat the city centre as a private business. In Manchester, the founding chair was also the head of Bruntwood, a major local property developer. The wishes or needs of local electors assumed second place.

Originally a concept from the United States, it had acquired popularity in Britain thanks to growing interest from the New Labour government. In 1995, Jack Straw, as Shadow Home Secretary, had paid a visit to New York to learn about Mayor Rudy Giuliani's new policing strategies. He'd been particularly interested in Giuliani's "Police Strategy No 5", issued in 1994 and dedicated to "reclaiming the public spaces of New York" from the "homeless, panhandlers, prostitutes, squeegee cleaners, squatters, graffiti artists, 'reckless bicyclists' and unruly youths". Two years later, now in government, another delegation of Labour MPs, including John Prescott, made another trip to New York to study BIDs. They concluded they should come to the UK. In journalist and academic Anna Minton's assessment, the arrival of BIDs "marked the beginning of private government and the decline of local democracy".[7] These pseudo-public spaces proliferated across the country, but Manchester, in the aftermath of the bomb, can lay claim to be the originator.

BIDs aimed to attract high-net earners — "ABC1s" — to the city centre to spend their money. In the aftermath of the bomb, this was seen as even more of a priority. Throughout the 1990s people had been travelling to out-of-town shopping centres, drawn by their sanitised, "clean and safe" environments — a consequence of their private ownership and management. Faced with the threat of the Trafford Centre, and given a golden opportunity to reshape the centre, Manchester enacted the BID with gusto. The effect was the gradual ejection of "undesirable" elements from the city centre, a similar list to that identified by Giuliani. The tool of choice was the antisocial behaviour order, or ASBO — another New Labour innovation, a key part of the wider stigmatisation of "undesirables" during the 2000s. By 2007 Manchester had the dubious accolade of being the ASBO capital of Britain, with 659 orders issued between 1999 and 2007, and condemned by the ombudsman for a "shocking abuse of power".[8]

Assessing the reconstruction of the centre five years after the bomb, the veteran Labour MP for Manchester Gorton, Gerald Kaufman, drew the ire of the city leaders when he described it as "an opportunity for revolutionary urban renewal that was ultimately wasted".[9] After the bomb, he claimed, he had advised patience, to "take all the time needed" to turn the city into "an object lesson in Town Planning". Instead, spooked by "a shopping mall in the suburbs" and "impelled by a spirit of urgency" they'd rushed headlong into reconstruction. The results, according to Kaufman, were underwhelming:

I have just received a glossy brochure from Manchester City Centre Management Company. It claims that "a programme of major project completions have changed the character of Manchester for ever". What a daft boast! The character of Manchester is great — a historic city inhabited by sturdy, independent, generous-minded citizens. What was needed was a reconstruction programme that would express that historic character in a new, exciting way. As it turns out, the brochure is a great deal more glossy than the reality... honestly, the presence of DKNY, Armani, Boss, Calvin Klein and Bang & Olufsen (and the arrival of a multiplex cinema together with an IMAX screen, several years after Bradford's) are not exactly groundbreaking evidence of new ideas in urban planning.

In the years since, the bomb has been described by some as the crucial moment which kickstarted the Council's regeneration of Manchester. This is a myth — the roots of the "Manchester Model" stretch back a decade prior, with their origins in the Olympic bids, Hulme Regeneration and the Central Manchester Development Corporation. The response to the bomb — "Millennium Manchester Ltd" — was a continuation of this, a repetition of some of the structures, methods and key personnel who had been working together in some cases for nearly a decade. It was an accelerator, not a catalyst. However, with the formation of the BID, we can certainly point to the post-bomb reconstruction as marking the start of the city centre's transformation into a consumption playground for the wealthy. It also had a profound effect by cementing in place the leadership duopoly that would steer the city's trajectory for the next two decades: Richard Leese and Howard Bernstein.

Leese was first elected to the Council in 1984. A former mathematics teacher and youth worker, his was a key voice in the aftermath of 1987 urging for a change of tack and constructive engagement with the private sector:

What we had found out was that although municipal socialism could take on the government if it wished, it could not win…. There was no get out of jail card. We had gambled on Labour winning the election and we lost.[10]

He had been the author of an influential positioning paper which argued that the Council had to turn to the private sector to create the jobs needed to dig the city out of its crisis,[11] followed by a number of positioning papers across the late 1980s on the new economic strategy.[12] In 1990 he became Deputy Leader of the Council and Chair of the Finance Committee, a position he held for five years. Along with Housing Chair Dave Lunts and Stringer, he sat on the board of Hulme Regeneration Ltd. He was increasingly seen as Stringer's heir-apparent, in public united to a common strategy, in private increasingly frustrated by his leadership style. In 1996 Leese insisted that Stringer stand down, and he was elected in his place, his only rival the former chair of the Equalities Committee Val Stevens, who attracted only 17 votes.[13]

Bernstein too was intimately bound with this agenda. Joining the Council as a junior clerk in 1971, as a highly competent administrator he had ascended through the ranks. In the mid-1980s he oversaw transport — working with Stringer on the establishment of the Airport Group. By the end of the decade he was Deputy Chief Executive, closely involved in the delivery of the tram network, the Olympics bid, the Velodrome, Arena and Stadium, the CMDC and the Bridgewater Hall and Manchester Millennium Ltd. In 1998 he became Chief Executive of the Council, a position he held until 2017. He had, in Alan Cockshaw's assessment, the confidence of not only the city, but the private sector.[14] Together, Leese and Bernstein would bring to the heart of policy a management competence, a proven ability to secure government grants and most importantly their firm belief in the overriding centrality of the private sector in urban development. This direction, borne out of the long trajectory since the late 1980s, was cemented as the central governing principle in the aftermath of the bomb — a mere six weeks into the leadership of Richard Leese. Beyond the city centre, however, the key district where the new philosophies would be enacted, was in its ex-industrial east.

New East Manchester

Until 1968, East Manchester was one of the most economically productive zones in the city. Home to a coal mine, Stuart Street Power Station, huge gasometers and a number of engineering works, including the massive Beyer, Peacock and Company locomotive plant, it was, as we have seen, the city's industrial core. But then began its decline, and between 1975 and 1985 it lost 60% of its economic base. By 1999 its economic activity fell to 62% — 10% below the national average. Unemployment was at 8.2%, double the Greater Manchester and national average.[15] The apocalypse of deindustrialisation didn't fall evenly on the city — East Manchester was its epicentre. It was also the area with the longest fidelity to the Labour Party, with Beswick the ward which elected the first ever Independent Labour Party candidate in 1894, followed swiftly by Bradford and Openshaw. Arresting this decline through job creation and a revitalisation of the built environment had been a Council priority since the early 1980s.

From the time of the second Olympic bid, Bernstein and

others at the Council insisted on leveraging the investment into the regeneration of the area. In 1992 the East Manchester Regeneration Strategy was launched, with a vision of a "Sportcity", rising like a phoenix out of the derelict zone, at its core. The ultimate success in hosting the Commonwealth Games in 2002 bore this out; a stadium, velodrome and tram line were to follow. It was heralded as the first "regeneration games", the model that underpinned London's bid for the Olympics in 2012. It was estimated that 450 jobs were created, and after Manchester City FC inherited the stadium in 2003, this was sustained. Much of this employment, however, was in part-time and casual contracts, for instance matchday stewarding. After the acquisition of Manchester City by Abu Dhabi in 2008, the new owners undertook a major investment programme in the area surrounding the stadium, building up the club's football academy and, as we shall see, entering the housing market. Eddie Smith, Director of Growth and Development for Manchester City Council, claimed "the first wave of East Manchester regeneration has been done by the public sector, and the second wave is hopefully going to be undertaken by the football club".[16] The gambit of sport into wider investment appeared to have paid off. Yet this is only a part of the story of East Manchester — we must situate it within the wider urban agenda of the New Labour government.

Urban regeneration was a high priority for New Labour. The first speech Blair made as Prime Minister was in the Aylesbury Estate in the London Borough of Southwark,[17] where he claimed the biggest employer was the drugs industry. In the speech, he pledged the end to "no hope areas" and promised to bring back the "will to win" among the "workless classes".[18] The focus was not only on regeneration of the built environment, but to tackle social exclusion as well — building strong "communities" to cultivate active and responsible citizens. Restrictions on welfare were used to cajole people into work. The flagship urban policy launched in 1998 was the "New Deal for Communities", ten-year programmes of area-specific investment, £50m each for 39 deprived neighbourhoods in England. Alongside them sat the "Urban Regeneration Companies" (URCs), public-private companies established to oversee the physical transformation of their areas through master planning and coordinating financial assistance. These programmes pursued the model of the public-private partnership, stimulating urban land markets. In significant ways they were a continuation of the urban policy taken under John Major's government, and there was a strong feeling in Manchester that the policies of the Blair government were simply building on Manchester's experience across the 1990s. Lord Rogers, the author of the report which set out the strategy of the URCs, was known to have visited the city on multiple occasions when drawing up his recommendations.[19] The major problem with both these schemes, aside from the largely unaccountable structure of their delivery vehicles, was that the state funding provided was nowhere near adequate for the massive task at hand. Pound for pound they were less well-resourced than some of the initiatives of the Thatcher era.[20] But, perhaps most controversial of all were the "Pathfinder" programmes, so-called "housing market renewal", designed to kickstart housing markets in areas of "low demand". In total, 850,000 homes, usually in perfectly fine condition, were slated for demolition across the North and Midlands. There was some in Manchester, but far larger swaths in Oldham and Salford were targeted. It prompted fierce resistance, as the ghosts of the 1960s returned.[21] In Owen Hatherley's assessment, Pathfinder represented "slum clearance without the socialism".[22] This verdict could have applied to New Labour's urban policy *in toto*.

East Manchester was a focus for all these government schemes throughout the 2000s. The regeneration was delivered and governed by an array of structures, with complex overlapping jurisdictions and interrelations. At the heart of it was an Urban Regeneration Company, New East Manchester Ltd, a three-way joint venture between Manchester City Council, the North West Development Agency and English Partnerships. It was the second such URC created in England. Bernstein became its secretary, while Alan Cockshaw took the chair, also at that time the Chair of English Partnerships. On taking the role he drew direct reference to his recent work on the post-bomb reconstructions:

> I can say without doubt that the model of the urban task force is a highly successful vehicle to drive forward radical change. I have seen the city centre task force pull together various interested parties to unite them in a partnership far stronger than any of their individual efforts. I am sure East Manchester will enjoy similar unity and we all look forward to the challenge ahead of us.[23]

Its strategy document, *A New Town in the City*, made plain the ambitions of the programme. Richard Leese, also on the board of New East Manchester Ltd, said: "We must applaud those families who have stayed, who have kept the community going in the face of incredible difficulties. They are the base on which a renewed East Manchester can be built."[24] It was a laudable ambition.

New East Manchester set out to deliver on a range of projects, including boosting employment, skills training, transport improvement and housing redevelopment. Assessment of its success in sober academic studies drew, perhaps unsurprisingly, a mixed picture. New employment, where it did occur, tended to be in low-wage sectors such as supermarkets and match stewarding, with temporary and part-time contracts proliferating. The Blair-era plans for the super-casino, cancelled in 2007 by Gordon Brown, would have been much the same. It was never a like-for-like replacement for the old industrial employment — in the assessment of academics Blakeley and Evans, "unemployment remained unsatisfactory".[25] Yet, they cautioned, the assessment shouldn't be too harsh — the constraints in place in East Manchester always meant that the attempts to revive the economy were going to be an uphill struggle, one not helped by the 2008 recession and then the subsequent cutting of funding for the inner-city programmes by the coalition government. However, one area where they highlighted a range of negative outputs was housing, and no section of the redevelopment zone was more controversial than the Cardroom Estate, Ancoats.

Urban Splash and New Islington

Consistent with the wider aims of New Labour's urban regeneration projects, one aim of New East Manchester was the stimulation of physical regeneration and tenure-mixing — new-build homes for market rent or sale. This agenda dovetailed with the Council's own strategy for the city centre, a "new urbanist" strategy of developing urban living. The land identified was adjacent to Great Ancoats Street, on the edge of the growing Northern Quarter. The master planners envisaged the areas as a corridor, carrying development from the city centre to the peripheral zones in the east. In a press release from the time, New East Manchester stated that the 25-acre area to be redeveloped "incorporates the former Ancoats Hospital site, the former St Jude's Primary School and disused industrial site".[26] It failed to mention the 1970s Cardroom Estate, around 200 houses. At the time, around 100 residents still lived there. The company selected to redevelop the estate was Urban Splash.

The estate, named after the room in which the first stage of raw cotton processing began, was built in the aftermath of the slum clearances of the 1960s. Many of its oldest residents had worked in the cotton mills when they were younger. Their families had lived in the area for three generations — they were a living link with the working class that had built the city. One elderly resident, Agnes, had been born on 24 Pollard Street, opposite Bazeley's Mill. She was one of the many residents interviewed and photographed for *Cardroom Voices,* a project by photographer Len Grant.[27] Agnes remembered being woken up each morning "to the sounds of the machines starting off and the clogs coming up the street. It was marvellous." She'd been moved by the Council to Cardroom in the 1970s, and recounted the first time she laid eyes on it with two other girls from work. "It was like a palace, and I had a porch at the front. To me, it was the loveliest house we had ever been in. It was marvellous. Really lovely."[28]

Over time, disinvestment and a lack of repairs as well as the use of some of the homes for unstable temporary accommodation saw the estate start to run down. "Then the drugs came on, but nobody came to sort drugs out", Agnes explained. "We were just left there, having to face everything. Nobody bothered. So everybody just gave up hope." By the early 2000s it was stigmatised as a major "problem estate" and "no-go zone". Despite this, many of the residents interviewed for the *Cardroom Voices* project emphasised the deep sense of resilience in the community.

Of all the property developers working in the city, it was Urban Splash that most came to represent the peculiar post-rave exuberance and macho posturing of Manchester between the bomb and the crash. Its founder, Tom Bloxham, was an 80s ex-raver who moved from selling music and posters to apartments, founding the company in 1993. He'd made a name for himself by pioneering a kind of Manhattan-esque "loft living" for Manchester and Liverpool, with redevelopments in ex-industrial buildings in the 1990s. The Cardroom redevelopment, quickly rebranded as "New Islington" after an old mill in the area, was their biggest project yet. In the promotional video from 2002, still available on their YouTube channel, a peroxide Bloxham paces, frantically, words staccato: "Look at this! The canals! Aren't they fantastic? The Ashton, the Rochdale! Let's put in some new canals, let's reinvigorate the old canals. And let's create a New Amsterdam, a New East Manchester-dam, a really special place in the city."[29]

It's a weird scene. To the sparse drum beat and bass guitar of the Fall's "Jerusalem", Bloxham, perched atop the roof of the old Ancoats Dispensary, surveys his new domain. "Here we are, top of the world, or at least on top of Ancoats hospital, and overlooking the Cardroom estate. We want to turn this, this dereliction, into a world exposition… to really show what can be done with urban regeneration *in these kind of areas.*" We then see footage of the community consultations at the Cob O'Coal, a pub now long demolished. Here, Nick Johnson, the development director, explains to a room of stony-faced residents how he has the day-to-day responsibility of what is going to happen to Cardroom for the next five-ten years.

The architect, working for master planner, Will Allsop, introduces a few ideas — "Do you want to keep the pub?" (Yes!) "Hairdresser? Betting shop?" (Yes! Yes!) "Ah, you want everything." Johnson chimes in, "We can't guarantee that everything you say you want you will get". The architect again, "Would you like to have more water on the site? Like, linking the two canals together?" (No!! Too dangerous!). It goes on like this. At some point, the music changes, it's Hubert Parry's "Jerusalem" now. Plans are unveiled and pored over. One woman asks, "Where are the houses going to be to accommodate us?" Another: "I want to know where my house is going to be!" There was no clear answer. Then there's a strange scene, where Johnson is locked in an argument with a resident, exasperated, pointed finger jabbing: "I can only go off the stuff we're building at the moment in Castlefield and the provision we are making — that's what you're getting!" His interlocutor responds: "Yous have made your mind up what you're going to do, let's have it right. You have." The footage, taken at the very beginning of the process, clearly shows how deep community scepticism was from the start.

Liam, a Cardroom resident, later explained:

It was quite good to begin with, we thought "great, we're getting a voice, we can stand in there, and give our point of view…" but when we objected to certain things, it was very rare we got anything cause they'd already made the plans for what they were doing to this area. We wanted selective demolition, we wanted certain houses keeping… but they said no, it's complete demolition.[30]

In 2006 all six members of the community steering group resigned, one of the first public signs of the community's deep dissatisfaction with the urban renewal programme. Urban Splash continued regardless. Few of their promises were ever kept, and by the time the crash happened in 2008, only the new clinic and the so-called "Chips" building (in an homage to the area it was designed to look like "a plate of chips") had been completed.

It belies something of the supreme confidence of Urban Splash that the video is still on their YouTube channel. The narrative of the cut seems to discredit their entire consultation process as one big sham. In the end what the residents thought or said didn't really matter. The condemned estate was to be demolished, the people moved out. Agnes, who lost little Bobby, one of her three cats, as the removal men came to take her from her home, put it as follows:

> Do they understand what they're doing when they pull these houses down? What they're doing to people? Now, ok they have a lovely name for it now, "regeneration". But in the old days they would have called that a slum clearance. At the bitter end it was terrible. We didn't want to go, but we had to move.[31]

Another resident moved out of the area, to Openshaw, was a woman called Jackie Marston. She'd lived in her house for 42 years. Her home was on the edge of the Miles Platting Private Finance Initiative (PFI), despite her considering it Ancoats. PFIs were another government-backed means of regenerating estates during the New Labour years, exchanging part privatisation for private investment.[32] In Colin Stone and Rachael Gibbons' film *Working Class Heroes*, she told the story of how she found out her house was condemned:

> On arriving home from work one day there was a leaflet through the door that was telling me about the regeneration

of Miles Platting. I rang up and I said to him, what have I got this leaflet for? I don't live in Miles Platting, I live in Ancoats, M4! The first meeting I went to there was this great big map on the table, and on this map of the whole area were these purple splodges. And I said, can you tell me what that's about, what are they on there for? They are the demolition sites. And unfortunately my house was underneath one of these purple splodges. Due to the redevelopment of Ancoats or "regeneration" unfortunately I was in one of the houses they wanted to get rid of. It was on prime land. It was so upsetting to move, to leave what I thought was a lovely home. It wasn't a house, it was a home.[33]

In the end, owing to problems with the PFI following the financial crash, the land her house was on was never developed. To this day it remains a patch of grass. Later in the film, she walks past the place she used to live.

When I pass here, I could cry. Every time I pass in the car or if I come home from town on the bus, it turns around this corner — as soon as I see this, I still get upset. Nine years later. It is still a plot of grass. There is nothing on it. So why did we have to go at that time? I just feel sick. I feel empty. I think the Council have treated us diabolically. Absolutely diabolically.

Marston and her neighbours were to form the core of a bitter campaign to save the Ancoats Dispensary from demolition. This had been the building that Bloxham had stood atop of in the original film, confidently claiming, "If I get this wrong, I'll never work in the city again". It was historic — the place from which J.P. Kay had conducted his cholera surveys in the nineteenth century; a pre-NHS health centre, somewhere which almost everyone locally had an intimate memory of. It had been a working hospital until 1996 — saved from proposed closure in 1987 by a 200-day sit-in by residents of the Cardroom. It seemed unclear what Urban Splash's intentions for the site were. In 2010 Urban Splash removed the roof, hastening its deterioration. When funding was pulled with the abolition of the North West Development Agency by the Coalition government, progress on the site stalled and Urban Splash mothballed it. A year later they filed an application for its demolition. In response, residents formed the Ancoats Dispensary Trust to fight a campaign for the building's preservation and reuse. Linda Carver, who became its chair, explained the moment it became clear what Urban Splash's true intentions were:

And as I looked at this presentation, it all looked very sort of... how can I put it? European. Cafes outside, people drinking, you know, families playing, the houseboats. It was all very colourful, but I couldn't see the building of the Ancoats dispensary. And so I just happened to ask the question: where is the dispensary in all of this regeneration? And you could have heard a pin drop... I realised that I said something that was quite controversial. And then there was a bit of mumbling going on between the Urban Splash development team and then I heard the words "Mum, I think it's going to be demolished"... I thought to myself: over my dead body.[34]

In 2012 the community launched two interconnected initiatives to save the hospital from imminent demolition: a daily vigil outside the building and a people's history project, in which oral histories of the hospital were gathered. The vigil continued for four years. Eventually, the force of the campaign staved off demolition, and the community were given the opportunity by the Council to bid for the building. For a few years it looked like it would be repurposed for community use. But, owing to the roof's removal, the building was just a shell and the costs required to renovate it were too great for the community to muster. It reverted to the Council in 2018, and today is set to be developed into social housing. Reflecting on its significance as a building, Carver said:

> The Dispensary was almost the last building standing from a period of history of Manchester when things were being taken away all the time, houses demolished, people re-homed elsewhere, outside in the suburbs, where all the social services and community things had gone, like the New Islington Baths: demolished; Ardwick Lads Club: demolished; Women's Shelter: demolished; The Girls Home: demolished. It was kind of, everything had gone, all the social agencies that had held this together, a cohesiveness had disappeared and the only thing left was the Ancoats Dispensary. So, well I certainly felt, it's like a whole piece of heritage is being wiped out without a whimper, and what's replacing it, what's replacing it?[35]

Richard Leese had opened the regeneration programme with the rhetoric that those who had stayed would be the base upon which the New East Manchester would be built. In *Working Class Heroes*, Jackie Marston delivered her verdict on these ambitions in clear terms. "They've ripped the heart out of the community. Just ordinary, working class people. They're not wanted now." It's hard to see what happened to the Cardroom as anything other than social cleansing.

Original Modern

Bloxham, with his peculiar trajectory, captured the spirit of the moment in 2000s Manchester. His swaggering, arrogant braggadocio made him and his business partner Nick Johnson the Oasis of the property world. They claimed their inspiration for Urban Splash had been the Sex Pistols gig at the Free Trade Hall (when they would have been 13 and ten, respectively), and that the "energy of rock and roll can now be found in regeneration".[36] In a talk in 2008 to an assembled audience at the Tate, Johnson said he had learnt three key things from his experience at New Islington: "You need to be unprofessional, you need to be unaccountable and you need to be irresponsible".[37]

Another figure who slid seamlessly out of the music world of the 1990s into the business of selling the city's real estate boom in the 2000s was Colin Sinclair.[38] Sinclair had been the owner of the Boardwalk, a nightclub in the centre of town, until 1999 when he'd closed the club. By 2005 he was heading up MIDAS, the inward investment agency funded by the ten Greater Manchester councils. It was a sort of CLES for the new age. Sinclair was a key member of the team that brokered the deal for Bank of New York Mellon to open a department in Manchester. To mark the occasion, the City Council renamed "York Street", where the offices would be located, to "New York Street".

Come the new millennium, so many of the "Madchester" generation made the shift into civic boosterism. Peter Saville, the director of a London-based design agency who had once made the sleeves and posters for Factory, was appointed the City Council's "Creative Director" in 2004, a role he held until austerity started to bite in 2011. He was tasked with coming up with a concept for the city, an identity to bind and brand it. His idea was "Original Modern". It was a neat concept. Unfortunately, any insinuation that modern aspirations might include things like public housing were lost on the city's leaders. Instead the concept was boiled down into the idea of Manchester as the "city of firsts" (first place to split the atom, build a computer, invent graphene, etc.)

Armed with such concepts, the city representatives, including officers from MIDAS, headed to MIPIM, the annual "property professionals" jamboree held in Cannes. Here Manchester does lay great claim to being a pioneer. MIPIM, today more high profile than ever and with a degree of public controversy attached to it, had been attended by representatives of Manchester since the early 2000s. Howard Bernstein and Richard Leese were frequent attenders. Tom Bloxham often played wingman. Andy Spinoza, a frequent attender in his capacity as PR man for agencies like MIDAS and various property developers (he had worked on the original pitch for Urban Splash to take on the Cardroom estate) provides us with a useful insider account:

Flights to Cannes were filled with business people who worked with the Council, all expectant of a private meeting with the regeneration king, Sir Howard Bernstein. Rising younger hopefuls were often challenged by their boss to win their spurs, by getting a chat with the man whose encouragement, they believed, could make their company's project fly. At the Manchester stand at MIPIM, "SHB" was in his element, as assistants cued up his presentations and kept the coffees and canapés flowing.[39]

In 2006 New Labour broke with 90 years of political tradition and spurned its traditional conference town,

Blackpool, and selected Manchester as the host city instead. It was a fitting accolade for the city which in many ways had prefigured the Third Way.

The Financial Crash and Aftermath

The 12 years between the bomb and the crash were marked by the continuation and extension of a growth regime that had been forged in the late 1980s and early 1990s, grounded in the belief that economic success would lead to a decline in social exclusion. Yet the data collected on the eve of the finanicial crisis demonstrated that result had been in many cases the opposite — that the city's growth model had resulted in stark patterns of uneven development, with two Manchesters — one rich, one poor — rubbing up against one another but rarely crossing, much as had been the case in Engels' day. Two reports published in 2009 which examined social deprivation across the city showed an extreme polarisation of wealth and poverty. One of the studies, by Centre for Cities, showed that of the 56 English cities studied, Manchester was the most unequal in terms of the gap between rich and poor.[40]

The city's uneven development, a patchy and incomplete response to the catastrophe of deindustrialisation, would receive its most severe challenge yet with the onset of the global financial crisis. The immediate effects of the crash on the city's property market — the mainstay of its economic engine — were dramatic. In 2008 house prices fell by 10%, with an 8% fall concentrated in the final quarter. In the speculative apartments market, the decline was even greater — 15% in the city centre and up to 30% in the north of the conurbation. Overall, sales were down by 75% by 2009 from their peak in 2006-7. Prestige projects, such as the Albany and Piccadilly Towers were shelved indefinitely. A report by Deloitte ten years after the crash noted its dramatic impact: from a pre-crash peak of 4,000 residential units in the development pipeline in 2006, the flow dropped dramatically to less than 500 units in 2010, 2011 and 2012.[41]

The Thin Veneer of Democracy

The most unusual critique of Manchester in the years of high Blairism was created by the art collective UHC, based out of the old Dunlop Factory on the edge of Hulme. Recalling it sometime later, journalist Danny Moran remembered UHC, and in particular its "lynchpin" Jai Redman whose "various paintings, happenings and interventions — calling on experiences at the tree-dwelling end of political activism — belie a subtle knowledge of the nature of power, rooted as they are in a world where state and citizen engage each other in semi-permanent low-level conflict".[42] It was called "The Thin Veneer of Democracy", a 16-foot oak table etched with a diagram, mapping power relations between key interests associated with the regeneration of Manchester.[43] In etched and burnished wood it laid plain the dense web of interests at play in the new Manchester, revealing the lines of power that bound the city's elite together.

The decline of local democracy and the rise of private government went hand in hand with the fate of that great emblem of the city's democracy and culture — the Free Trade Hall. The site of Peterloo, built by Cobden; draped in black by the city's workers to mark the assassination of Abraham Lincoln; the site of rallies for women's suffrage; where Maurice Levine had chanted down Mosley's Blackshirts; the Hallé had performed countless concerts; Dylan had gone electric; the Sex Pistols had performed *that* gig; Stringer had convinced 1,800 council workers of the need to embrace the market.

Rebuilt in the 1950s following its bombing in the war, it would not survive Manchester's entrepreneurial turn.

In 1997, one year after the bomb, the Council sold it off to howls of protest from the Manchester Civic Society, and it became a Radisson Hotel. This sell-off represented a severing of the New Manchester from its past. It is said that Blair enjoyed staying in it, hoping perhaps some electric Dylan chic would rub off on him. Some years later, at a memorial day of discussion and talks to mark one year since Tony Wilson's death, someone heckled Leese from the floor: "Reclaim the Radisson!" He retorted with a response about the Free Trade Hall having poor acoustics and being a 1950s rip-off building. "No doubt believing", the heckler reflected later, "I wished to enshrine some tacky memorial to the Sex Pistols or something, rather than the betrayal by the Council in terms of ownership and meaning of Peterloo".[44]

Chapter 6
From Homes to Assets

The regeneration started in Ancoats, then it came to Beswick, now we have come here. And we basically get the land from the Council, build open market houses, they are all open market, and we sell to first time buyers. So we change the demographics of the area. This was a pretty run down place, high unemployment, high crime. So naturally the more we build the more the area has regenerated.

Property salesperson, Manctopia

There is something inherently stupid about gentrified thinking. It's a dumbing down and smoothing over of what people are actually like. It's a social position rooted in received wisdom, with aesthetics blindly selected from the presorted offerings of marketing and without information or awareness about the structures that create its own delusional sense of infallibility.

Sarah Schulman, *The Gentrification of the Mind*

"Ladies and gentlemen, can I bring everyone to order, as it were." It was the last day of the property fair MIPIM, held annually in Cannes on the French Riviera, and Howard Bernstein took to the stage in the Manchester pavilion, about to introduce his delegation's keynote guest. Somebody "who I spent a long time booing when he was playing football, but who since, actually, I have come to respect. Not only as a very entertaining analyst about football on TV, but a guy who has quite a profound sense of place and understands property, and who will become one of Manchester's influential leaders going forward. I genuinely believe that."[1]

The year was 2014 and ex-United footballer turned pundit and property developer Gary Neville was the star turn. He was being interviewed by Mike Emmerich, head of the Manchester City Council thinktank New Economy, and "our Bamber Gascoigne", according to Bernstein, due to the way he'd chaired the first day's session on the importance of agglomeration economics and cities to global economic development. In a session lasting just under half an hour, Neville fielded questions on the relative fortunes of the two Manchester clubs, his own property ambitions — including his recently opened "Hotel Football" — and the comparable leadership styles of Bernstein and Sir Alex Ferguson. Top of the agenda, however, was Manchester's nascent new property boom. "Cranes are now returning to the city's skyline", he noted. "Everything's a lot more vibrant than it was two or three years ago."

Neville wasn't just there to promote his home city, however. At play too were his own ambitions as a property developer. He'd long sought to develop the site near the Town Hall known as Jackson's Row, acquiring land there sometime previously. But he'd hit several obstacles — not least Greater Manchester Police's ownership of their old HQ on Bootle Street. Figures close to Bernstein presented Neville with a solution: the Council would buy the police station from GMP and lease it back to Neville, so that a complete land plot would be available for development. Over rosé-fuelled receptions in the spring sunshine the deal was struck. Six months later the Council's executive approved a joint-vehicle with Neville's Jackson Row

Development Company, and the Council bought the land the following year for £2.5m.[2] Little did Neville know, however, that this would be only the first hurdle — there was a wave of public backlash over the scheme still to come.

The Manchester presence at MIPIM in March 2014 seems in retrospect a crucial moment in the post-crash revival of its property industry. The following years saw a flurry of important announcements take place. Two months later, the deal with Abu Dhabi United Group was struck to continue the regeneration of Ancoats. In June 2014 at the city's Museum of Science and Industry, the then Chancellor George Osborne announced the launch of the "Northern Powerhouse", outlining his vision to build a "supercity" in the North of England with Manchester at its core. In a speech which praised Bernstein, "that brilliant star of city government", he drew on the same ideas that had been presented by Emmerich at MIPIM earlier that year.[3] Property-led regeneration, leveraging universities and attracting the all-important "creative class" were all themes of his speech. In a way, the "Manchester Model" had become national state policy. In November, Osborne signed off the most substantial devolution of powers to an English region in a generation. Central government funding was signed off for the Factory, while New Order's Peter Hook wondered aloud whether Osborne had once been a Haçienda raver himself.[4]

The following year saw the government sign off a £300m fund to Greater Manchester to invest in housing, aimed to provide loan capital to private developments struggling for liquidity on the open market. By September, Osborne, fresh from securing the first majority for the Tory Party in 23 years, led a trade delegation to China, banging the drum for his "Northern Powerhouse" project. Accompanying him was Richard Leese, who said there was an enormous opportunity for "massive investment" in Manchester over the following decade. A month later, Xi Jinping himself visited Manchester, as investments in the airport, in Salford's Middlewood Locks housing development and a host of other projects were confirmed.[5] Manchester, for a few brief years until the aftermath of the Brexit Referendum saw the Cameron/Osborne government collapse, was at the heart of national economic policy. In May 2016, Ian Simpson, who'd worked in the city since the reconstruction after the 1996 bomb, was presenting his designs for the new skyscraper cluster at the end of Deansgate, and emphasised the need for state money to be concentrated on Manchester, arguing that after it would all "flow out, exactly as happened when we rebuilt the city after the bomb".[6] By summer 2017, with Bernstein having stepped down and Andy Burnham being elected as inaugural mayor for the city-region, the results of the previous years were clear. Chair of Manchester's Planning Committee, Dave Ellison, remarked that Manchester was at the start of a "Chinese style" building boom.

Kickback

Of course, Osborne's newfound love for cities was a trend concurrent with austerity, the policy that had defined his whole time as Chancellor. Local government had been a key site of cutbacks, and Manchester, like many Labour-held urban administrations, was hit harder by the loss of direct grants than most. By 2015, austerity was having dramatic social and political effects. In Manchester, a wave of protests had erupted over the homelessness crisis — rough sleeping had increased tenfold since 2010.[7] In April that year, the activist group Homeless Rights of Justice pitched tents outside the gates of the Town Hall to draw attention to the rising crisis.

Soup kitchens were set up. More protesters arrived, and the tension rose. Groups from across the anti-austerity movement were present. A more militant section detached themselves and tried to force their way inside the Town Hall, but were blocked from doing so.[8] A few days later the Council acquired a court injunction to move the protestors on.

Across the summer, as the activists set up "tent cities" across the city centre, moving from high-profile spot to high-profile spot, the Council acquired an injunction each time to move them on. Eventually, at the end of July, the Council acquired a city-wide injunction on anybody pitching a tent. Councillor Nigel Murphy, deputy leader, welcomed the ruling,

> The court found in our favour after listening to the evidence we presented about the amount of disruption these camps have caused to residents and businesses… We will now be working with Greater Manchester Police and court bailiffs to regain possession of the site as soon as possible.[9]

By the following year, the "tent cities" had moved to sites on the peripheries of the city centre. In the centre itself, the activists had changed tactics and started to squat buildings instead.

In October 2015 Gary Neville had his own confrontation with squatters in his building, the old Stock Exchange, which he and fellow ex-United player Ryan Giggs had plans to turn into a hotel. The squatters' spokesperson, Wesley Hall, announced that they'd renamed the building the "Sock Exchange", and had plans to operate a homeless hub from the building across the winter. Surprisingly, Neville agreed, telling the squatters he had no need of the building until the following spring and would be happy to work with them to house the street homeless over the weekend.[10] It's likely that Neville had an eye on the good publicity his act would generate — at the time concerns were rising over the future of the Peterloo-era pub the Sir Ralph Abercromby, which was likely to be demolished under his plans for Jackson's Row. The fight to save that pub would dominate headlines for years, as Neville's scheme garnered massive opposition, being rejected at planning a number of times for its "overbearing" twin towers and the demolition of the pub. Eventually he rowed back on his initial masterplan, and brought forward another in 2017 that included the retention of the pub and the façade of the Bootle Street police station. Still to go, however, was the city centre's only synagogue, a beautiful piece of Modernist architecture that saw its last service at the end of 2022.

Over the following years, from 2015, the pattern of the tent cities was repeated with the squatters. For over two years, the squatters and the authorities were locked in a game of cat-and-mouse — they broke into buildings and claimed squatters rights, and pushed the landowners to go through the legal process of gaining court injunctions to evict them. By 2018 police figures showed that there had been over 40 squat evictions in that time.[11] Many of the buildings squatted were on sites primed for development, including the Ducie Bridge pub, part of the Co-operative Group's NOMA redevelopment masterplan and now demolished. From there the squatters were violently evicted, resulting in one of them, Chris Blaine, being put in prison for eight weeks. Another was the so-called "Cosy Dragon", in an ex-mill on the site of U&I's £1.4bn Mayfield development, now 100,000 square foot of office space.[12] By far the highest profile, however, was the squat which took over the Cornerhouse Cinema, one of Bob Scott's old projects. The cinema, recently closed and amalgamated with the Library Theatre into HOME, the new arts anchor for the Council's "First Street" masterplan, had lain empty for a couple of years. In February 2017 a crew of squatters took it, and the following month threw open its doors for a week-long arts festival called Loose Space, all centred around the idea of "home". The squat stayed open until September, when its owner secured an eviction notice.

Coming at a crucial time, over the period of the first mayoral election and with its significant location, the Cornerhouse Cinema squat served to force political attention on the housing and homelessness crisis more than anything else. When in April of that year, the mayoral candidates assembled for a housing hustings organised by the campaign group Greater Manchester Housing Action at St Phillip's Church in Salford, a crew from the Cornerhouse set up tents outside and grilled the candidates on their housing policies. Burnham later reflected to Helen Pidd at the *Guardian* that the hustings had been "the most explosive I've ever seen".[13] Housing and homelessness had become the lightning-rod issue for the campaign, and Burnham's focus on eliminating rough sleeping the direct result of the pressure applied during it:

> There was an anger about housing policy in Greater Manchester and a sense that Greater Manchester hasn't been focused enough on affordable housing. I agree, and that's got to change. There's cranes in the sky building luxury apartments while the numbers in the doorways are going up all the time.[14]

Tents and Towers

Those years between the MIPIM conference in 2014 and the housing hustings in 2017 saw the revival of the "Manchester Model", as the city's leaders grappled with the economic fallout of the 2008 crash. The years after saw increased contestation, with an increasingly well organised housing movement and a small but growing bloc of left councillors during Jeremy Corbyn's leadership of the national Labour Party beginning to challenge the leadership's direction. Despite this, the general trajectory continued.

Today the results of those years are clear. Anyone visiting Manchester with prior knowledge of the city would be shocked by the transformation of its centre in the last decade. Clusters of skyscrapers break the skyline, injecting a verticality into the backdrop of what had always been a predominantly low-rise city. The towers, in gleaming corporate style, are angular blocks against the skyline. From the suburbs they stand in striking silhouette, by night, their white sparkle is ringed by red lamps, providing an unambiguous point of orientation. Less dramatic than these, but with greater consequence, are the blocks of flats erected at pace and now home to scores of young professionals. Most of these flats are private rentals, with a single, corporate landlord. This is the result of the "Chinese-style" growth, Osborne's "Northern Powerhouse" and the City Council's own leadership's canny manoeuvring of city towards investment in its land and property assets.

How did this happen? We have already seen in vignette some of the details of the deals struck by major figures in the Council, and the ways in which investors were sourced to buy into the Manchester Model. But to properly understand what is going on, a more systemic approach is required. Here, it is helpful to borrow a concept from Harvey Molotch and think of the city as a "growth machine" — a regime of capital accumulation through the empowerment of the rentier.

What follows relies on a body of critical research produced

over the last five years. During this time, a series of reports were published by a network of academics and organisers centred around the campaign group Greater Manchester Housing Action.[15] Taken as a whole, the body of work tracked and critiqued the post-crash revival of the city's property-led regeneration model in real-time. Its impact was extensive — covered by the media, discussed in public meetings, Labour Party branches and with small groups of allied councillors. For many it was clear, the research confirmed what they had already intuited, adding statistical weight to the widely held opinion that Manchester was being sold off. Getting to grips with and synthesising this body of research gives us the tools we need to get beneath the hood of the growth machine and demystify the arrival of the towers.

Post-Crash Accumulation Strategies

First though, we need a basic theoretical grounding. As we explored at the start, capital has always tended to "switch" investment from production into real estate. Crises in the capitalist system result in the overaccumulation of capital, leading to pools of surplus capital, unable to find an outlet in productive sectors of the economy, fixing themselves in investments in infrastructure and real estate (the "secondary circuit"). This absorption of capital surplus temporarily solves the problem of overaccumulation and at the same time creates an expanded and improved built environment for future capital accumulation. Since the 1980s — after the "Big Bang" in the financial sector — the secondary circuit has taken on an increasingly important structural role within economies in the Global North.

In the aftermath of the financial crisis, a "wall of capital" has flooded into property and real estate as a secure outlet for surpluses. This has created a process of the financialisation of housing, whereby housing has increasingly operated as a core asset in the portfolios of investors. Financial actors have become direct players in the entire production process of new housing. Asset managers increasingly move as active participants in not only the construction of housing, but also its operation. They hold the new properties as fixed rental assets and draw a fixed income from them in perpetuity. The United Nations, in a report to its Secretariat in 2017, described housing financialisation as "Structural changes in housing and financial markets and global investment, whereby housing is treated as a commodity, a means of accumulating wealth, and often as security for the financial instruments traded and sold on the global market."[16]

The city leaders were operating in an environment where investors were increasingly looking to place their investments into cities — their housing and urban land. These were investments of a very particular sort. Asset managers were investing with a clear financial purpose — they were buying up the right to extract wealth through the development of real estate. They were investing to become rentiers.

The research done by academics Richard Golding, Jonathan Silver and Adam Leaver into the property boom — analysing over 45,000 housing units built or granted planning permission between 2012-2020 — shows us that these trends are very much evident within the Greater Manchester urban core.[17] What emerges, strikingly, is the growth in build-to-rent. A favoured housing product by asset managers and a key indicator of financialised housing markets, build-to-rent properties are constructed for permanent rental. Their presence in Britain's private rented sector is a novel post-crash development, as historically this sector had been dominated by small-scale buy-to-let landlords. High-density rental-residential owned by institutional investors accounts for just over a quarter of all properties above five storeys built since 2008. Just over half of these are in London. However, in Manchester, over half of all housing units granted planning permission in the city centre since 2012 are build-to-rent.

Another tell-tale sign that the process of financialisation is well underway in Manchester is the increased presence of professionally managed investment funds: almost half of all developments were financed this way. They come in different forms, such as pension and insurance funds, limited real estate funds, real estate investment trusts or direct investment from banks and hedge funds. There are also private funds — pools of capital in the ownership of one individual or family. Within the context of the professionally managed funds, build-to-rent is particularly favoured. The city's property market has become attractive to a wider and deeper pool of capital, marking a stark departure from the pre-crash era in the city, where homes were largely being built for sale.

Manchester has also seen the proliferation of novel forms of rental housing. Purpose-built student accommodation (PBSA) and co-living are both types of apartments that are characterised by low build standards and high yield. They can circumvent minimum space standards — structured more like hotels, with living spaces below what would be allowed for ordinary rental accommodation, as multiple non-related adults share a single living space with rooms off the side of it. PBSA is looked on as "asset class" investment on the part of institutional investors — with return on investments well over 10% and sometimes up to 20%.[18]

Almost a third of the development boom in Manchester has been financed by capital coming from overseas.

Professionally managed funds tend to be more international, while international finance tends to favour build-to-rent by a factor of 2-1 over build to sell. A full 41.5% of all the build-to-rent developments in Greater Manchester since 2012 is financed by overseas money. This shows us the attractiveness of this as a fungible asset class to investors wanting to park their money somewhere.

These three forms of rental housing — PBSA, co-living and build-to-rent — ought to be understood as three prongs in the same process: the building of a new renter subject. Taken together they form a pipeline of new renters that can be relied upon to continue paying rents and be used to the practice of renting from a corporate landlord. Wider shifts in housing, particularly the growing inability of a section of the middle class to gain access to the property ladder, has led to investors realising that there is a reliable pool of potential wealthy renters that will not exit the sector for a long time — if ever.

While build-to-rent remains a marginal part of the rental sector nationwide, its growth in recent years has been impressive: by the end of 2022, it accounted for over 240,000 units built or under construction in the UK.[19] Property group Savills predicts that this will increase fivefold over the next decade, with the sector set to be worth £170bn by 2032.[20] What kind of society is being built? To gain an insight into this question, we might look to Manchester, where the rise of the rentier is stark.

Manchester City Council, through the deals struck in the middle years of the last decade, handed over the extraction rights to a broad class of corporate landlords, who extract rent from their tenants and often take this wealth offshore. Manchester has become a pre-eminent example of the *real estate state*. This is the symbiotic relationship between politicians, the institutions of the local state and the property lobby. It amounts to a form of state capture by a sectional interest of the capitalist class. Coined by American urban theorist Samuel Stein, the "real estate state" refers to

> The growing centrality of urban real estate to capital's global growth strategy. Through this process, the price of land becomes a central economic determinate and a dominant political issue, determining both which social groups have access to urban life and what kinds of economic activities can survive. The clunky term "gentrification" becomes a household word and displacement an everyday fact of life. Housing becomes a globally traded financial asset, creating the conditions for synchronised bubbles and crashes.[21]

We will now explore how we got here, by examining four interrelated aspects in turn: the public-private partnerships struck by the Council; the privatisation of public land; the use of financial incentives like the Housing Investment Fund and the relaxing of the usual levies on developers; and finally the exercise of raw political power through the planning process to get certain developments through.

Public-Private Partnerships: The Case of Manchester Life

We have already encountered the use of public-private partnerships by the Council to facilitate development in the case of Gary Neville's proposals for the Jackson Row site, which Jen Williams in the *Evening News* described at the time as "not an unusual move for a town hall long known for its willingness to work with the private sector".[22] What is perhaps more unusual — and certainly the deal to have attracted the greatest amount of critical attention — is that struck between the Council and the Abu Dhabi United Group (ADUG), owners of Manchester City, to build rental housing: Manchester Life.

To trace its origins we have to return to Ancoats. After the farcical failure of Urban Splash to deliver anything like it promised, the land reverted to the Council, which was looking for a new strategy for its development. The purchasing of Manchester City by ADUG in 2008 provided an interesting alternative. As we have seen, the Council had posited the new owners as an alternative source of capital for development from the end of the East Manchester regeneration project. Since 2010, the seemingly limitless oil wealth of the emirate has become a key prop for the Council's vision to transform East Manchester. This process is ongoing, with a masterplan vision laid out for the neighbourhoods around the stadium stretching to 2027. At the heart of it is Manchester Life.

To date, Manchester Life has delivered 1,468 housing units located within Ancoats. The total value of all of Manchester Life's assets stands at around £350m. The land upon which these housing blocks are built was once owned by the Council. In 2014 ownership was transferred to a series of subsidiary companies of "Loom Holdings Ltd", a Jersey-based company owned by the ADUG. While the Council maintained ownership of the freehold (the permanent ownership of the land), the leaseholds (the right to use the land) were handed over for 999 years, making this a *de facto* privatisation.[23] The report "Manchester Offshored" delved deep into the nature of the deal, and we can gain a clear view inside the workings of the partnership. It provides us with an invaluable snapshot into the inner workings of a company so symbolic of the contemporary neoliberal city.

Manchester Life is a joint development vehicle between Manchester City Council and the ADUG. Its developments consist mainly of flats, but some townhouses have been built too. Of the completed units, the majority (1,073) have been built to rent, while 395 have been sold. The company adopts what it terms a "through life" approach — it manages the project from initial conception, to assembling the finance, land and labour in the construction state, all the way through to letting and sales and ultimately, in the case of the rental homes, acting as the landlord and managing company of the blocks. On the surface it seems straightforward. On the one hand, the Council has land assets and control over planning, as well as its regeneration agenda in East Manchester. On the other, Abu Dhabi, with its deep financial reserves, needs to find both a productive outlet for its capital in order to diversify its income in the face of peak oil and burnish its reputation in the West through soft power initiatives.[24]

But, like many modern corporate entities, Manchester Life is not a single "corporation" in the traditional sense. Rather than being a single organisation, it is a complex nested set of companies with varying lines of ownership and control. These are linked through financial and legal relationships, and all held under the common umbrella of "Manchester Life". It is better understood as an assemblage of entities, all performing different functions, including development, rental, management and sales. By examining the percentage of shares held in the joint vehicle and the differing right to appoint directors, it is clear that the Council is the junior partner.

Once the buildings are complete, their ownership is transferred to a set of Jersey-based entities owned by "Loom Holdings", itself registered in Jersey. So, for example, Smiths Yard is owned by "Blossom Iron Developments", Cotton Field Wharf by "Silk Glass Developments" and One Cutting Room Square by "Loom Cotton Developments". These companies each own a physical asset, and together they also own "Manchester Life Management Ltd" — the company, registered in the UK, that employs the sales and management teams and collects the rent. In 2021 this rental income amounted to £10.1m. But all taxation liability is mitigated by balancing the sales revenue by an equal amount of "administrative expense". This means in practice that the rental income from apartments that were built through a joint vehicle between the Council and Abu Dhabi, on public land, is routed offshore, through Jersey and back to Abu Dhabi itself.

Manchester Life has several key novelties. In it we see the Council acting more like a commercial developer than a public authority. The local state has gone beyond simply providing the supportive policy context for development or acting as an *enabler* to being an *executor* of development. Through the partnership the Council has intervened directly into land and property markets — expanding and accelerating processes of state-led gentrification on the eastern edge of the city centre. This marks out a second novelty — the privatisation of regeneration. No longer the business of the local state, not even in its New Labour iteration with significant private partnerships, it feels the Council has wholly outsourced the regeneration to private interests.

The Privatisation of Public Land

The privatisation of public land was another lever the Council was able to pull to shape development. By the early 1980s, the City Council's land ownership reached a historic high — with one estimate placing its ownership at almost two-thirds of the city's total area.[25] At the dawn of the city's neoliberal era, the

Council owned over half the land in the city. There has thus been a plentiful supply of this resource to shape development.

This privatisation of public land assets is not a phenomenon unique to Manchester. In his work *The New Enclosure*, Brett Christophers argues that the privatisation of public land ought to be popularly understood as the single greatest privatisation of the neoliberal era. Since Thatcher's time, the government has consistently argued that the public ownership of land is inefficient, and through a combination of incentives, targets and funding cuts has chivvied councils and other public bodies to sell "surplus" land to the private sector. He estimates that, as a result, 10% of Britain's total land mass has been privatised since the 1970s, equivalent to land worth £40bn.

Tom Gillespie and Jonathan Silver's research into the disposal of public land in Manchester gives us a sense of the deployment of this tool by the Council. Freedom of Information requests they made revealed that in the post-crash period (2009-2019) the Council has disposed of 36 freeholds and 298 leaseholds across the central wards of the city. These have either been sold to a private body or transferred into a joint vehicle — like Manchester Life. Out of these disposals, the Council has made a total of £9.03m from the freehold sales, and £33.4m from the "premium" generated on the disposal of the leasehold land. In total, the Council has made £42.4m in income from the disposal of public land in the decade following the crash.

Drilling down further, Gillespie and Silver take as their case study the neighbourhood of Ancoats, which as we have already seen has been the centre of the developments of Manchester Life. This neighbourhood had already been the site of significant land disposals in the previous decade, with Urban Splash the principal beneficiary. Their failure to deliver on the full development site meant that by the mid-2010s, the Council retained significant interest in the site. The beneficiaries of this land have been Manchester Life, the largest single beneficiary, and several private developers. These include UK developers McCauls, developer of "The Point", a 117-unit luxury apartment complex near the Ancoats Marina, built on land received on a 999-year lease for £0, and General Projects, who have been granted the land south of the Ashton Canal, so-called "New Islington Green" — for a total of £2.38m — or £528,000 per acre. The total value recouped from land disposals in this neighbourhood by the Council appears to be £6.12m.

The character of the developments that have arisen on the former public land in Ancoats is emblematic of the city boom as a whole. 1,996 apartments have been built on the 15.75 acres of privatised public land since 2014. On top of this, 400 units were built by Urban Splash in the pre-crash era. Based on a conservative estimate, the total development value of this land may now exceed £400m.[26] The majority of these are build-to-rent. Assuming the standard operating margin for the developers is between 15-20% of the total development value, this suggests that these schemes may have generated £80m in profit — dwarfing by many margins the £6.12m recouped in land sales by the Council. Aside from the 37 social rented homes built by Urban Splash in the 2000s to replace the 163 units lost with the demolition of the Cardroom, there have been no affordable homes built in the neighbourhood. Neither have any of the developments appeared to have contributed Section 106 payments to the Council for their construction elsewhere.

The research into land disposals in the ward of Ancoats and Beswick shines a useful light on the granular processes of development in the city. A picture emerges of the Council strategically deploying its land assets to create a certain kind of development — often at a loss to itself, as the land appears to have been sold in many instances for prices below its true value. We can only assume that the loss on true land values was accepted as a price worth paying to kickstart the development of the district. The results of this process represent a particular form of urban development; of financialised, high-yield rental; and the creation of what academics at the University of Manchester Business School identified as "a kind of parallel private new town, the central city".[27]

Financial Incentives

Financial subsidy is most clearly tied to the devolution agenda in the form of the Housing Investment Fund, initially a £300m loan from the central government, and administered by the Greater Manchester Combined Authority (GMCA). As part of the devolution package agreed in 2014, this pot of money was then used by the GMCA to loan to developers, to provide additional capital liquidity to developments at a time when accessing the finance on the open market was more difficult — in the immediate half decade after the crash. Where difficulties arose for developers in terms of accessing the finance they needed to move projects forward, the Housing Investment Fund (HIF) stepped in. It has thus played a key strategic role in the development of the property boom, acting as a source of bridging capital to de-risk build-to-rent schemes from the perspective of the developers. In its initial round, it lent out £167m to one mixed and five build-to-rent schemes, a total of 3033 units — 67.7% of the total of 4483 supported by the scheme.

One developer above all has been the receipt of these funds. Its name is Renaker, and it is the actor most responsible for the clearest indication of the change in Manchester over the last decade, its changing skyline. An FOI request put in by journalist James Graham to the HIF confirmed that half of the entire £400m fund had gone to Renaker.[28] The changing skyline has been made possible through the financial support of the state.

Another form of financial subsidy, insofar as the lifting of levies that would otherwise be charged acts as a bung to developers, is the lifting of the affordable housing requirements that can be negotiated with developers under Section 106 of the Town and Country Planning Act 1990. The Act would normally enable Councils to compel developers, as a condition of planning consent, either to provide a quotient of on-site affordable housing or infrastructure improvements; or to give a cash donation towards the construction of such housing or infrastructure elsewhere. It represents a sort of clawback or tax that the local state can make upon the vast flows of capital coursing through the build environment of the city. But, it is a tool that has gone largely unused by the planning department in Manchester.

The measure of how little this tool has been taken up can be reached by comparing the total value of the developments that have taken place in the city core, against the clawback that the local councils have been able to secure from it. Conservative estimates put the gross development value of the 45,000 units at a total of £8.3bn.[29] From this, the total S106 payments that have been secured amount to £33.3m, or around 0.4% of the total development value that has been captured. Of this, £20.9m has been channelled towards infrastructural improvements, while only £15.4m has been for affordable housing contributions, representing 0.2% of the total value.

Furthermore, figures comparing the three boroughs of Greater Manchester who have presence in the core, show that Manchester has been particularly lax. Across the three boroughs, the total figures are broken down as follows: Manchester, £9.2m; Salford, £4.4m and Trafford £1.9m. It's immediately clear from these figures that Manchester is lax in collecting levies on developers, when compared to its neighbouring boroughs. These figures are particularly stark when one considers the volume of the development to have taken place in this area. Section 106 may also be paid with in-kind affordable house building on site. Yet, judging by this metric the clawback from developers is even more paltry. The database shows only 192 affordable homes were provided this way, 0.4% of all the housing units built in the city over this period.

The relaxation of planning restraints in the post-crash period was, in the Council's view, a deliberate strategy designed to further significant development proposals critical to economic growth. We might alternatively understand it as a critical incentive provided to bring the rentier city into being.

Politicised Planning

By way of an introduction, let's consider the battle that raged for almost four years over the future of a derelict warehouse on Soap Street, home of the Manchester "rice and three" institution This and That, a legacy from when the area was home to hundreds of South Asian textile workers. Situated on the edge of the Northern Quarter, where the trendy district collides with Shudehill, the site had been acquired by property developers Salboy, owned by local-boy-done-good and founder of the Betfred gambling empire, Fred Done. The Northern Quarter is the area with the most listed buildings in the city, while Shudehill has its own ragged charm — home to a few old-school boozers, dirty mag shops, a cult bookstore, a mysteriously empty "safe shop" and the transport interchange. It was a sensitive site for future development.

In the summer of 2017, Salboy put forward plans to construct a 13-storey "aparthotel" on the site — demolishing the existing building and constructing a faux-brick tower in its place, to be managed by "Zoku", an Amsterdam-based aparthotel operator. The site was analysed in a case study in the *Homes to Assets* report as indicative of the growing short-term lettings market in the city.[30] Compared to equivalent yield for long-term rental, the report estimated that the 122-room aparthotel would draw an additional £2.46m in rental income for the owners. There was therefore a clear business case for the developers, and from the planners' perspective the site represented an opportunity to uplift a corner of the city centre that had thus far seemed immune from redevelopment. It seemed nailed on that the planning committee would grant approval, as they had done for so many earlier schemes.

Yet, it wasn't to be. Influenced by changing political winds in the city and country at large, the scheme attracted a degree of opposition that took Salboy by surprise. Almost immediately concerns were raised over the size and scale of the development, particularly on the Shudehill side. Some labelled the proposal a "sore thumb". Councillor Davies, who sat on the Planning Committee, called it "a giraffe among hamsters". Scores of residents wrote in with their objections.

Part of Manchester's planning process is the need for the Planning Committee to give multiple refusals. The initial refusal of any development is a verdict that the Committee is "minded" to refuse. A second vote is required to confirm refusal. However, in the meantime the developer then can work with the planning department to meet the concerns of the Committee and bring it back. If it comes back, then it is classed as a new proposal — meaning the Committee can only be "minded to refuse" as it's classed once more as the first vote on a proposal. This means that final refusal always seems elusive, and the developer has in practice unlimited opportunities to bring a project back.

The Committee was due to hear the proposal on the 16th November 2017, but postponed a vote pending a site visit. The following month they passed a motion that they were "minded to refuse". In January 2018 the developers brought back a slightly amended proposal. It was rejected, but owing to the fact this was not the version rejected in December, it had to come back for a second time again. Finally, in February 2018 the refusal was sealed with a third vote. Simon Ismail, a director at Salboy, admitted in that meeting that they "had not anticipated that the scheme would cause so many concerns". These three votes to refuse had each gone against the recommendation of the planning officers to approve the site; as the councillors had stood firm to their convictions and voted the scheme down. It felt like a turning point. But what came next stands as an object lesson in the realities of the city's planning machine under the late Leese period.

Rather than filing an appeal with the planning inspectorate to overturn the Council's decision, Salboy returned to the drawing board. By September that year, the company opened a consultation on a new design for the site. "Dirty tactics on Soap Street", cried journalist Hayley Flynn, covering the supposed "consultation" event that ended with announcement of the imminent demolition of one part of the existing building on the site, due to "safety concerns" — actioned the following morning. This came on top of earlier demolitions in May that year, and contributed to a sense of ratcheting tension over the site — and the notion that the development was becoming

ISAAC ROSE

emblematic of the transformations of the neighbourhood. By Christmas that year plans were unveiled — a glass tower now 17 storeys tall on the Shudehill side, with apartments. In a sop to local opinion, frontage from the old warehouses was maintained and a so-called "pocket park" (a single cherry tree) was added to the plans. None of the apartments, unsurprisingly, were to be affordable.

The plans were finally approved by the Committee in June 2019, by a vote of 8-5. Residents, who had turned up expecting a victory, left in tears. Salboy's people high-fived in the chamber. Questions hung over the verdict — one commentator asking whether it signified the "end" of the Northern Quarter as it had been, while others pointed to irregularities on the Committee — the fact that there were two councillors on it from Crumpsall, the same ward as Council leader Richard Leese. By the end of the year another fact emerged — Fred Done had personally donated £6m to a YouthZone in East Manchester, something which at the very least can't have hurt his chances of getting the proposals through. In a last-ditch attempt, campaigners — including the ward councillors where the development sat, who had consistently opposed the proposals — sought to halt the disposal of a small piece of public land in the middle of the site necessary for its development. But by 2021 they conceded defeat — the land had been signed away on a 250-year lease, in exchange for funding for social housing, while the Council executive had approved a change from apartments to "tech hub" offices during the years of the pandemic.

The list of proposals that were the flashpoint of opposition is long. Examples include PBSA developments such as the "Tombstone", a 55-storey skyscraper south of the city centre, which residents ultimately took to a judicial review and lost; as well as the "Church Inn" development in Hulme, rejected

218

multiple times by the Committee and then approved by Joanne Roney, the new Chief Executive of the Council, during the Covid-19 lockdown under delegated powers. A similar case is the Smith's Arms in Ancoats, the neighbourhood's oldest pub, dating back to 1775, a true survivor of many eras of change. There was a campaign to save it, but it was in vain — the pub was demolished in 2016 to make way for Manchester Life's development "Smiths Yard". Today the doorway of the pub has been repurposed as a fireplace in the lobby of the flats.

Over the decade and a half since the crash, the only real way residents have been able to push back against the rentier city's rollout has been through the Planning Committee. Absent any sort of coherent political pushback — for instance, a significant bloc of oppositional councillors — attempts to shape, direct or just block the walls of capital have been condensed into this key committee. What's more, these tussles over planning permissions confined their opposition to couching their objections within strict guardrails: the "material" considerations that were legally the only ground for refusing applications. It wasn't possible to argue that this or that development was bad because of gentrification or the nature of urban development it engendered. Rather, objections had to be couched in less political, more supposedly objective terms: height and mass, impact on sunlight, overshadowing, impact on waste management and street parking, etc.

Pressure could be countered by the political control the leadership had within the Labour Party — which held all or nearly all seats on the Council throughout this period. They could use the whip to discipline rebellious councillors or rearrange committees, removing dissenting voices, applying political pressure and contorting the system to get "their" developments through. Of course, these manipulations were never in view of the public and always within the realm of plausible deniability. We can only surmise that they took place based on the snippets of information that were leaked into the public sphere. And for observers of the Planning Committee, there was none more tantalising than that of Councillor Marcia Hutchinson, who in conversation with journalist Danny Moran shared a memory. "I remember people picketing outside…" she said:

I remember going in and thinking "you're picketing the wrong meeting". The decision on how we're all going to vote has been made earlier…In one case I was told "yeah, good Marcia, it'll be good to have somebody sounding a bit of opposition in the meeting…" It was almost a rehearsal.[31]

Hutchinson would later resign as Councillor, citing racism and targeted bullying within the Labour group.

Struggles over Land in the Heart of the City

Where much of this came together in a particularly interesting way was in the battle fought by the campaign "Trees Not Cars" between 2019 and 2021. The story of this fight takes us back to Ancoats — only the residents now fighting the Council were primarily people from "new" Ancoats, those living in the new buildings that had been built since the mid-2000s. This time the struggle was over a large site of prime development land, the former Central Retail Park, sandwiched between Urban Splash's arena and Great Ancoats Street. That retail park had once been an attempt to "regenerate" the area, but had fallen on hard times with the collapse of retail and by 2015 was largely empty. The Council spotted an opportunity for strategic intervention.

In 2017 the Council bought the 10.5 acre site for £37m. Its long-term plan was for office space and residential development, with a possible role for the ADUG. In contrast, many in the city saw the site as an opportunity for an alternative vision, with space for a city centre park to address air quality and carbon-neutral public housing to tackle Manchester's growing housing crisis. However, there was little scope for any kind of coherent challenge to the Council's plans. This all changed in 2019 when the Council announced, on the same day it declared a "climate emergency", that the meanwhile use of the site would be for a temporary car park. In response, members of the surrounding community established a campaign, Trees Not Cars, and began to cohere opposition. Its lead organisers were two women, who had both experienced the detrimental effects of their neighbourhood's high air pollution: Gemma Cameron, who since moving to the city from Nottingham in 2011 had felt her asthma getting worse, resulting in a first-time hospitalisation, and Julia Kovaliova, a mother of three, two of whom attend the primary school next to the site, and one of whom, the eldest, then 11, had developed asthma five years earlier.

Across 2019 Trees Not Cars led a vibrant summer of action, amassing over 12,000 signatures on its petition and holding regular demos and protests. They took direct action, digging up the concrete and planting saplings as a form of "guerrilla gardening" and engaged architecture students at the University of Manchester to craft alternative proposals for the site. In September, the campaign drew strength as large climate mobilisations brought hundreds of people down to the site in opposition to the Council's plans. As well as the popular mobilisations, the campaign also had the support of all three of the ward's Labour councillors and wider sympathies within the Party across the city.

The focus of the campaign was, again, the Planning Committee, whose members would have the power to reject the Council's plans — but when the critical vote came on 17th October 2019, the car park proposals passed by 7-3. But it appeared that the leadership of the Council had manipulated the Committee in order to get the vote through. In a statement on their website, the campaigners noted that "prior to the crucial planning meeting the Leader of the Council and Councillor Pat Karney wrote emails suggestive of seeking to influence the planning committee's decision".[32] Furthermore, in the days leading up to the meeting, Karney, then Labour Group Whip, Chair of the Constitutional and Nomination Committee and Executive Member for the City Centre, reconstituted the planning committee. One of the councillors added to the committee on 8th October, a mere nine days before the decision was to be made, was Councillor John Flanagan, who had been part of an executive group that worked on the purchase of the site with the ADUG in 2017.

The campaigners launched a judicial review. To defend itself, the Council spent an estimated £70,000 on a team of lawyers led by Christopher Katakowski QC, a London-based barrister, one of the leading planning specialists in the country and a key architect of the controversial government planning reforms. But the Council's efforts were fruitless. On the 19th February 2021 the Court of Appeal ruled in favour of the campaign and overturned the planning permissions. In his ruling, Judge Bird found that the Council had failed to consider both the impact of the development on air quality in the local area and what effect a 440-space car park would have next to a primary school. It was also found that Council officers had "misled" members of the Planning Committee by providing erroneous analysis of the air-quality impact of the proposals. Cameron, responding to the ruling, said,

> We have stopped the Council from putting a car park next to a primary school. This is the first time we are aware of a community group beating the Council in a legal challenge… The Council instructed probably the most expensive planning barristers in England in an attempt to crush a community group fighting for clean air for children. It's time that Sir Richard Leese retire.[33]

The victory of Trees Not Cars in the courts meant that for four years plans were stalled on the site. In late 2022 it was announced that the Home Office had expressed an interest in developing the site to relocate parts of the civil service north, and a draft plan was announced — including a small city centre park.

What Is the City but Its People?

There is a risk that by only focussing upon the global dimension of the investors — particularly in the case of the Manchester Life deal and its partnership with Abu Dhabi — that only a moral and ethical critique of the partnership is advanced. Manchester Life is bad because the people the deal was struck with are bad. The risk is twofold, first that Manchester Life is seen as anomalous and set apart from the wider structural transformations at play. Second, is that it runs the risk of falling into the trap of saying that the investment is bad merely because it is global, as if what was happening would be good if only the investors were based in Britain. Or, relatedly, that what is happening in Manchester today is bad and novel because it is global.

Of course, there is nothing novel about Manchester being integrated into the circuits of the global economy. As we have seen throughout this book, Manchester has for hundreds of years been a city drawing upon a wider, global and imperial economy. The recent post-crash boom is a *reintegration* of Manchester into the global economy after a period of separation following the collapse of industry and the closure of the docks.

What is new, though, is that the city now exhibits a broad class of corporate landlords who extract rent from their tenants and often take this wealth offshore. The *rentierisation* of the city functions as an enormous extractive machine, valorising the balance sheets of investors all over the globe. Manchester has re-entered the circuits of global capital circulation, but now the secondary circuit of real estate and land speculation is predominant. In this way it is like many other cities worldwide where global capital has entered the land and property markets.

Yet perhaps what makes Manchester stand out — certainly compared to London, the only other city in the UK with similar levels of institutional landlordism — is that these new rental blocs aren't tucked away in distant suburbs or along waterfronts. Rather, they sit in the heart of the city, transforming the entire feel of the place. Additionally, their relative mass is greater — Manchester is a far smaller city, but its build-to-rent sector is about a third the size of London's. A casual observer of the city can witness the changes merely from passing through it on the train.

The efforts made to create this rentier city have birthed their own contradictions. The example of Trees Not Cars stands as an important illustration of these, as they unfold within the city as the development model rolls on. Its leaders were largely residents of "New" Ancoats — precisely the people that a decade of development had been designed to attract. In a way they were the gentrifiers. Yet their interests were rapidly hurtling into conflict with the demands of the development machine for more construction, for squeezing profit margins out of every inch of space. Social amenities, green space and places for children to play — in other words, the kinds of areas necessary in a neighbourhood where people are meant to actually live, rather than just consume — were not being built.

This example is just one of many in the city, which is increasingly oriented as a "growth machine" where the interests of capital accumulation through the built environment and the production of spaces of consumption is at odds with the kinds of things a city requires for social reproduction of its people — for people to live there. Parks are illustrative — as public, non-commercial spaces they hold an important and now rare space within our cities. But after over a decade of austerity this kind of public space, public service and public amenity is increasingly vanishing. The city's working class is at a crisis point, and the question of housing is more and more having an effect outside the city centre.

The huge upswing in development in the city centre is bursting its boundaries and putting rents under pressure in the neighbouring districts, the traditional ring of working-class neighbourhoods that surrounded the urban core. The housing crisis might be understood as the modality through which the urban crisis is lived. It is to the mechanics of the city's housing crisis that we now turn.

Chapter 7
The Gentrification Frontier

*If you're born and raised in the middle of the city — Hulme,
Ardwick, Rusholme — within eye view, as soon as you get to any
of the major roads, you can see two things popping up. To the
north: towers. To the south: to let signs.*

Jamil Keating

*Times have changed for tower dwellers,
We don't have city lives now we are pushed to the outside,
To the margins in overspill estates,
The city closed firmly we were forced out by the back gate.*

Tina Cribbin

Members of the Moss Side Tenants Union meet twice a month.
One regular meeting is a housing rights and advice drop-in at
the Millennium Windrush Centre, situated in the heart of the
Alexandra Park estate. The sessions, running since late 2022,
provide a sort of mirror to the conditions tenants, both public
and private, are struggling with in the inner south of the city.
"It's concerning", says union organiser and neighbourhood
tenant Thirza Amina Asanga-Rae, "just when you think you
have heard something shocking or dumbfounding, someone
walks in and tells us their story. And leaves us puzzled with
how to solve it."[1] Disrepair is a common condition that
people are struggling with. Leaks, mould, damp and vermin

infestations mark daily life for many tenants across Moss Side. This is something Asanga-Rae has personal experience of, having previously faced extreme water leaks through the roof of her social tenancy into the bedrooms and the kitchen. The housing association was slow to act, despite many attempts to raise the alarm. The engineers sent out merely advised her not to use the water or shower. When eventually the alarm was raised right to the top, the association finally acted, decanting her family from the home to make the necessary repairs. Her story is not unusual. "As part of my role I visit properties and gather evidence", Asanga-Rae says. "I have to be frank, people are living in squalor. It's not just one, it's not an isolated incident and dotted — it is a pandemic." The culprit is long-term neglect and underinvestment by the social housing providers.

Paradoxically, the social tenants are comparatively lucky. Also presenting themselves at the drop-ins are tenants in the private rented sector (PRS). Here, as well as disrepair and mould being common, the major issues are exorbitant rent rises and evictions. Manchester is one of the places in Britain where rents are accelerating the fastest. Research from summer 2023 showed that the average rent in the city had increased by 20% in the last year, a repeat of the same figure the year before.[2] But this effect isn't uniform across the city. Rather it is spatially concentrated, with much higher rent rises in particular districts. Moss Side and its surrounding areas, for reasons we will explore, is one of the places where rent racketeering is most acute. Over the last year, the union has frequently encountered rent rises of over 100%, doubling, or even tripling. Families, previously paying around £600 per month for a two- or three-bedroom house are being faced with rents of well over £1000, in certain cases even higher. Most of the time, this is way beyond the limit of what they can afford, and the landlord hands them their eviction notice.

Unable to find affordable lets in the private sector, they're faced with homelessness, presenting themselves to the Council for re-housing. The problem then is the total lack of social housing, particularly in the area they are being evicted from. This is particularly difficult for people who rely on support networks in the neighbourhood. Asanga-Rae explains:

> some of them have come over as refugees, they have made Moss Side and the surrounding areas their home and built networks to support their lives here. Being uprooted, literally being told you can't afford to live here anymore, or even if we rehouse you it won't be in the same area, it's heart wrenching.

A week after the drop-ins each month, the union members meet again at the St James' Church on the Princess Road. The church has been a centre of housing action stretching back to the 1970s and the resistance to the slum clearances. Here, members assess the presentations the week before and plan strategic campaigns and interventions into the wider picture in the neighbourhood. Top of the agenda, for over five years, has been the preservation of family homes and the protection of social housing. In 2018 the union found out that social housing provider Jigsaw had been selling off its homes to the private market, advertising two homes on Leslie Street and Seedley Street on Rightmove for private sale. It fought a campaign, raised the alarm and the practice was stopped. But Jigsaw confirmed it had sold 40 properties in this way over the previous three years, including six in Moss Side.[3]

But these selloffs are a comparatively minor threat. Something else has been of far greater impact. Another member, Matt, sketched it out. "Over the past, say 25 years, there's been a phenomenal shift here from long-term families to HMOs [houses of multiple occupation] and more recently Airbnbs."[4] The intensity of this change is striking. "From about 2010-2011, nearly all the house sales that took place right towards the Whitworth Park area of Moss Side went to private landlords." In almost every case, these new landlords let to students, a process identified in academic literature as "studentification".[5] The impact has been profound. "It's completely changing the area because it makes it become a neighbourhood of strangers", says Matt. "It means that those of us who are growing up here, we lose that sense of community. The next generation have no hope of living in the area." This switch has had a direct impact on rents:

> A private landlord who lets to families will think, "Well, I should charge the families at least £1200". Whereas actually the average income for this area is very, very low. People don't look at what the local income is and think how can we fix rents according to that, they think "What sort of rents are the other landlords getting? What's the biggest income they're bringing with their houses? — I'll have that too." You just think, where are the poorer people supposed to go?

The situation in Moss Side shows unmistakable signs of what we might term "the gentrification frontier" in action. Yet, unlike in other parts of the city, this isn't something with the drama of clearances and massive newbuilds imposed from above. It's more subtle — the seeping into the community of multiple pressures and changing social forces. Rents and house prices rise. Families get dispersed as children can't afford to live near their parents, who may remain in social housing, but for a younger generation this is largely inaccessible. Former family homes get converted to HMOs and Airbnbs. Social housing providers fail to invest in stock, diverting their resources to newbuilds, usually on significantly more expensive and less secure tenure types. In this way, we see what Leslie Kern has called the "slow violence" of displacement. Not something that happens overnight, but the gradual, gnawing and relentless pressures that drive neighbourhood change.

The View from the North

On the other side of the city, at the border between Collyhurst and Harpurhey, on the Rochdale Road, sits the Manchester Communication Academy. A secondary school established

View to the city centre from Moss Side

in 2010, it has 1,200 pupils drawn from the local area and a further 400 in its linked primary school. When built, it was the first secondary school in the area for over 50 years — its predecessor closed in the 1960s when the area was slum cleared. The school itself is state of the art, built to the cost of £32m by the New Labour government. But the reality for children when they get home from school is quite different. The area, hammered by deindustrialisation and compounded by long-term neglect and disinvestment, is in the top 100 most deprived wards in the country. In 2022 it was estimated that three quarters of the pupils were living in absolute poverty.[6] It's only up the road from Manchester's gleaming towers, but it feels a world away. The contrasts are extreme. "It's almost like society's offering them a double life", Patsy Hodson, vice-principal of the school, said, "half affluent and half destitute". The investment in the school was presenting the image that the neighbourhood was OK; but for three quarters of the students, that sense of affluence disappeared as soon as they went home. "The hidden destitution is dangerous as it's so easy for it to be swept under the carpet and hidden."[7]

In 2019, Hodson and her colleague Vicky Leigh began to uncover how housing was very often at the root of the problems they were identifying, such as attendance, health or behaviour. It was precipitated by a handful of families in crisis, who had just been moved into hotels after evictions. Extending investigations, they began to realise that many of them were going home to the most appalling circumstances. Situations where families had so much damp the walls were black were not uncommon. Leaks forced them to put buckets out in the rain. Rats and other vermin ran uncontrolled through the neighbourhood, waking the children up in their sleep. The key issue had been temporary accommodation, families housed by the Council in homes run by racketeering private landlords, who had in some cases bought up whole streets nearby. But it became clear that the problem was far broader, rooted in the poor quality of the PRS as a whole. Leigh explained:

> the poor standards of properties in the PRS and the massive rise in rents as well, these things combined were putting people at risk of homelessness — being unable to pay their rent or complaining to their landlord about the state of the property only to be told, "OK you might as well leave, I will put the rent up and get someone in who will pay more for it".[8]

Resolving to do something about it, the school put a callout to parents facing housing issues. Within a year, Hodson and Leigh were dealing with 100 cases.

Elsewhere in the neighbourhood, at the local community centre, the Harpurhey Tenants Union have been meeting weekly. They run a regular pay-as-you-feel cafe and advice drop-in, and have encountered many issues. Top of the list though has been the failures of the social housing provider over the last decade to maintain and upkeep their property. Until 2021 the housing provider had been Northwoods, an arm's length management company (ALMO) owned by the Council, which was established in 2005 around the time of stock transfer. In 2021, citing poor performance, the Council closed the ALMO and brought its 13,000 properties back under direct control. But any immediate improvement was difficult to see. One union member described the situation as a "slow and deliberately mismanaged decline".

There is, however, one massive change that is coming to the neighbourhood. South from the school, down the Rochdale Road to the edge of the city centre, is the development zone formerly known as "The Northern Gateway", now called "Victoria North". But to everyone who lives there the area is called Collyhurst. The area is facing redevelopment, with the Council partnering with the Far East Consortium to deliver 15,000 new housing units in the neighbourhood over the next 15 years. It's the largest area of redevelopment in Britain today. At each end of it, work has already begun. Near the city centre are the new towers of private flats, while at the top, work is underway to build the first phase of "Collyhurst Village" — 130 social rented homes, and around double that number of private lets. The new social housing is undoubtedly welcome, but it comes against a backdrop of demolitions of older social housing across the last decade to prepare the district for redevelopment. Amanda, who works as an archivist and oral historian at the school, running regular community groups for older residents, said: "They have knocked hundreds of houses down. They weren't all empty. The people living in them will have just been rehoused where and whenever."[9] For her, the demolitions are personal, having been forced to move herself 12 years ago. She doesn't call it regeneration, though, but modern day slum clearance:

> I lived on Whitley Road, just off Collyhurst Street. In the maisonettes, but they were deemed not fit for purpose. But I loved living there. My neighbours, you know, you hear all these horrible things about the inner city, but my neighbours were great.

This is an all-too-familiar lament from social housing residents displaced from demolished estates.[10]

The new clearances, Collyhurst

Where Do We View the Boom from?

These two pictures from the inner city, one in the south and one in the north of Manchester, allow us to gain a new perspective on the issues analysed in the previous chapter. They permit us to consider the question — where do we view the city centre property boom from? To both its champions and critics, the rapid growth of the city centre has been an alluring magnet of attention. To an extent, it has been considered a zone apart, a special case, acting in parallel but with no wider effect on the city. Defenders of the boom often point to the fact that 40 years ago "city centre living" was an alien concept in Manchester. The argument they make goes like this: "Nobody lived there, the warehouses stood underused or empty; the city centre was essentially a dead zone — the remains of industry after the economic tide had gone out. Increasing density in the city centre avoided urban sprawl elsewhere, accommodating new populations as the city grew. There haven't been widespread estate demolitions, and the new populations have settled in alongside the old" — if, some will eventually admit, not always comfortably.

But is this right — is the property boom in the core really an island apart from the rest of the city? To answer this we need to look at the boom from outside the perspective of the new town it is building at the city core. Its concerns — pedestrianisation, green space, liveability — appear lessened from outside, replaced instead by the more basic question of finding an affordable place to call home. To see how these things are linked, we will have to consider the outward ripple effect of land value rises that result from the city centre's development. We need, then, a more sophisticated understanding of the dynamics of urban development to try and understand the picture. In short, we need a theory of gentrification.

Before we proceed, however, a note of caution is required. This term "gentrification" is often plagued with a host of misunderstandings. This is deliberate. It is the direct consequence of the dominance of the property lobby — Britain's number one industry — in the discourse of public life. This industry is laced with its own ideology; a justifying set of logics and narratives which shore up the mobilisation of public resources in its favour. Private development is seen as virtuous while public investment — in the context of austerity — is shied away from. Its cheerleaders are many and deploy their solutions as a *fait accompli*, their prognostics as simple common sense. They present a "false choice" — between private-capital-led redevelopment (and associated but under-identified) gentrification on one hand, and on the other doing nothing — allowing neighbourhoods to decline. All this adds up to a powerful set of justifying logics which marshal swaths of public opinion behind the redevelopment machine. Taken together, this powerful developer ideology amounts to what the geographer Tom Slater has termed "agnotology", or the production of ignorance.[11] Here it's hoped we can dispel some of that ignorance and arrive at a far more robust understanding of what is happening to our cities.

What these investigations will show is that there is a profound in-built logic to the dynamics of urban development that are now underway in Manchester. This logic is rooted in the political economy of capital circulation through the built environment. Richard Leese retired as Leader of Council in 2021, and the more reformist Bev Craig took his place. Moves have been made to foreground the construction of social housing and focus policy attention away from the city centre. However, the interests of the developers and their investors have independent capacity to shape the city — and the legacy of the last decade has been a concentration of power in the city in this sector. Under current conditions, absent additional powers being granted to local governments such as grants for social housing or rent control, the gentrification logic will continue.

The Economics of Gentrification

In the popular press, and to an extent also in the popular mind, gentrification conjures up a set of images and concerns which draw attention to the cultural symptoms of neighbourhood change. Forms of shops selling particular products are often dwelt upon excessively, either in condemnation or in celebration. Shoreditch's notorious Cereal Killer Cafe was an extreme example of this. Gentrification is boiled down to matters of consumer taste and habit — where and how middle-class people want to live, what they want to buy and how they identify as urban or city-dwellers. This conception confuses and elides more than it reveals — "gentrification" is nothing more than changing tastes and fashions. Its use is strategic. For gentrification's apologists and cheerleaders, of which Manchester has scores, it is a great boon.[12]

Here, we need to shift our focus away from these symbolic, surface-level signs of neighbourhood change towards the base economic shifts in land and property markets, capital flows and rental yields. Through this new focus a new set of actors emerge — not so much the consumers of gentrification, but its producers. Journalistic focus on "hipsters" and the weight of scholarly consternation over the preferences and lifestyles of middle-class gentrifiers recede into the background as we question the political relevance of such a focus.[13] Instead, let us ask another question. Who and what makes urban land profitable for redevelopment?[14]

First, we must land on a workable definition of gentrification. The origins of the term lie with Ruth Glass's famous observations of the children of the middle class taking over formerly working-class housing of inner-city London, in her case Islington, in the 1960s.[15] Through their own financial resources, sweat equity and personal preferences for renovated houses, they gradually transformed the neighbourhood. Removed from the specificities of 1960s London, Glass identified at root an expansion of housing options for the middle class and the parallel shrinkage of those for the working class.

Yet, from today's perspective, Glass's observations and her focus upon the impact of middle-class homeowners seem, as Paul Watt has argued, almost quaint.[16] Today's agents of gentrification are on another scale and altogether more powerful: property developers, investors, the super-rich (in

Manchester's case footballers like Gary Neville are a clear example of this) and, crucially, the state. Gentrification, state-led and global, is a process for the wholesale remaking of urban space. As an event, a process and a strategy it has become a signal feature of urbanisation in the last 50 years. Here, it is essential to focus on the role of the local state in pushing gentrification as a strategy for urban development. Rather than gentrified urban change being the inevitable outcome of raw market forces, it is shaped, corralled and helped along by a local state orientated to the creation of favourable conditions for private accumulation.

We can recall Engels' observation from *The Housing Question* on "Haussmann" — the making of "breaches in the working class quarters of big towns, particularly in those which are centrally situated… the scandalous alleys and lanes disappear to the accompaniment of lavish self-paise from the bourgeoisie… but they appear immediately somewhere else."[17] How are we to make sense of this? One concept offers a useful aid to grasping the fundamental structural dynamics of gentrification — "the rent gap".

Gentrification and the Rent Gap
First theorised by Scottish geographer Neil Smith, the rent gap is a disarmingly simple idea whose application acts as the key to gaining a more robust understanding of urban land markets and gentrification.[18] It is indispensable in unpacking the dynamic interrelation between the city centre property boom and its relation with the surrounding inner city. It is the most useful tool available to us not only to understand the political economy of gentrification, but to respond to its apologists. At its heart, the theory concerns the interrelationship between capital and land.

ISAAC ROSE

Consider a plot of land, whose owner is likely deriving some income from it. Say an old industrial building sits there. When the structure was built, it represented the "highest and best use" of that land. Investment flowed into the site, the labour of the builders was put into the construction and the function of the building created a surplus for its owner. Over time, this value declines, through natural deterioration and through the changing fortunes of the original use. Roofs leak, walls crumble, wood rots. Ageing technologies employed on site become outmoded and unproductive, in an old factory for example. The use of the building declines and the value deteriorates.

This value decay may also be produced by the actions of the local state: neighbourhood disinvestment, the cutbacks of public services, the mobilisation of stigma towards the area in which the building sits. This often takes the form of a very active process. The Cardroom Estate provides us with an unambiguous example of this. First, the Council stopped doing repairs. Then services were cut back. Finally, stigma was mobilised to present it as the "worst estate in Britain" — an all-too-familiar label applied to several estates across the country. Its demolition and the dispersal of its people was seen as the only possible response at that point.

In the Victoria North development zone today we see these same processes at work. Long-term lack of investment in the housing stock runs down its quality. A cutback of services sees social problems intensify in neighbourhoods already struggling with the generational impacts of deindustrialisation. Selective demolitions, of maisonettes or of condemned houses, leave gaping holes in the streetscape, giving a sense of abandonment. Public opinion is mobilised through the media to condemn the place as a "problem" area. Leigh explained how one BBC documentary, *People Like Us*, released in 2013, did exactly this in Harpurhey. "Its premise was 'what's it like to live in the number one most deprived area in the UK?' There was a lot of negativity and the people who lived here were very upset about the way it was portrayed. This type of media representation is harmful", she added, "I'm totally against it".

Finally, landlords themselves can play a part in forced degeneration by, for example, leaving the building exposed to the elements, failing to carry out repairs or in extreme cases partial demolition. All these factors combine to create the gradual decline of value of the land and the building on it, or, as Smith would term it, it's "actual ground rent".

Yet in concert with this downward pressure on values, the landowner is presented with a second option, the "potential ground rent". This is the potential, higher rent from the building that can be unlocked with the mobilisation of investment capital. For example, a building's owner may choose to repurpose it — converting an old factory into flats. This requires a capital outlay, but promises higher yields. Alternatively, the building may be demolished and something constructed on the site anew.

On a smaller, almost micro scale, we can see individual repurposing of family housing into HMOs or Airbnbs as an example of the exploitation of the rent gap too. Minimal investments might be required to do this: extending a back room, partitioning existing rooms or converting the ground floor to add new bedrooms. We should understand these function shifts within the framework of landlords exploiting rent gaps. Sometimes, though, the landowner or landlord may just choose to sell the site, with the new owner buying with intent to develop.

This process happens all the time. In gentrifying neighbourhoods one can quite literally watch it unfold. This is "the rent gap" — the gap between the declining actual rent and the potential rent that could be captured with capital investment. When this gap grows to large enough, capital floods into the site and the gap is closed and gentrification takes place.

These rent gaps exist at a wider scale than individual buildings. Sometimes they cover entire neighbourhoods. So when enough buildings or parcels of land in an area are brought up to their potential rents, then the rest of the (yet unchanged) neighbourhood exhibits a rent gap. These gaps are systematically closed through the repurposing of buildings, demolitions and evictions to make way for higher rent-payers. The process doesn't necessarily happen in a linear fashion, but rather jumps from plot to plot non-sequentially. But, true to its logic, it tends to move in waves across a city. Smith described this process as the advance of gentrification "frontier", a "policy of revenge" by the elite against minorities, working people and the poor.[19]

Rent gaps (1)

The very business of property developers and estate agents is to identify and close rent gaps, although of course they do not describe it in such terms. Often they are the actors doing it on behalf of the owners of land and capital. For our purposes, it is an invaluable concept for understanding the processes of urban change. By focussing on our attention on the flows of capital in and out of land, and the developers, landlords and state actors which act in concert with this flow, it draws our eye away from the oft-traced "cultural" signifiers of gentrification, demystifying it and placing it upon the firmer terrain of political economy.

Gentrification and Displacement
The process of closing a rent gap will almost always necessarily result in displacement, albeit to variable degrees. As old uses of space are repurposed and recapitalised, the old inhabitants are

Rent gaps (2)

displaced to make way for the new. These could be residents evicted to make way for higher rents or a slum cleared to make way for development. They could alternatively be businesses, moved out of a place ready for its demolition and repurposing in favour of higher yields. This is a process that is shaped and structured by class- and race-based inequalities.

In Glass's initial coining of gentrification she identified displacement with this process, writing "altogether there has been a great deal of displacement... all those who cannot hold their own, the small enterprises, the lower ranks of people, the odd men out, are being pushed away".[20] Indeed, connection between cycles of urban change and the ejection of the workers from their neighbourhoods goes back further still, with Engels identifying, near 100 years prior to Glass, how housing speculation had negative consequences for the working class:

> The result is that the workers are forced out of the centre of the towns, towards the outskirts; that workers' dwellings and small dwellings in particular become rare and expensive and often altogether, for under these circumstances the building industry, which is offered a much better field for speculation by more expensive dwelling houses, builds worker dwellings only by way of exception.[21]

Working in New York City in the 1980s, Peter Marcuse began to conceptualise and theorise displacement as a process of urban change. He provides us with a typology of displacement and identified multiple ways in which gentrification was responsible for displacement. He grouped them into two broad categories: direct displacement, where families, individuals and communities are literally forced —

sometimes physically — from their homes by demolitions, evictions or landlord violence; and indirect displacement, where residents, despite not leaving an area, no longer feel at home there due to the changing feel of the neighbourhood.[22] He wrote of such displacement pressure:

> When a family sees the neighbourhood around it changing; when their friends are leaving the neighbourhood, when the stores they patronise are liquidating and new stores for other clientele are taking their places, and when changes in public facilities, in transportation patterns, and in support services all clearly are making the area less and less liveable, then the pressure of displacement is already severe. Its actuality is only a matter of time. Families living under these circumstances move as soon as they can, rather than wait for the inevitable. Nonetheless, they are displaced.

Some have termed this process "un-homing", plainly, the loss of home, a term that covers both psychological and physical displacement.[23] It happens over a range of timescales, not just the fast, dramatic moment of the eviction or demolition, but the "slow violence" of rent rises and seeing a neighbourhood gradually stripped away.[24] Gentrification, as its scholars have written, "is never a one off event, but a series of attritional micro events, that unfold over time, generating different emotional and mental states for those affected: anxiety, hope, confusion, fear, dislocation, loss, anticipation, dread and so on".[25]

Whatever the cause, whether someone has been forced to move or not, gentrification can be tied indelibly to displacement. Academic or policy apologists for the wealthy can and have tried to hide this fact, but as Marcuse said; "if the pain of displacement is not the central component of what we are dealing with… we are not just missing one factor in a multi factor equation, we are missing the central point that needs to be addressed".[26] In a sober summary of the debates in *Geography Compass*, researcher Kate Shaw concluded that "there are no serious studies demonstrating that displacement doesn't occur at all".[27]

Rent gaps induce displacement through one of two means — through rent rises, until the point where an area becomes unaffordable for its previous residents, and through direct demolition and redevelopment — dispersing a community through what is in effect modern-day "slum clearance". Both these processes are at work in Manchester today, as land and rental values rise, emanating outwards from the city centre. In turn, we will return to the areas explored in the opening vignettes to see the rent gap in action in these two examples.

South Central

Moss Side, where we began, is one of four wards that comprise the heart of south-central Manchester. Alongside it are Hulme, Ardwick and Rusholme, totalling a combined population of 80,000. Yet, rather than consider these as separate spaces, it makes sense to consider the area as the broad popular district of the south of the city. Jamil Keating, an actor, community worker and lifelong resident of Ardwick, has an acronym or "poetic framework" for it, which he calls the "Village of Harm". Speaking to me beneath a tree in the yard of the Old Abbey Taphouse — the very pub in Hulme where Len Johnson broke the colour bar nearly 70 years previously — he explains its twentieth-century history:

Once upon a time, this area was one slum. If you go back before the creation of the NHS in 1948 and the expansion of the university and hospital over the second half of the twentieth century, the area was known originally called Chorlton upon Medlock. It was a white Irish working-class slum that primarily housed the workers who built this city in the mills, the factories and the textile industries. And then the generations of Irish communities who came here and settled here were told they were no longer viable once the textile industry had died. And were evicted in immediate, swift evictions and moved into overspill estates across the north, east and south of Manchester. They were then replaced by Black communities primarily from the Caribbean. And then there were successive waves of immigration, building on previous waves of immigration from Bangladesh, India, and later Pakistan. Then in the 1990s, during the civil war, from Somalia. [28]

Today the neighbourhood is sliced up by three roads — Oxford Road, Stockport Road and Princess Road — which give rise to the area having among the worst air quality in Britain. And at the heart of the village are the major institutions which have an outsized effect on the area around it — the hospitals and two universities: the University of Manchester and Manchester Metropolitan University (MMU). These are the main sites of employment, as well as the reason that the area is, each year, home to around 70,000 students. "It's an incredibly multicultural area", Keating explains, "mismanaged generationally to serve the major players of this city. We are their labour stock. Their cattle. And the village of Harm as a community is moved around at will, whenever people decide we need a new gallery department, building, office."

It is also a district of renters, with over three quarters of the population paying rent to a landlord — 41% social, 36.5%

private. This balance is not evenly spread, with Ardwick and Moss Side maintaining a majority of social renting, while Rusholme and Hulme are characterised by the dominance of private landlords. Social housing to an extent offers a bulwark to its inhabitants from the pressure of rising rents. Outside it, in the PRS, tenants are exposed to the whims of an unregulated landlord class and the vicissitudes of the market. The pressure of rising rents, as we saw earlier, is acute. Private rents, increasingly orientated towards students and middle-class professionals, are influenced by the growing rental market in the city centre. In the city centre, the arrival of corporate landlords has marked a clear professionalisation of the private lettings market in the city. One of the ways which this has split out into the inner city is through the transformation of the landscape of estate agents. Here, we can focus on one in particular, Thornley Groves.

Thornley Groves is an estate agent founded in 1991 in the affluent township of Altrincham, a suburban satellite to Manchester's south. It began with a single office, and by 2013 it had eight offices and managed a portfolio of 1,600 properties on behalf of landlords. That year, it was bought out by Lomond Capital for an undisclosed sum.[29] Chief Executive of Lomond Capital, Stuart Pender, explained the motivations behind the acquisition: "Manchester has a very attractive property market offering, with the largest private rental sector outside London". The acquisition of an estate agent was happening in concert with the proliferation of institutional investors in direct development. But it didn't stop there. In 2020, with private equity funding from Lloyds Development Capital, the investment arm of Lloyds Bank, Lomond Capital merged with Linley & Simpson, a Scottish estate agent, with £100m of finance behind the deal. The new organisation was the Lomond Group, but it maintained Thornley Groves as the name of its local, Manchester and North West subsidiary. Over the following two years, Thornley Groves went on a major acquisitions spree — by the start of 2022 it had tripled its holdings from 2,400 to 6,000.[30] One by one, it swallowed up different estate agents, consolidating its market control over the private rental market in Manchester.

Backed with significant pools of investor capital, Thornley Groves has been able to monopolise its position over a wide swath of the private rental sector in Manchester. They aren't distinct or separate from the city centre boom, but part of the same process — two heads of the same industry. Their employees move between them, as with the transfer of their Sales and New Homes Manager Stephen Clayton from Thornley Groves to the Far East Consortium in 2021.[31] The development of the private rental market in the city centre with newbuilds, and the monopolisation of estate agents in the suburbs and inner city, is happening in concert.

The often immediate impact after Thornley Groves has taken over a smaller estate agent is that they raise the rent to a position near the market level. James Varney, the Secretary of the Hulme Tenants Union, is one such case. His old estate agent was bought out by Thornley Groves at the end of 2022. Despite there being a clause in his contract that the rent wouldn't rise by more than 7.5% annually, in early 2023 he and his housemates were presented with a 40% rent rise. They attempted to negotiate, pointing out the many issues with the property. The letting agent wouldn't move from a 30% rise and eventually issued a Section 21 no fault eviction notice instead. The notice was incorrectly filed, as is common, and was pointed out to the letting agent by a solicitor at the Law Centre. It was dropped, but by autumn the estate agent had come back with a Section 13 rent rise notice instead, demanding a 60% rise. This story is not unusual. Each year, estate agents calculate the new market rate and set the rent to that. They are literally professionals at exploiting rent gaps. The result has been rapid rent rises, which tenants — in the absence of rent control — have had few avenues to resist. Inevitably, as rent goes up while wages fail to keep up, and as rents are set at a level almost three times the housing benefit level, displacement occurs. A failure to build social housing in the city means that tenants rely on the private rented sector to find affordable rents. But this is being closed off as an avenue. So, they tend to fall out of the bottom and then are homeless — either sofa-surfing or trapped in "temporary" accommodation for many years.[32]

There is, then, a long-term pattern of generational expulsion of the working class from the inner city. Keating, who is now 29, describes what he has witnessed growing up in the area. He recalled the impact of the PFI redevelopment in the Blair years of his estate in Ardwick:

All the kids who I grew up with, whose parents lived here, were not going to be allocated social housing on that estate, because there wasn't any. And you couldn't afford to buy any of the newbuilds. So therefore many of the kids who I grew up with who wanted to have families had to move to social housing in Gorton or Denton, wherever there was available housing, they were pushed eastwards or northwards. Anyone who still lives here is either living in their parents' addresses or are struggling to exist in and amongst their community, families and neighbours in private rental accommodation.

The Impact of the University

The question remains, however: what exactly is driving the opening of the rent gap in south-central Manchester? Landlords and letting agents are exploiting it, raising rents as they spot the opportunity in the market, but is there a more fundamental cause? We have already noted the impact of the centre boom, but there is something far more proximate — the university district, which splits the village of Harm in two. Together, Manchester's two city universities create one of the largest higher education campuses in Europe. Almost 70,000 students study there and there are almost 60,000 jobs in education, healthcare and professional services. It's the economic powerhouse of the city, accounting for 20% of its economic output over the last five years.[33] In the eyes of the city planners, this zone is designated as "the Corridor" and is a key focus of the city's economic growth strategy. Established

Campus at Birley Fields

in 2007, the Corridor is a typical Mancunian formulation — a partnership with presence from the major public institutions as well as anchor private developers such as the commercial property developer Bruntwood. Parts of it are designated an Enterprise Zone. Over the last decade its boundaries have extended, with the construction of major new university assets. The Corridor partnership describes the area as "Manchester's cosmopolitan hub and world-class innovation district, where talented people from the city and across the world learn, create, work, socialise, live and do business; contributing to the economic and social dynamism of one of Europe's leading cities".[34]

Principal among these has been MMU's new campus in Birley Fields in Hulme. The site, left vacant after the City Challenge programme, was selected by MMU in 2011 as the site for their campus consolidation after the alternative — in bourgeois Didsbury — was torpedoed by affluent residents' threats of "open warfare" were the plans to go ahead.[35] Some Hulme people launched a campaign, "Save Birley Fields", but their weight was less than those of affluent Didsbury and the campus opened in 2014, extending the campus and zone of student housing deep into the heart of Hulme. The university and residents are uneasy neighbours, with residents struggling with the effects of the huge student numbers, including noise, late-night drinking and persistent rubbish. Another concern heard again and again is the issue of "transience". Each year a new cohort arrives, destabilising the neighbourhood. Perhaps most significant, however, has been the impact on accelerating development in the neighbourhood. Since 2018 three high-rise PBSA blocks have been built in Hulme — one, controversially, on the site of an old pub, the Church Inn, which was waved through during the pandemic when the Planning Committee was suspended. Another pub, the Salutation, was taken over by the Student Union and some regulars were barred by the new owners. At the same time, private landlords in the area reorientated their lettings towards the (higher paying) student market. Workers in the area can rarely get a look in. It all adds up to clear displacement pressure. For many, to paraphrase Marcuse, its actuality feels only a matter of time.

The presence of the huge universities, right up against the ethnically diverse working-class neighbourhoods of the inner city, feels at times more akin to the situation found in major American cities than anything in Britain. Davarian Baldwin, who has studied extensively the interrelations between US universities and their host cities, has termed this the rise of the "UniverCity". He traces how universities came to acquire an increasingly important role in post-industrial urban strategy. At the same time planners were beginning to view the campus as the model of a "palatable and profitable version of a safe urban experience", the universities themselves were increasingly adopting a "for-profit" approach to their urban surroundings, forced in part by the marketisation of higher education.[36]

While the situation in Manchester is perhaps not as extreme as that of the University of Chicago's presence on the South Side of Chicago or Columbia's encroachment into Harlem, there are unmistakable echoes. Keating recounts a story of a time he was sitting on the campus with his friend, a Black man, over 50 with long dreads, and they attracted the attention of two police officers:

They walked over to us and one of them said, "Excuse me, what are you doing?" And we were both just sat there, two non-white people, on the bench. "We are sitting here", we say. "You can't sit here, it's a student area." I was about to kick off, before my friend, who was a very calm and tempered person let loose, and said, "How dare you! Exactly where I am sitting, I used to sit 13 floors above at my friend's house running nights in the 90s and 80s!"

Realising they'd overstepped, the police backed off. But the message from them, and the new campus, appears clear enough.

On the other side of the Corridor, where it borders Ardwick on the eastern flank, another urban development outrage is looming. In the summer of 2023 proposals were submitted by a consortium of developers to turn a disused strip of car garages and showrooms into a huge complex of student accommodation and office space. The vision is for almost 1,800 student bed spaces, and office space for nearly the same number of workers. Most concerning of all for residents of the nearby Brunswick estate is a proposed 42-storey student tower block. If approved, it would mark the first time that buildings of this height cross the inner ring road, the symbolic boundary of the city centre. As well as casting their park into darkness, the fear is that this would set a precedent — opening the neighbourhood up to similar high-rise development. In response, a campaign has sprung up, "Ardwick Against the Monster". One of its members, musician Gareth Smith, a.k.a. Vanishing, spoke to the *Quietus* in 2023 and raised the issue of the development. "People's ability to influence change in any meaningful way is becoming less and less tangible. I get the sense that there's not been any meaningful attempt to address the concerns of the public."[37]

Gentrification's ideology made plain

It's clear from the interview that the estate is a special, valuable place. "I love living here. It's near town, it's accessible. It's a working-class estate and there's a community. People spend their whole lives living in places like this — it's not got that transitory population." But it feels like it's under threat, siege almost. "I just hope it's able to carry on being like this. With so much change, nothing is ever certain." In late spring that year, a poster had been spotted all along the Oxford and Stockport roads. It was advertising the soon-to-open developments on the eastern end of Brunswick Street, not on the neighbourhood's Corridor side, but its opposite. Intentionally or not, the poster revealed, clear as day, the mentality of the people behind the scheme — and, perhaps by extension, the property industry as a whole. In big, bold letters, the word "ANCOATS" was crossed out. In its place, beneath, was "ARDWICK". The new frontier. "It is violent." Keating said,

> It's cruel and vicious. It is even worse when you go on their website, and follow the link from that poster, the copy on their website is evil. It says — Ardwick is an up and coming area for development, similar to Bushwick in New York. As opposed to being a place we have lived here for generations. It is an act of colonialism, literally — we are striking out the old world and here is the new. Like, this is the place we are going to invade because we can no longer afford to live here. It is evil.[38]

The New Clearances

If you were to look at a satellite image of Collyhurst, one thing that would immediately become clear is the number of empty plots of land. The street layout is there, but where houses should be there's just grass. It brings to mind the old maps of the city fringes in the early nineteenth century, as speculative landowners laid out road patterns, awaiting the construction of the jerry-built back-to-backs. In one sense, there is a similarity. In both cases speculation on the land is taking place. But there's a crucial difference. Here, the vacant plots have been created not by laying roads over green fields, but by demolishing what previously stood in the gaps. This is

Topographies of speculation, Collyhurst

the new slum clearance. It's worth briefly tracing something of the trajectory of the neighbourhood since the 2000s.

Under the last New Labour government, Collyhurst, like other areas of the city we have encountered — Brunswick, Miles Platting — was due to be part of a PFI scheme, announced in 2006. The £250m investment would have seen 1,300 homes built as one of the largest such schemes in Britain. One of the early actions of the coalition government was to scrap these PFI programmes, withdrawing nearly £2bn of investment.[39] Ray Fisher, chairman of the Collyhurst South Tenants' Association, said: "It's disgusting that the scheme isn't going ahead".[40] At that point, some demolitions had already taken place in preparation for the PFI, while the three tower blocks on the estate had been handed over to Urban Splash in 2008 by the Council for their "3Towers" project — the recladding and rebranding, in a tip to "radical Manchester", after the three

Pankhursts. Local rumour has it that Bloxham acquired these towers for a tenner. The flats were all for private sale.

The Council wanted to push ahead with the redevelopment, despite the axed PFI funding. In 2011, to prepare the ground still further, the Council pressed ahead with demolitions, securing a grant from central government to do so. 13 maisonette blocks were demolished, along with several houses. Around 350 units of social housing were lost and 190 households had to be relocated. In 2012 the Council, along with Network Rail, another major landholder in the area, announced they were on the hunt for a development partner. The balance of public home improvements to new private construction had tipped — with 2,000 private homes in the proposed master plan, rather than the previous 1,500, a ratio of 2:1 to public housing. This was explicitly done to make the offer more appealing to a private developer.[41] John Laing was selected as the development partner that year, but pulled out a year later, leaving the neighbourhood in limbo-land.[42] The Council went back to the drawing board, producing new spatial masterplans and separating the Irk Valley from Collyhurst proper as a development opportunity on the fringes of the city centre.

In 2017 the Far East Consortium (FEC) was announced as the development partner with the Council, on a joint-venture basis. Like with the Manchester Life partnership, a deal was struck with the public sector providing land assets, development frameworks and planning powers, and public funding to pump-prime the development, with the private sector providing additional finance, managing delivery and, ultimately, owning the rental assets. The FEC is an international real estate company, incorporated in the Cayman Islands and listed on the Hong Kong Stock Exchange. Its previous developments include high-end apartments in Hong Kong, car parks and hotels across south Asia and a casino in Australia.

The signing of the deal in 2017 with the FEC led to the restarting of the project in earnest. This deal led to the production of a masterplan in 2018. The proposal laid out is to construct 15,000 housing units over the next 15 years in a 155-hectare site stretching north from the city centre, with a total estimated value of investment in the billions of pounds.

Direct and racialised displacement occurred in 2022, when the Traveller site in the Redbank area of the development — the land formerly owned by Network Rail — was cleared.[43] Formerly situated on a meander of the Irk River, it was one of the sole dedicated Traveller sites in the city. Because its location was prone to flooding, and very limited maintenance was put in place by the authorities, the site was allowed to fall into extreme disrepair. It was earmarked for the development

Clearing the frontier, Red Bank

"Victoria Riverside", scheduled for completion in 2024. This residential-led development includes a landmark 37-storey building, Crown View, on the corner of Gould Street and Dantzic Street, as well as two sister towers. None were affordable. The site was cleared, with no alternative Traveller site found.

Over the last decade, the vision for Collyhurst has undergone a dramatic shift. Initial plans to refurbish some of the social housing stock, and in-fill with a few thousand private developments, have been replaced by the wholesale reimagining of the district as a vast extension to the city centre. This has been shaped in part by the dictates of a national policy landscape, the impact of austerity and the cutting back of state funding. But it also appears to us the outgrowth of a series of strategic partnerships with the property industry that Manchester City Council has made in the last decade, as they have come to embrace wholesale "residential-led regeneration", handing vast swaths of the city to a corporate rentier elite. In the estate itself, fears over the future abound. The current wave of redevelopment for many older residents is the third time in living memory that demolition has happened. The ghosts of the slum clearances and the breakup of the community that followed are the unavoidable comparisons drawn

The Council, aware of the potential political sensitivity of the forced clearance of its tenants, has promised that everybody who wants to stay in the area will be able to. The regeneration of "Collyhurst Village" is seen as one of the early stages of the plan, and the buy-in from the community for this stage is seen as crucial for the wider success of the project. Yet to date only 130 new council homes are planned in the development — which given the earlier loss of 300 represents a net loss of public housing in the area. Over the long-term, the plan is for 20% of new housing built through the partnership to be "affordable". However, only one third of this will be social housing, only 7% will be a like-for-like replacement in terms of tenure and rent levels.

This has amounted to a managed process of demolitions and decline over a period of a decade. As part of the process of "regeneration", Collyhurst and the people living there have been put through forced *de*-generation, as blocks of housing are cleared and swaths of the estate stands as waste.[44] Processes which unfolded in the previous decade on the Cardroom Estate have been repeated here — only on a grander scale.

Return to Cropper Street

And so, our story ends where it began — on Cropper Street. This street, the city's most radical in the early nineteenth century, has seen many changes over the course of the last two centuries. In the early 1840s it was bisected by two railway lines. In 1845 it was renamed by the Improvement Committee to "Osborne Street", a name it still bears today.[45] The back-to-backs on this street were demolished in the mid-twentieth century as part of the slum clearance programme. At the start of the 1970s a new estate was built there, at the same time as Eastford Square, at one end of Osborne Street. Its history is one of the rise, euthanasia and rise again of the rentier.

Osborne Street, and the handful of streets around it, was a central location in the 2020 BBC documentary *Manctopia*. The film followed a handful of residents there who were contending with their uncertain futures in the face of Victoria North — and specifically if there was a direct threat of demolition of their estate. One story arc in Episode Four follows two residents, Donna and her auntie Anne, who examine the maps of the plans for the area.[46] Seeing the streets where Anne lives, they see nothing but a grey splodge and a single asterisk on the map. The asterisk, it is revealed, represents an "opportunity for a distinctive landmark building with a focus on height".

At the "consultation" later Donna challenges the representative of Victoria North. "My auntie's home and my dad's home are only 48 years old. Why would they want to demolish good standard living homes? Is it," she asked, "because they're quite near to town and the land is quite valuable?"

The consultant, visibly under pressure, fumbles her answer. "It's... it's more about looking at the layout of these communities. Whether there might be a way of redesigning these neighbourhoods to make a more welcoming, successful neighbourhood." Donna replies, "Most people on my dad's estate, the homeowners in particular, they don't want to go. At this moment in time you really can't say that the Osborne Street estate won't be coming down?"

"I'm sorry", is the response, "I can't really say at this time when Osborne Street would be looked at." After the meeting away from the consultants, Donna says:

> If they continue to not spend any money in the area, leave it to look like a rubbish tip, it gives them a reason to blight the area and say — look at the state of it. It's going to have to go, we are building all these swazzy properties that are going to be x number of hundred thousand pounds and these are the type of people you're going to move in. And it doesn't really matter that you have a community spirit, it doesn't really matter whether it affects you mentally if you are carted out of your home. There has to be change and there has to be development, but it's not necessary that

it has to be at the price of completely ripping an existing community apart.

Victoria North appears to us today, as we watch it unfold, as the apotheosis of the Manchester Model of urban development. State-led gentrification has become the strategy for developing the city, as public land and finance are mobilised to create the conditions for private gain. Over the coming decade, this development — above all others — will profoundly change the social and economic geography of the city. Amounting to the building of a parallel, luxury, new town on a massive scale, jutting up into the disinvested and stigmatised neighbourhoods of north Manchester, Victoria North is set to trigger a frenzy of private speculation, displacements and clearances as a new frontier for closing rent gaps opens. This is no mere conjecture but, if you look at the long-range planning documents for the north of the city, with their euphemistic referrals to housing market "drag" from the expanding city centre, the plainly stated plan.

Conclusion
Militant Particularism in the Rentier City

Cities are battlefields.

Walter Benjamin

"Working-class houses for working-class people in Hulme!" It's a balmy summer afternoon, the Friday closest to midsummer, late June 2021. For an hour, over the school run, a picket assembles outside a closed pub called the Gamecock on a busy bus route on the Aquarius Estate, Hulme. Each week for the last month the protestors have been meeting at the same time, same place; Boundary Lane, the literal boundary of the Corridor, the place where two visions of one neighbourhood collide. "Hulme is for the needy — not for the greedy!" On the megaphone, leading the chants, is local poet, tenant and community leader, Tina Cribbin.

The pub was built at the end of the 1960s, at the same time as the neighbouring tower block, Hopton Court. Both buildings are survivors from another era. Being far more solidly built than the system-build maisonettes constructed around them, they were spared the bulldozers in the 1990s and today Hopton Court remains social housing. The pub, closed in the early 2000s, has for the last decade and a half been the site of a lengthy battle as various developers have submitted plans to turn the site into

Blocking the Block

purpose-built student flats. In both 2008 and 2012 proposals were rejected. In 2020 a new developer, Curlew Opportunities, tried again, proposing a 13-storey, over 200 bedspace project onto the tiny plot where the old pub stood.

Residents were keenly aware of the multiple losses that their community had suffered over the previous decades. The violence of austerity had fallen heavily on the neighbourhood. Care homes, pubs, community-orientated shops and social spaces had all closed, turned over to the university or to private developers. One, the nearby Church Inn, was demolished to make way for student housing in April 2021 in the face of widespread resident opposition. For many who had lived in Hulme for most or all their lives, this feeling of displacement pressure was best articulated when one of the tenants in Hopton Court said to Cribbin one day, "We're just a community of ghosts".[1]

Speaking to an audience sometime later who were watching a documentary film made about the campaign, Cribbin explained the wider context for the fight. "There are no care homes in Hulme anymore. People are hiding in their homes scared to tell anyone they're ill in case they get moved away from their community. These are people from Ireland, Jamaica, other places. Their whole support system is here. It's not just about a pub. It's about the destruction of a culture, the destruction of a way of life. It got so bad," she added, "I had to become a poet."

The leadership of the campaign, called Block the Block, which emerged to try and fight off developers' and advance their own vision of age-friendly social housing, have led lives that are woven through the story of modern Manchester. Two of the campaign's spokespeople, who went before the Planning Committee and made their community's case, are exemplary in this regard. Sally Casey moved to Chorlton-on-Medlock from Dublin in 1963 and then into the Aquarius Estate in Hulme in 1969 when Chorlton-on-Medlock was slum cleared. She's lived there ever since and has been a major figure within the cycles of tenant struggles there dating back to the mid-1970s — but particularly in the period of resisting the Housing Action Trust and working with the Council during City Challenge. Another is Roy Bennett, who was born off the Stretford Road in Hulme in 1954 and whose father worked at Trafford Park. His whose family have lived in Hulme since the early twentieth century. After slum clearance, he moved into the maisonettes. Bennett then had a long working life for the Council as a caretaker on the Crescents, where it was his job to clean the graffiti off the walls with a giant pressurised hose.

Their memories and experience stretch back over the decades, informing a scepticism towards the grand dreams of city planners. Their lives encompass the failures of the system-build era, as young people they experienced slum clearance, then, in the 1990s, were witness to everything being demolished and rebuilt again. Today they see it all under threat once more from private developers and Council planners. They brought to the campaign a great moral weight, garnering support from a wide range of quarters — the local housing associations, GPs, the ward councillors and MP and even, verbally in a meeting, the new leader of the Council, Bev Craig. This, combined with robust ground-level organisation, brought hundreds of residents on side, and ensured that the campaign secured four victories over the years 2021-2023, with the Planning Committee knocking back the plans three times. In the case of Manchester's planning system, though, it is near impossible to secure a final refusal, and every victory is, sadly, contingent. But Block the Block demonstrates how the energies of historic tenant struggles are not dead or inert but living — drawn upon in the present to bolster a continuation of struggle. Their militancy is the refusal to disappear.

Hulme is perhaps a highly pronounced case of the multiple makings and remakings of the inner city, due to the "flagship" role attributed to its many redevelopments: the Crescents, City Challenge and to an extent also its current refashioning as an "outer city centre" campus district. But this pattern is visible across Manchester's inner city too. Its central motif is the "slum clearance". This phrase and process of state-directed urban transformation emerges again and again in our story. There is a powerful case, then, that this is *the* central motif of British urbanism over the last 150 years.

If the experience of "slum clearance" has a constancy for the working class of the inner city, we ought to be attendant to the differences too. Space and place, as Doreen Massey has argued, is a product *of* and imbued *with* social power. In her essay on Wythenshawe, she alerts us to the risks of always glorifying "resistance" and assuming that it is always ranged against "domination". She cautions us against organising our rhetoric uncritically on the resisters' behalf, without attendant scrutiny of the crystallisation of social forces within the "authority" that is being resisted. "It is", she wrote,

> a way of thinking that reads "power" as necessarily negative... There are few, if any, abstract or universal "spatial rules." Local people are not always the bearers of the most progressive values, "resisters" though they may be. Battles over space and place are always battles (usually complex) over spatialized social power.[2]

She takes as her example the battle for Wythenshawe and the fight that Manchester City Council had to win against the Cheshire residents to secure incorporation of the area into the Council authority. The residents were commuters who depended upon Manchester for their livelihoods but wanted nothing to do with the consequences of their large incomes: the higher taxes of the city and the necessity of living among the poor. As in Engels' day, they were content to travel in and out of the city along thoroughfares that concealed the reality of the social structure. They wanted a life apart. They were, Massey wrote, "defenders of a local way of life that included property and privilege". Ranged against them was "the state, the planners, the system, here a collection of socialists and progressives battling to win more, and healthier, space for the city's working class".[3]

Massey's insights help us a great deal when assessing the history of clearance. What social forces were crystallised within the authority that was driving the clearances? Were they the same "then" (i.e., between the late nineteenth and mid-twentieth centuries) as they are "now" in the neoliberal era? Of course, the excesses of the original version of the slum clearances — the lack of consultation, the demolition of perfectly good houses and the sense of an overmighty state clearing and moving working-class communities, creates a sense of continuity with the same story today. But while this is certainly a key strand, it is also only one facet. Subjecting this motif of slum clearance to a wider analytical lens shows us, quite clearly, that there is a radical discontinuity. The class orientation of the clearances has dramatically reversed. Whereas once the ambition (if in reality it fell short) was to clear in order build higher-quality *public* housing for the working class, today we see clearances as part of a broader strategy of private accumulation by dispossession. At the heart of this shift is the return of the rentier.

The Return of the Rentier

Over the course of our analysis, we have traced the rise, euthanasia and return of the rentier. We have also posited Manchester as the paradigmatic city to understand this process.

The provision of housing for workers in the industrial city was the business of the speculative landlord. We have seen how developers bought up strips of land and crammed them full of poorly built and badly maintained houses, designed only to last for a few decades. The use of the buildings lasted much longer than their designed lifespan, as their landlords extracted as much rent as they could from their long-suffering tenants. In *Love on the Dole*, Walter Greenwood describes vividly one of these working-class districts that were still typical across the city in the 1930s:

> The identical houses of yesterday remain, still valuable in the estate market even though the cost of their building has been paid for over and over again by successive tenants... Places where men and women are born, live, love and die and pay preposterous rents for the privilege of calling the grimy houses "home".[4]

This pattern of speculative house provision was not solely for the working classes, but in the building of middle-class suburbia too. Housing provision was entirely controlled by a speculative landlord class.

The social degradation that resulted from this birthed a powerful reform movement from the late nineteenth century onwards. It had multiple strands — liberal, socialist, Fabian, communist — but it was unambiguous in its attempts to secure a better lot for the working class. At the heart of this deeply modern project was the euthanasia of the rentier. So it was that the impulse of slum clearance, garden cities and high-rise flats for the working class secured to a great extent a world without the rentier and land speculator. The provision of housing was subsumed into the local democratic state. Prefigured on a municipal level throughout the interwar years, this became national state policy in the aftermath of World War II.

The disintegration of this postwar world, under the weight of its own contradictions and, more importantly, under the sustained ideological assault from the New Right, paved the way for the return of the rentier. The powers and independence of local government were attacked under the guise of combatting the "loony left". Right to Buy struck at the foundations of the settlement; austerity, the reduction of direct grants and the imposition of fiscal limits constricted municipal room for manoeuvre. Enterprise Zones and the Urban Development Corporations created spaces outside democratic control. Wider transformations — the strategic goals of the 1986 Big Bang and the 1988 Housing Act — released the shackles that had been placed on both financial and land rentiers. These were possible only after the defeat and decomposition of Thatcher's most significant enemies: inner-city Black communities, the trade union movement and local authorities. The message for local government was adapt or be defeated. Manchester provides a near unique example of a leadership that adapted to the new reality — a continuity of personnel from the era of the challenge to the Thatcherite project through to its acceptance and implementation.

The role of the state was refashioned into the facilitator of private accumulation, which has been a gradual process. Throughout the 1990s and 2000s as the rollout of neoliberalism expanded, the role of the private sector in delivering what had previously been public goods grew. The impact of the financial crisis and the subsequent austerity regime accelerated this. In the post-crash era a "wall of capital" has flooded into property markets, generating housing financialisation and an acute housing crisis. So we return to the question from the start, posed by Gilbert and Williams, "Who won the twentieth century?" It seems clear that in Britain the group which has benefited most from the political regimes that have governed the country since 1979 are landlords and property developers.

We see this trend unfold most clearly in Manchester. With the highest proportion of renters in any of the major British cities, it is also the city that has most vigorously — and effectively — pursued a policy of property-led regeneration. The forces of the state have been deployed over a period of decades to engineer a housing crisis. The relative weight of build-to-rent and corporate landlordism is greatest here and set only to increase as more rental apartments come online over the following decade. The city has become a byword for cynical accumulation by dispossession — and it prefigures the wider transformation of our cities over the coming decades, should the broad balance of class forces remain as they are.

The question in Manchester is whether this can be changed. Our analysis has focussed upon a leadership cadre which emerged out of the conflicts of the 1980s, who pioneered an embrace of urban entrepreneurialism and developed the "Manchester Model", the effects of which we see so clearly today. But they have now passed into history, replaced by a new leadership which appears to be of a more reformist bent — both in the city region, with Andy Burnham as Mayor, and in Manchester itself with Bev Craig its new Council leader. Under Craig there's a stronger emphasis on social housing and a desire to focus policy across the city, not just the booming centre. It remains too early to say whether this will result in a meaningful change for the city and its peoples, but one thing is already clear — there will be no dramatic confrontation with the development machine. In an assessment of the first year of Bev Craig's leadership in *Place North West* at the end of 2022, Dan Whelan wrote that "any concerns that the left-leaning leader would make things difficult for the property industry have been quashed".[5] In light of this, any major shift seems unlikely.

Militant Particularism

In his great reading of the literary and philosophical works of socialist theorist Raymond Williams, David Harvey draws out Williams' concept of "militant particularism" as of crucial importance to his thought. This Harvey defines as "ideals formed out of the affirmative experience of solidarities in one place get generalised and universalized as a working model of a new form of society that will benefit all of humanity".[6] In other words, how very particular places create localised militancies around certain issues — in Harvey's case, his exploration of Williams was prompted by his own involvement in the support of the Cowley car plant strikes as part of a struggle against deindustrialisation. Indeed, Harvey says, convincingly, "the socialist cause in Britain has always been powered by militant particularisms".

Harvey is grappling with the central challenge of how these militancies might be scaled up to a greater level of abstraction and universality. In his words,

the move from tangible solidarities understood as patterns of social life organised in affective and knowable communities to a more abstract set of conceptions that would have universal purchase involved from one level of abstraction — attached to place — to another level of abstractions capable of reaching out across space.[7]

This question is strangely unresolved, Harvey following Williams' own Brechtian device of a lack of closure, with perpetually unresolved tensions which the audience is invited to consider.

In this regard "Block the Block" was a militant particularism. A specific neighbourhood history and identity was brought to bear in a campaign that attempted to foreclose a particular future envisioned by developers. Such militant particularisms have been an enduring motif in our story — in both tenant and workplace struggles across the centuries. The challenge today is how such militant particularisms might be generalised. Identifying the contours of the rentier city should help us in this goal.

Manchester offers us a framework for understanding the conditions that many of us find ourselves living in today. It is a city whose struggles are particular to a place, but which illuminate a more universal story. The "local" out of which militant particularisms are generated is never in and of itself entirely local.[8] They are always produced in and through relationalities of a global nature. In Manchester, this means wrestling closely with how histories of empire have produced formations of capital, class, racialisation and gendering that still shape the city and the ongoing struggles within it.

It seems clear that solutions to the crisis can be found in the lessons of this history. If the trajectory of our times is from homes to assets, then we must throw this process into reverse. Urban land markets must be brought under democratic control. Private landlords should be squeezed out of the market by rent controls, secure tenancies and taxation, as they once were. True public housing — affordable to all at the point of need — must be our central goal; our wider vision an old one: a world so beautiful and so unobtrusive that all people can become human.

The question, then, is who is this "we"? Who could deliver this transformation? To my mind, this is currently a question without an answer. While forces do exist which are contesting the rentierisation of our cities, they remain relatively weak, certainly when compared to the concentrated might of the real estate state. Walter Benjamin, in his commentary on Brecht's *Handbook for City Dwellers*, noted that cities were battlegrounds, but today it seems only one side is really on the offensive. It is my hope in writing this book that it can contribute towards the crystallisation of a general force that could again wrest our cities back from the hands of the rentier, landlord and speculator.

Notes

Introduction

1   With thanks to *Modern Mooch* for the exhaustive detail on the
     Mitchell totems.

2   Natalie Bradbury, "William Mitchell: Artist, Designer, Inventor",
     The Modernist, Issue Nº 2 (Brilliant), September 2011.

3   "Northern Gateway rebrands as Victoria North", *Place North West*,
     16 March 2021.

4   "Manchester Approves Thousands of Homes at Huge Meeting",
     Place North West, 31 August 2023.

5   Brett Christophers, *Rentier Capitalism: Who Owns the Economy
     and Who Pays for It?* (London: Verso, 2020).

6   Jeremy Gilbert and Alex Williams, *Hegemony Now: How Big
     Tech and Wall Street Won the World (And How We Win it Back)*,
     (London: Verso, 2022).

7   The central text is David Harvey, *The Limits to Capital*, (London:
     Verso, 1982).

8   Manchester breakdown by Tenure in the 2021 Census is as
     follows: Owned outright (16.5%), Owned with a mortgage or
     shared ownership (21.5%), Social renting (29.5%) and Private
     renting or lives rent free (32.5%).

9   Figures taken from 2021 Census data show the following
     percentages who rent either privately or in social housing:
     Sheffield (41.3%), Leeds (42.2%), Bristol (44.9%) Birmingham
     (46.5%), Newcastle (50.3%), Liverpool, (52.6%).

10 "The Rise of Corporate Landlords: How They Are Swallowing City Centres Like Manchester One Block Of Flats at a Time" *The Conversation*, February 1 2023.

11 "New Study Shows That Manchester Is Now More Expensive to Live in Than London", *ITV News*, 18 September 2023

12 "Temporary Accommodation at Crisis Point", The Smith Institute, October 2022, p. 12.

13 Doreen Massey, "Places and their Pasts" in *Selected Political Writings*, (London: Lawrence and Wishart, 2023), 165.

Part One: The Primary Circuit

Chapter 1: Shock City

1 This account of Cropper Street, Manchester is drawn from Katrina Navickas' extraordinarily rich account in her book *Protest and the Politics of Space and Place, 1789-1848*, (Manchester: Manchester University Press, 2016), 106-117.

2 Howard Platt, *Shock Cities: The Environmental Transformation and Reform of Manchester and Chicago*, (Chicago: The University of Chicago Press, 2005), 31.

3 *Ibid.*, pp 32-3

4 Fredrich Engels, *The Condition of the Working Class in England*, (Oxford: Oxford University Press, 2009), 21.

5 Mervyn Busteed, *The Irish in Manchester c. 1750-1921: Resistance, Adaptation and Identity*, (Manchester: Manchester University Press, 2016).

6 Alan Kidd, *Manchester: A History*, (London: Carnegie Publishing Ltd, 2007), 5.

7 The analysis of Manchester in Ed Soja in *Postmetropolis: Critical Studies of Cities and Regions*, (Oxford: Blackwells, 2000) has been particularly useful to this account.

8   Sven Beckert, *Empire of Cotton: A Global History,* (London: Vintage, 2015), 30.

9   See *Ibid*, pp. 41, 121 for graphs showing volume of cotton by source of production.

10   This point is made effectively in Mark Harvey, "Slavery, Indenture and the Development of British Industrial Capitalism", *History Workshop Journal*, Vol. 88, 66-88.

11   This phrase, attributed to the Marxist Ecologist Jason W. Moore appears in Nancy Fraser's *Cannibal Capitalism: How our System is Devouring Democracy, Care, and the Planet – and What We Can Do About It,* (London: Verso, 2022).

12   C.L.R. James, *The Black Jacobins: Toussaint L'Ouverture and the San Domingo Revolution*, (London: Allison & Busby, 1980), 86.

13   Sidney Mintz, *Sweetness and Power: The Place of Sugar in Modern History*, (London: Penguin, 1985), 47.

14   J. A. Hobson, quoted in Tom Hazeldine, *The Northern Question: A History of a Divided Country*, (London: Verso, 2020), 74.

15   Recent scholarship has reinforced these arguments, see Maxine Berg and Pat Hudson, *Slavery, Capitalism and the Industrial Revolution*, (London: Polity, 2023).

16   Platt, *Shock Cities*, 36.

17   Léon Faucher, *Manchester in 1844: Its Present Condition and Future Prospects*, (1845), 92.

18   Andreas Malm, *Fossil Capital: The Rise of Steam Power and the Roots of Global Warming*, (London: Verso, 2016).

19   Faucher, *Manchester in 1844*, 93.

20   Platt, *Shock Cities*, 41.

21   Karl Marx, *Capital vol. 1,* (London: Penguin, 1976), 503.

22   Royal Commission on the conditions of the poorer classes in Ireland. Quoted in Hazeldine, *The Northern Question*, 48.

23   Quotes from Asa Briggs, *Victorian Cities*, (London Penguin, 1963), 89.

24 Thomas Carlyle, quoted in Stephen Marcus, *Engels, Manchester and the Working Class*, (New York: Random House, 1974), 32.

25 E.P. Thompson and Eileen Yeo, *The Unknown Mayhew*, (London: Merlin Press, 1971), 23.

26 Quoted in Briggs, *Victorian Cities,* 115.

27 Faucher, *Manchester in 1844,* 15-16.

28 Quoted in Mark Crinson, *Shock City,* (London: Yale University Press, 2023) 21.

29 Engels, *The Condition of the Working Class in England*, 9.

30 *Ibid.*, 87.

31 *Ibid.*, 36, emphasis original.

32 Andy Merrifield, in *Metromarxism* (London: Routledge, 2002), provides us a fantastic introduction to the series of different strands of urban Marxism, including a very worthwhile chapter on Engels. Another useful overview is S. Holgersen, "The Urban" in *The SAGE Handbook of Marxism* (2021). N. de Noronha and J. Silver use Engels' urban theory to great effect in their interlinked chapters on the district of Ancoats, "The Housing Question in the District of Ancoats", in S. Burgum and K. Higgins (eds), *How the Other Half Lives: Interconnecting Socio-Spatial Inequalities*, (Manchester: Manchester University Press, 2022).

33 Engels, *The Condition of the Working Class in England,* 70

34 Account drawn from E.D. Simon and J. Inman, *The Rebuilding of Manchester*, (London: Longmans, 1935), 4

35 Briggs, *Victorian Cities*, 101.

36 Kidd, *Manchester: A History*, 42.

37 Angus Reach, *A Cotton-Fibre Halo: Manchester and the Textile Districts in 1849*, (Royd Press: 2008), 21.

38 Busteed, *The Irish in Manchester*, 22

39 *Ibid.*, 31.

40 Over time Engels came to develop a more sophisticated understanding of the position of the Irish as colonial subjects

within the British system. See John Newsinger and Seán Byers, "The Irish Lever", *Tribune*, 5 August 2020.

41   *Ibid.*, pp 104-112.

42   Navikas, *Protest and the Politics of Public Space,* 32-5

43   Clive Behagg, "Secrecy, Ritual and Folk Violence: The Opacity of the Workplace in the First Half of the Nineteenth Century", in R.D. Storch (ed), *Popular Culture and Custom in Nineteenth Century England*, (London: Routledge, 1982), 154-179.

44   Ian Taylor et al, *A Tale of Two Cities*, (London: Routledge, 1996), 58.

45   Elizabeth Gaskell, *Mary Barton*, (London: Penguin, 2003), 58.

46   Robert Fishman, *Bourgeois Utopias: The Rise and Fall of Suburbia,* (New York: Basic Books, 1989) *75.*

47   *Ibid.*, 90. The economics of suburbanisation are laid out in 84-90.

48   *Ibid.*, 91.

49   *Ibid.*, 82

50   Engels, *The Condition of the Working Class in England*, 56.

51   E.P. Thompson, *The Making of the English Working Class,* (London: Penguin, 2013), 124.

52   *Ibid.*, p. 752.

53   A good overview of the links between the English and Irish working-class movements can be found in Busteed, *The Irish in Manchester*, ch. 5 "Revolution and Reform", 169.

54   Quoted in *Ibid.*, p. 18.

55   Dorothy Thompson, *The Chartists*, (London: Breviary Stuff Publications, 2013), 67.

56   This account is drawn from Busteed, *The Irish in Manchester,* 156.

57   See Thompson, *The Chartists*, 193-4 for discussion on the approach of the Chartists toward free trade.

58   Quote in Hazeldine, *The Northern Question,* 64.

59   Worth noting that there were dissenters to this line — some of the Chartists sought to work with law enforcement to suppress

the strikes during the Great Strike. See Navickas, *Protest and the Politics of Public Space.*

60 Quoted in Thompson, *The Chartists*, 208.

61 Catherine Howe, *Halifax, 1842: A Year of Crisis* (London: Breviary Stuff Publications, 2014).

62 Matthew Roberts, "Women and Late Chartism: Women's Rights in Mid-Victorian England", *The English Historical Review*, August 2021; considers in interesting detail the role played by women's organisation during the Chartist period and its legacy in Sheffield's Women's Rights Association.

63 The narrative for the fight for incorporation is drawn from Shena Simon's *A Century of City Government* (London: G. Allen & Unwin Limited, 1938).

64 *Ibid.*, p. 84

65 Crinson has a set of interesting reflections on the machine-like architecture of the Town Hall in his chapter on the subject in *Shock City* (2023).

66 Beatrice Webb characterised Manchester's ruling elite as such in 1899.

67 Gary Messinger, *Manchester in the Victorian Age*, (Manchester: Manchester University Press, Manchester University Press), 157-8.

68 Briggs, *Victorian Cities*, 90.

69 Cobden was a supporter of the Confederacy during the Civil War. John Bright, in contrast, supported the North. *Ibid.*, 80.

70 Michael Taylor, "The Limits of Liberalism in the Kingdom of Cotton", *The Guardian*, 29 March 2023.

71 David Featherstone, *Solidarity: Hidden Histories and Geographies of Internationalism*, (London: Zed Books 2012), 1.

72 "Remond, [Sarah Parker]" *Manchester Weekly Times* (Manchester: 17 September 1859), Black Abolitionist Archives, Doc. No. 21048

Chapter 2: Modernity and Apocalypse

1   Walter Greenwood, *Love on the Dole*, (London: Jonathan Cape, 1893), 157-8

2   Marshall Berman, *All That Is Solid Melts into Air: The Experience of Modernity*, (London: Verso, 1982), section 4 "Petersburg: The Modernism of Uunderdevelopment", 173-286.

3   Ian Hartford, "The Ship Canal: Raising the Standard for Popular Capitalism", *Manchester Region History Review*, 1994, Vol 8.

4   Messinger, *Manchester in the Victorian Age*, 165.

5   David Paton, "The Manchester Ship Canal", *Good Words*, London Vol 33, (Jan 1892) : 100-107.

6   Jaqueline Jenkinson, *Black 1919*, (Liverpool: Liverpool University Press, 2008), 14.

7   *Ibid.*, p. 17.

8   This section is drawn from N. de Noronha and J. Silver, 'From Emergence to Clearance: The Housing Question in the District of Ancoats' in S. Burgum and K. Higgins (eds), *How the Other Half Lives* (2022), pp. 14-16.

9   Hansard, 1902, quote in *Ibid.*

10 Quoted in I. McIntosh, "'It was worse than Alcatraz': Working for Ford on Trafford Park, *Manchester Region History Review*.

11 D.A. Farne, *The Manchester Ship Canal and the Rise of the Port of Manchester*, 1.

12 McIntosh, "'It was worse than Alcatraz'", 69

13 *Ibid.*, 130.

14 *Ibid.*, 75.

15 *Ibid.*, 71

16 Peter Shapeley, *The Politics of Housing: Power, Consumers and Urban Culture*, (Manchester: Manchester University Press, 2014), 97.

17 De Noronha and Silver, :From Emergence to Clearance", 17.

18 See Neil Gray, *Rent and its Discontents* (London: Rowman and Littlefield, 2018) which clearly presents the argument that it was working class mobilisation, principally on Clydeside, but nationwide too that forced the hand of the government to introduce major tenant reforms.

19 E.D. Simon and Inman wrote celebratorily of this in *The Rebuilding of Manchester* (1933).

20 Doreen Massey gives us some interesting reflections on the contestation between the Manchester planners and the Parish Councils of Cheshire, and much else, in her chapter "Living in Wythenshawe" in I. Borden et al (eds), *The Unknown City: Contesting Architecture and Social Space*, (Cambridge, MA: MIT Press, 2001).

21 See Owen Hatherley, *Red Metropolis*, (London: Repeater, 2020) for a survey of the interwar reformers in London.

22 C. Wildman, "Urban Transformation in Liverpool and Manchester, 1918-1939", *The Historical Journal*, (2012).

23 Shapely, *The Politics of Housing*, 112.

24 Simon and Inman, *The Rebuilding of Manchester,*17.

25 Shapely, *The Politics of Housing*, 113.

26 De Noronha and Silver, "From Emergence to Clearance", 19.

27 Shapely, *The Politics of Housing,* 115

28 *Ibid.* 120.

29 De Noronha and Silver, "From Emergence to Clearance", 19

30 Shapely, *The Politics of Housing*, 121

31 *Ibid.*, 118.

32 *Ibid.*, 123.

33 *Ibid.*, 125-127.

34 Manchester Communism is still waiting for its historian. Michael Crowley's *Comrades Come Rally! Manchester Communists in the 1930s and 1940s,* (London: Bookmarks Publications, 2022) is a useful overview and goldmine of information, but the peculiar

omission of Len Johnson prevents it from being the definitive word on the matter. Nevertheless, much of the information presented below is from this text.

35 The Social Democratic Federation, Britain's first Marxist party, took over the three-storey building in Liverpool that became Hyndman Hall in 1906, renaming it after their founder, the notorious Henry Hyndman. In his account of working-class life in Edwardian Salford, *The Classic Slum*, Robert Roberts wrote, "Hyndman Hall remained for us mysteriously aloof and through the years had, in fact, as much political impact as the near-by gasworks." There are reasons to dispute this assessment however, at least by the 1930s, with both Walter Greenwood and Joe Norman crediting social trips to the Workers' Arts Club there as instrumental to their politicisation.

36 Crowley, *Comrades Come Rally!*. 67.

37 *Ibid.*, 69.

38 *Ibid.*, 62.

39 G. Fugazzotto, "Processes of Black Subjectivation in Great Britain: The Mobilization Against the Italian Invasion of Ethiopia, 1935-36", in Bellia et al (eds), *Conflicting Subjects*, (Pavia: Pavia University Press 2022), 54.

40 Crowley, *Comrades Come Rally!,* 96.

41 *Ibid.*, 158.

42 *Ibid.*, 161.

43 *Ibid.*, 246-254.

44 *Ibid.*, 256-262.

45 Accounts of these years are to be found in E. MacColl, *Journeyman* (Manchester: Manchester University Press, 2009) and "Theatre of Action", in R. Samuel (ed), *Theatres of the Left*, (London: Routledge, 1985), 223.

46 Piratin's activities fighting Moseley's blackshirts in London and in the Stepney Tenants' Defence League are detailed in his essential

memoir *Our Flag Stays Red*, (London: Lawrence and Wishart, 1948).

47 Shapeley, *The Politics of Housing*, 166

48 Details of Johnson's political life are drawn from S. Hirsch and G. Brown, "Breaking the Colour Bar: Len Johnson, Manchester and Anti-Racism", *Race and Class*, 2023, Vol 64(3), 36-58.

49 Ras Makonnen, *Pan Africanism from Within*, (London: Diasporic Africa Press, 2016), 147.

50 *Ibid.*, 138 detail about Kath Locke in Hirsch and Brown, "Breaking the Colour Bar".

51 Makonnen, *Pan Africanism from Within*, 164.

52 Hakim Adi and Marika Sherwood, The 1945 Manchester Pan-African Congress Revisited, (London: New Beacon Books, 1995).

53 Makonnen, *Pan Africanism from Within*. 164

54 *Ibid.* 164

55 These sections are drawn from the highly suggestive article by John McLeod, "A Night at 'The Cosmopolitan': Axes of Transnational Encounter in the 1930s and 1940s", *interventions*, 2002, Vol. 4(1) 53-67.

56 Makonnen, *Pan Africanism From Within*, 138.

57 Manchester City Council, *City of Manchester Plan 1945*, p. 1.

58 *Ibid.*, 4

59 *Ibid.*, p. iii

60 MacColl, "Theatre of Action, Manchester", 221-2

61 David Edgerton, *The Rise and Fall of the British Nation: A Twentieth-Century History*, (London: Penguin, 2018)

62 MacColl, *Journeyman*, 181.

63 Sophie Atkinson, "Unsolved Mysteries", *The Baffler Magazine*, 30 August 2021.

64 Tebbutt, M and Bourne, D (2014) "Shebeens and black music culture in Moss Side, Manchester, in the 1950s and 1960s." *Manchester Region History Review*, 25. pp. 21-34.

65 Alexander Goehr, *Finding the Key*, (London: Faber, 1997), 279. All autobiographical detail relating to Manchester drawn from his reminisces in chapter 2 "Manchester Years" and the last chapter, "Finding the Key".

66 This point is made well by Alex Niven in *The North Will Rise Again,* (London: Bloomsbury, 2023). For a musicological exploration of New Music Manchester, see P. Rupperecht, *British Musical Modernism: The Manchester Group and their Contemporaries*, (Cambridge: Cambridge University Press, 2015).

67 W.G. Sebald, *The Emigrants*, (London: Harville, 1992), 151.

68 *Ibid.*, 157

69 *Ibid.*, 159-160.

70 *Ibid.*, 157.

Part Two: The Interregnum

Chapter 3: The Rise and Crisis of the New Urban Left

1 Details of the occupation have been taken from "The FAC Book", Manchester Archives, GB3228 5/5/4-17

2 (Resident, quoted in report FAC into conditions in the maisonettes 3228 5/5/29

3 MASHA Newsletter no. 4, 1976. Manchester Archives, MSC 331/833 MASHA

4 "Squatters, Slums & the Mouse", *Red Weekly*, 26 October 1974.

5 MASHA Newsletter no. 3, June 1975. Manchester Archives, MSC 331/833 MASHA

6 Interview. "Gus John and the Moss Side Defence Committee", *Manchester's Radical History,* October 1, 2011.

7 Shapely, *The Politics of Housing*, 167.

8 Laurence Brown and Niall Cunningham, "The Inner Geographies of a Migrant Gateway: Mapping the Built Environment and the

Dynamics of Caribbean Mobility in Manchester, 1951-2011",
Social Science History, 2016.

9   Joe Pemberton, *Forever and Ever Amen*, (London: Headline
Review, 2000), 51.

10   Robin Ward, (1975) "Residential Succession and Race Relations
in Moss Side, Manchester", Unpublished PhD Thesis, University
of Manchester.

11   *Moss Side News*, issue no 7, 1969. Manchester Archives, GB3228
5/3/48.

12   *Moss Side News* issue no. 15, March 1970. Manchester Archives,
GB3228.5/3/54.

13   MASHA Newsletter No. 5, 1977. Manchester Archives, MSC
331/833 MASHA

14   MASHA Newsletter No 3, 1975. Manchester Archives, MSC
331/833 MASHA

15   Giordano and Twomey, "Economic Transitions: Restructuring
Local Labour Markets" in J. Peck and K. Ward (eds) *City of
Revolution: Restructuring Manchester,* (Manchester: Manchester
University Press, 2002) 53.

16   *Ibid.,* 51

17   John Gyford, *The Politics of Local Socialism*, (London: Harper
Collins, 1985). I am also indebted here to the work of Tom
Blackburn, in particular his essay "The Capacity to Imagine:
Labour in Local Government", *New Socialist* (2020).

18   Gyford, *The Politics of Local Socialism.*, 10.

19   *Ibid.,* 24-5.

20   The first "New Left" was that formed in the aftermath of the split
within the Communist Party in 1956 following the Soviet Union's
invasion of Hungary. The second was that which emerged in and
around the tumult of 1968. For an extended discussion of the
New Left(s) see S. Hall, "The First New Left: Life and Times" in

Selected Political Writings, (Duke: Duke University Press, 2017), 117-141.

21 Hatherley, *Red Metropolis*, 109.

22 Gyford, *The Politics of Local Socialism*, 42

23 Doreen Massey, with L. Segal and H. Wainwright, "The Great Male Moving Right Show" in *Selected Political Writings*, (London: Lawrence and Wishart, 2022) 103. Massey was writing in response to the analysis of Thatcherism put forward by Stuart Hall in 1979 in "The Great Moving Right Show", in *Selected Political Writings*, 172-186.

24 See, Hatherley, *Red Metropolis*; Diane Frost and Peter North, *Militant Liverpool: A City on the Edge*, (Liverpool: Liverpool University Press, 2013); Daisy Payling, *Socialist Republic: Remaking the British Left in 1980s Sheffield*, (Manchester: Manchester University Press, 2023); and Matthew Thompson, "Whatever Happened to Municipal Radicalism?", *Transactions of the Institute of British Geographers*, 48:3, 2023 for a good overview.

25 Kath Fry and Karen Cropper, *Manchester 1984*, was a self-published account of the takeover by the left of Manchester City Council. Exhaustive in its detail, it remains the most complete account of this time in the public domain and has been an indispensable source in drawing together this section. It can be accessed at https://manchester1984.uk/ [accessed 19 October 2023]

26 MASHA Newsletter no. 4, 1976. Manchester Archives, MSC 331/833 MASHA

27 Quoted in Ray King, *Detonation*, (London: Clear Publications Limited, 2006), 75

28 Tony Benn became the figurehead for the Labour left, its push for an alternative economic strategy and for greater party democratisation during the late 1970s and early 1980s. His near-

miss of the deputy leadership in 1981 was the high watermark of this movement. See Leo Panitch and Colin Leys, *The End of Parliamentary Socialism* (London: Verso, 2001) for the key text on the Labour left during this time.

29   Giordano and Twomey, "Economic Transitions", 53

30   In 1962 only 18% of Manchester Black workers were in unskilled work. Ward, 1975: 310.

31   Taylor et al, *A Tale of Two Cities*, 209.

32   Simon Peplow, *Race and Riots in Thatcher's Britain*, (Manchester: Manchester University Press, 2019), 159

33   *Ibid.*, 159

34   *Ibid.*, 160

35   Gus John interviewed in "'A Violent Eruption of Protest': Reflections on the 1981 Moss Side 'riots' Part One", *Manchester Mule*, 15 August 2011.

36   Peplow, *Race and Riots in Thatcher's Britain*, 160

37   *Ibid.*, p. 129

38   The Labour Party, "Labour's policy for Manchester 1984". 1984.

39   Quoted in *Manchester Magazine*, July 1984. Manchester Archives. Q 352.042 735 MA 8

40   Interview with John Clegg done by Annette Wright and shared with the author.

41   Fry and Cropper, *Manchester 1984*, Chapter 5.

42   Quoted in *Manchester Magazine*, March 1985. Manchester Archives. Q 352.042 735 MA 8

43   Doreen Massey and Hilary Wainwright, "Beyond the Coalfields" in Doreen Massey, *Selected Political Writings*, 111-132.

44   Gyford, *The Politics of Local Socialism*, 31

45   Margaret Thatcher, "Speech to 1922 Committee ('The Enemy Within')", 1984.

46   *Manchester Magazine*, March 1985. Manchester Archives. Manchester Archives. Q 352.042 735 MA 8.

47   Quoted in *Manchester 1984*.

48   In Nicholson's unpublished recollections of the time.

49   Quoted in the *Manchester Magazine*, May 1984.

50   Stephen Quilley, "Entrepreneurial Turns: Municipal Socialism and After" in *City of Revolution*, 82.

51   Available in the archives of CLES in Manchester.

52   Robin Murray, *Breaking with Bureaucracy: Ownership, Control and Nationalisation*, (Centre for Local Economic Strategies, 1987), 31.

53   Quoted in Quilley, "Entrepreneurial Turns", 83.

54   Doreen Massey, "Heartlands of Defeat" in Doreen Massey, *Selected Political Writings*, 60.

55   King, *Detonation*, 85.

56   Manchester Magazine. July 1985. Manchester Archives. Q352 042 733 MA 8

57   "The 1980s AIDS campaign", *BBC News*, 16 October 2005.

58   See the analysis of Quilley, in *City of Revolution* and elsewhere, as well as the accounts by King in *Detonation*, which also was the basis for Andy Spinoza, *Manchester Unspun: Pop Power and Politics in the Original Modern City*, (Manchester: Manchester University Press, 2023).

59   *Manchester Magazine*, November 1985, Manchester Archives. Q352 042 733 MA 8

60   *Ibid*.

Chapter 4: The Manchester Model

1   Andy Spinoza's *Manchester Unspun* (2023) puts the Haçienda (of which he was an early attendee/ member) at the heart of the story. Paul Morley's *From Manchester with Love* (London: Faber, 2022) also is a sprawling example of the endless exegesis of the Factory/ Tony Wilson story.

2   The centring of this act in the creation of the contemporary housing crisis is argued convincingly by Nick Bano in *Against Landlords* (London: Verso, 2024).

3   Allan Cochrane, Jamie Peck and Adam Tickell, "Olympic Dreams" in *City of Revolution*,115.

4   David Harvey, "From Managerialism to Entrepreneurialism: The Transformation in Urban Governance in Late Capitalism"' *Geografiska Annaler,* (1989) 3-17.

5   Biographical details of Scott and narrative drawn from his autobiography *Win a Few, Lose and Few*, (London: The Book Guild Ltd, 2022).

6   Scott, *Win a Few, Lose a Few*, 102.

7   *Ibid.,* 102.

8   Interview with Nicholson by the author 13 July 2023.

9   Fry, *Manchester 1984*, ch. 26

10 Cochrane et al, "Olympic Dreams", 98

11 *Ibid.,* 99

12 Sam Wetherell, "Freedom Planned: Enterprise Zones and Urban Non-Planning in Post-War Britain", *Twentieth-Century British History*, Volume 27, Issue 2, June 2016, 266–289.

13 See Quinn Slobodian, *Crack-Up Capitalism: Market Radicals and the Dream of a World Without Democracy* (London: Penguin, 2023) for the wider global politics of the "zone" within the context of neoliberalism.

14 Paradoxically perhaps, Howe drew his ideas from the New Left theorist Peter Hall's idea of the "non plan". See Wetherall, "Freedom Planned", 267.

15 Keith Joseph quoted in *Ibid.,* 278.

16 *Ibid.,* 278-9

17 Michael Heseltine, *Life in the Jungle*, (London: Hodder & Stoughton, 2000), 130.

18 *Ibid.,* 213.

19 In Ben Beach's unpublished MPhil thesis, "Riots, Regeneration & Resistance" (Cambridge, 2021), he makes the convincing argument the measure of the UDC was a technical response by capital towards the resistance of the working class as demonstrated by the uprisings of 1981.

20 Thatcher Conference speech 1987, available at https://www.margaretthatcher.org/document/106941 [accessed 24 August 2023].

21 Adam Tickell and Jamie Peck, "The Return of the Manchester Men: Men's Words and Men's Deeds in the Remaking of the Local State", *Transactions of the Institute of British Geographers*, 1996, 607.

22 Speaking later to the journalist Ray King in *Detonation*. 93.

23 *Ibid.* 93.

24 Text from Fry, *Manchester 1984*, Appendix 24b.

25 Quoted in King, *Detonation*, 108.

26 Rob Ramwell and Hilary Saltburn, *Trick or Treat?: City Challenge and the Regeneration of Hulme* (Manchester: North British Housing Association, 1998), 11.

27 Alan Harding, *City Challenge: Did It Work?* (Manchester: Manchester City Council, 1998).

28   Fry, *Manchester 1984*, Appendix 24c.

29 Detail in Dave Haslam, *Manchester: England: The Story of a Pop Cult City*, (London: 4th Estate, 1999), 10.

30 Bob Scott quoted in *Business Life*, quoted in Cochrane et al, "Olympic Dreams", 101.

31 *Ibid.*, 99.

32 Tickell and Peck, "The Return of the Manchester Men", 598.

33 *Ibid.*, 608.

34 *Ibid.*, 605.

35 *Ibid*, 611.

36 Quoted in Cochrane, "Olympic Dreams", 99.

37   Quoted in Spinoza, *Manchester Unspun*, 341.

38   The MULE Speaks to Owen Hatherley, part 2. Available at: http://
      manchestermule.com/article/featured-interview-mule-speaks-to-
      owen-hatherley-part-2 [accessed 27 August 2023]

39   In both *Manchester Unspun* and *From Manchester With Love* there
      is no reference to "The Reno". Earlier histories, such as Haslam's
      Manchester, England and writings by Greg Wilson are much better
      at acknowledging the debt their livelihoods owed to Black culture.

40   David Wilkinson, *Post-Punk, Politics and Pleasure in Britain*
      (London: Palgrave Macmillan, 2016).

41   Jeremy Gilbert's essay "White Noise" makes this point on the
      cultural counterrevolution of Britpop powerfully. A similar point
      was made by Mark Fisher.

42   Ross Beveridge and Allan Cochrane, "Exploring the Political
      Potential of the Local State: Building a Dialogue with Sheffield in
      the 1980s", *Antipode*, 55:3, 2023, 8.

Part Three: The Secondary Circuit

Chapter 5: From the Bomb to the Crash

1   Leese, quoted in King, *Detonation*, 42. King's book, written
      to mark the ten-year anniversary of the explosion, is a hugely
      detailed and valuable piece of reportage on its the immediate
      aftermath. Much of the narrative detail here is owed to this work.

2   Quoted in *Ibid.*, 54

3   Quoted in *Ibid.*, 49.

4   Quoted in *Ibid.*, 132.

5   *Ibid.*, 135.

6   The detail of the policy transfer of BIDs into British cities is
      covered, using Manchester as a key case study, by Anna Minton in
      her book *Ground Control*, (London: Penguin, 2009), 37-58.

7   Minton, *Ground Control*, 40.

8 "Asbo capital condemned for 'abuse of power'", The Guardian, 4 July 2007.

9 G. Kaufman, "Teaching the Big Apple", *Building*, 5 October 2001.

10 Quoted in King, *Detonation*, 84-5

11 Spinoza, *Manchester Unspun*, 97 contains recollections of Leese on the great debate of 1987.

12 See Fry, *Manchester Unspun*, Appendix 13A, "Balancing the Budget and Developing a Positive Political Programme" as an example of one of Leese's papers.

13 *Ibid.*, ch. 17.

14 King, *Detonation*, 134.

15 Georgina Blakeley and Brendan Evans, *Regenerating East Manchester: A Political Analysis*, (Manchester: Manchester University Press, 2013), 51.

16 *Ibid.*, 33

17 On the Aylesbury estate see Paul Watt, "Territorial Stigmatisation and Poor Housing at a London 'Sink Estate'", *Social Inclusion* (2020). Volume 8, No. 1, pp. 20–33.

18 "Blair's pledge to the dark estates", *The Independent*, 2 June 1997.

19 Blakeley and Evans, *The Regeneration of East Manchester*, 28.

20 Paul Watt, *Estate Regeneration and Its Discontents: Public Housing, Place and Inequality in London* (Bristol: Polity Press, 2021).

21 See: Chris Allen, *Housing Market Renewal and Social Class* (2008) and Minton, *Ground Control*, chapter 5 which contains a detailed discussion of the Pathfinder programmes.

22 Owen Hatherley, "Pathfinder was slum clearances without the socialism", *The Guardian*, 19 November 2010.

23 "East Manchester Gets a Taste of Urban Renaissance", *Local Government Chronicle*, 29 October 199.

24 *Ibid.*

25 Blakeley and Evans, *The Regeneration of East Manchester*, 103. The whole study is a detailed and invaluable resource assessing the entire decade of regeneration in east Manchester.

26   "Regeneration Plans for East Manchester Revealed", *Local Government Chronicle*, 29 March 2001.

27   Len Grant, *Cardroom Voices*, (Manchester: The New Islington Client Group, 2004) available at https://www.lengrant.co.uk/work/48-2/ [accessed 31 October 2023]

28   Quoted in *Cardroom Voices.*,

29   "Urban Splash - New Islington, Manchester", September 2002, available at https://youtu.be/Tc5BeUcl3Hs [accessed 27 August 2023]

30   Quoted in Nikki Luke and Maria Kaika, "Ripping the Heart out of Ancoats: Collective Action to Defend Infrastructures of Social Reproduction against Gentrification", *Antipode*, 51:2, 2019, 584.

31   Quoted in Grant, *Cardroom Voices.*

32   See, Stuart Hodkinson, *Safe as Houses* (Manchester: Manchester University Press, 2019) for detailed explanation of the PFI schemes under New Labour.

33   C. Stone and R. Gibbons, *Working Class Heroes*, (2018). Available at: https://youtu.be/cx2Rm7Wjfws. Marston's experiences were mirrored by many during the New Labour years who found out their house was to be compulsory purchased and demolished through a PFI scheme. See Watt, *Estate Regeneration and its Discontents* for a detailed study of the same pattern in London.

34   Interview with Linda Carver by filmmaker Joe Malamed, 2022.

35   Quoted in Luke and Kaika, "Ripping the Heart out of Ancoats", 587.

36   Owen Hatherley, *A Guide to The New Ruins of Great Britain*, (London: Verso, 2010).

37   "In Real Architecture Spring 2008: Nick Johnson/Urban Splash", available at: https://www.tate.org.uk/audio/real-architecture-spring-2008-nick-johnsonurban-splash. [accessed 3 November 2023] In the talk he also rubbishes the Cardroom Estate, "the worst estate in Manchester" and claims it was where *Shameless*

was filmed. This was a lie. He then goes on to talk about an exercise where Urban Splash had asked the residents to bring three things that represented favourite things in their life "as a means to engage them and find out what they were interested in", which he says he thought might have included "gardening gloves, twenty four cans of Stella or the neighbours TV". The well-heeled London audience laughed.

38 Detail from Spinoza, *Manchester Unspun*, 181-3

39 *Ibid.*, 199.

40 Alan Harding, Michael Harloe, James Rees, "Manchester's Bust Regime?", *International Journal of Urban and Regional Research*, 2010.

41 Deloitte, "Transforming the skyline, Manchester Crane Survey", 2017.

42 Danny Moran, 'How Corrupt Is Manchester?' October 15, 2022, *About Manchester.*

43 A photograph and some closeups of the table can be viewed on Jonathan Atkinson's blog, available at http://www.lowwintersun. info/thin-veneer-of-democracy-table/

44 Expletive Undeleted, The Tony Wilson Experience, 31 July 2007. Available at https://undeleted.wordpress.com/2008/07/31/feature-the-tony-wilson-experience/ [accessed 3 November 2023].

Chapter 6: From Homes to Assets

1 "Gary Neville: City are better than us", *The Manchester Evening News,* 13 March 2014.

2 "Here's the financial deal Gary Neville struck with Manchester council over his skyscraper plans", *Manchester Evening News*, 21 February 2017

3 George Osborne, "We need a Northern powerhouse", Available at https://www.gov.uk/government/speeches/chancellor-we-need-a-northern-powerhouse

4   "George Osborne the Hacienda raver? It's possible, says Peter Hook… we had all sorts in there!", *Manchester Evening News,* 4 December 2014.

5   "Chinese president set to unveil raft of northern investment during historic trip to Manchester", *Manchester Evening News,* 23 October 2023.

6   "Meet the man changing Manchester's skyline and helping our city keep its swagger", *Manchester Evening News,* 4 May 2016.

7   "Homelessness in Manchester increases ten-fold, figures show", *BBC News,* 31 October 2016.

8   "Manchester Town Hall in lockdown as anti-austerity demonstrators attempt to storm building", *Manchester Evening News,* 16 April 2015.

9   "Manchester council welcomes city centre wide ban against homelessness protest camp", *Manchester Evening News,* 29 October 2015.

10   "Giggs and Neville work with squatters to make occupied hotel safe", *The Guardian,* 20 October 2015.

11   Matt Broomfield, "The squatters and rough sleepers taking up the fight against homelessness in Manchester", *The New Statesman,* 16 January 2018.

12   Details of the squatting movement sourced from interview with Nick by author, 12 July 2023.

13   Helen Pidd, "Northern powerhouse or cardboard city — can a new mayor fix Manchester?", *The Guardian,* 3 May 2017.

14   Quoted in *ibid.*

15   The three key reports are: Jonathan Silver, "From Homes to Assets: Housing financialisaton in Greater Manchester" (2018), Working paper. Jonathan Silver and Richard Goulding, "From Homes to Assets: Housing financialisation in Greater, Update for Financial Year 2018/19" (2019). Working paper, and Tom Gillespie and Jonathan Silver, "Who Owns The City? The Privatisation of Public Land in Manchester" (2020).

16 "Report of the Special Rapporteur on adequate housing as a component of the right to an adequate standard of living, and on the right to non-discrimination in this context", United Nations, A/HRC/34/51, 2017.

17 The dataset covers all developments over 15 units in size in the city-regional core between 2012-2020, 155 developments or 45,069 housing units in total. Over half are in Manchester itself, with around two-fifths in Salford and a tiny 3.6% in Trafford. This section's data is presented in the academic article, Richard Goulding, Jonathan Silver, Adam Leaver, "From Homes to Assets: Transcalar Territorial Networks and the Financialisation of Build to Rent in Greater Manchester", *Environment and Planning A: Economy and Space*, 1-22, (2023).

18 Alice Reynolds, "Contesting the Financialization of Student Accommodation: Campaigns for the Right to Housing in Dublin, Ireland", *Housing Studies*, (2022).

19 "UK Build to Rent Market Update — Q3 2022", *Savills*, 8 November 2022.

20 "Build-to-rent market to grow five-fold during next decade", *Construction Enquirer*, 20 October 2022.

21 Samuel Stein, *Capital City: Gentrification and the Real Estate State* (London: Verso, 2019).

22 "Here's the financial deal Gary Neville struck with Manchester council over his skyscraper plans", *Manchester Evening News*, 21 February 2017.

23 Gillespie and Silver, "Who Owns the City?", 8.

24 The examination of the corporate structures of Manchester Life is drawn from the Centripetal City public interest report Richard Goulding, A. Leaver, and Jonathan Silver, "Manchester Off-shored", (2022).

25 Geographers estimated that the Council held 67623 hectares of land within its local authority boundaries in 1982 — equivalent to

57.9% of the total area of the city. P.T. Kivell and I. McKay, (1988) "Public Ownership of Urban Land", *Transactions of the Institute of British Geographers*, 165-178.

26 Based on the average market value of £200000 per unit — the actual figure will almost certainly be higher.

27 Peter Folkman, Julie Froud, Sukhdev Johal, John Tomaney, and Karel Williams, "Manchester Transformed: Why We Need a Reset of City Region Policy", *CRESC Public Interest Report*, 2016, 8.

28 James Graham FoI Request, "Loans to Renaker by the GM Housing Investment Loans Fund", 31 March 2023. Available at https://www.whatdotheyknow.com/request/loans_to_renaker_by_the_gm_housi#incoming-2320932 [Accessed 19 October 2023]

29 Goulding et al, "From Homes to Assets", 8.

30 Jonathan Silver, "From Homes to Assets: Housing financialisaton in Greater Manchester", 2018. Working paper.

31 Danny Moran, "Does the council's Planning Committee do rehearsals?", *About Manchester,* 14 February 2022.

32 "Trees Not Cars win judicial review against Manchester City Council", *Trees Not Cars*, February 2019 available at: https://www.treesnotcars.com/february-2021 [accessed 3 November 2023].

33 "Manchester council lose judicial review over Central Retail Park planning decision", *The Manchester Meteor*, 19 February 2021.

Chapter 7: The Gentrification Frontier

1 Interview with Thirza Asanga Rae by the author, 30 August 2023.

2 There have been two year-on-year 20% average rent rises in Manchester. For 2023 see: "Manchester rents are 20% more expensive than last year", *Place North West*, 21 August 2023. For 2022 see: "Private rents in UK reach record highs, with 20% rises in Manchester", *The Guardian*, 14 July 2022.

3 "The social housing being sold off on Rightmove while homelessness soars", *Manchester Evening News*, 25 October 2018.

4   Interview with Matt by the author, 9 August 2023.

5   For a good review of the studentification literature, see Takashi Nakazawa, "Expanding the Scope of Studentification Studies", (2017), *Geography Compass*.

6   "Cost of living: 'The toxic reality of pupils living in poverty'", *BBC News Online*, 12 July 2022.

7   "Mums on the edge, hunger and rats — the families trying to hold it together and the schools trying to help", *Manchester Evening News*, 19 December 2022.

8   Interview with Vicky Leigh by the author, 31 August 2023.

9   Interview with Amanda by the author, 31 August 2023.

10   See Watt, *Estate Regeneration and its Discontents* for a definitive mapping of the same processes as they have unfolded in London.

11   See Tom Slater, *Shaking Up the City: Ignorance, Inequality, and the Urban Question*, (Berkeley, CA: University of California Press, (2021), 19-23 for a powerful discussion on "agnotology".

12   It's common to see commentators in the city, hypnotised by the ever-growing skyline, breezily dismiss concerns over gentrification as almost a false bogeyman, conjured up by muttering defectors. See various articles in *Manchester Confidential* and *The Mill* for examples of this discourse.

13   Here I am indebted, among others, to the work of Tom Slater, one of the best critical urbanists working today, and of course the legacy of Neil Smith.

14   Slater, *Shaking Up the City*.

15   Ruth Glass, *London: Aspects of Change*, (MacGibbon & Kee, 1964).

16   See Watt, *Estate Regeneration and its Discontents*, 25.

17   Engels, *The Housing Question*.

18   See the following articles by Neil Smith, "Toward a Theory of Gentrification: A Back to the City Movement by Capital, Not People", *Journal of the American Planning Association* (1979),

"Gentrification and the Rent Gap", *Annals of the Association of American Geographers,* (1987) and "New Globalism, New Urbanism: Gentrification as Global Urban Strategy", *Antipode*, 34:3, (2002) as well as his indispensable book *The New Urban Frontier: Gentrification and the Revanchist City* (London: Routledge, 1996).

19   Smith, *The New Urban Frontier*, 1996.

20   Glass, *London: Aspects of Change*, quoted in Adam Elliot-Cooper, Phil Hubbard and Loretta Lees, "Moving beyond Marcuse: Moving beyond Marcuse: Gentrification, Displacement and the Violence of Un-Homing", *Progress in Human Geography*, 2020, Vol. 44(3) 494.

21   Engels, *The Housing Question*.

22   Peter Marcuse, "Gentrification, Abandonment, and Displacement: Connections, Causes, and Policy Responses in New York City", in Neil Smith and Peter Williams (eds), *Gentrification of the City.* (Boston: Allen and Unwin, 1986), 121–152.

23   Elliot-Cooper et al, "Moving Beyond Marcuse", 494.

24   L. Kern, "Rhythms of Gentrification: Eventfulness and Slow Violence in a Happening Neighbourhood", *Cultural Geographies* (2016).

25   Elliot-Cooper et al, "Moving beyond Marcuse", 502.

26   Peter Marcuse, "A Note from Peter Marcuse", *City* 14, (2010), 187–188.

27   Kate Shaw, "Gentrification: What It Is, Why It Is, and What Can Be Done about It", *Geography Compass*, (2008).

28   Interview with Jamil Keating by the author, 11 July 2023.

29   "Lomond Capital buys out Thornley Groves", *Manchester Evening News*, 16 September 2023.

30   "Fast-growing agency secures another brace of acquisitions", *Property Industry Eye*, February 21, 2022.

31   "FEC makes trio of hires", *Place North West*, 27 January 2021.

32　Analysis drawn from interview with housing caseworker at the GM Law Centre, 17 July 2023.

33　"Corridor Manchester: Strategic Vision to 2025", *Manchester City Council*, 2015.

34　*Ibid.*, p. 6

35　"Residents to declare 'open warfare' over 1,400 student campus", *Manchester Evening News*, 18 January 2007.

36　Davarian Baldwin, *In The Shadow of the Ivory Tower*, (New York: Bold Type Books, 2021).

37　"Vanishing's Gareth Smith: 'What Is A City If Not For Its People?'", *The Quietus*, 1 September 2023.

38　Keatings' point here finds echo in the fantastic article by Ida Danewid, "The Fire This Time: Grenfell, Racial Capitalism and the Urbanisation of Empire", *European Journal of International Relations*, (2019).

39　"Government withdraws £1.98 billion PFI funding", *Inside Housing*, 22 November 2010.

40　"£250m Collyhurst revamp is axed in cuts", *Manchester Evening News*, 29 November 2010.

41　"Collyhurst Redevelopment Partner Sought", *Manchester Confidentials*, 12 March 2012.

42　For an exploration of similar dynamics in Salford of neighbourhoods left in "limbo-land" when the wheel of capital stops turning, see Andrew Wallace, "Gentrification Interrupted in Salford, UK: From New Deal to 'Limbo-Land' in a Contemporary Urban Periphery", *Antipode*, 47:2, 2015.

43　Sean Benstead, "GRT History Month Should Reflect An Honest History: A History of Land Struggles and State Harassment", *Greater Manchester Housing Action*, 10 June 2021.

44　This point has been made comprehensively by Watt, *Estate Regeneration and its Discontents*.

45   See Katrina Navickas' blog "Locales: Cropper Street Manchester (1)", https://historyofpublicspace.uk/2018/01/13/locales-cropper-street-manchester-1/ [accessed 8 October 2023]

46   This Anne is a different person to Anne Worthington, who was one of the principal characters of Manctopia. Her more celebratory view of the redevelopment of Manchester, in particular the repurposing of old industrial buildings for flats, has been used by defenders of the Manchester Model as something of a proof that "real Mancs" are supportive of what has happened. This is far from clear from the film, her position is much more ambiguous when it comes to the clearance of the inner city — and her own estate. On the Victoria North development, she says in episode four: "It's absolutely gobsmacking, our Labour council signing off a loan to the multi-billion Far East Consortium… something stinks somewhere along the line there." By October 2023 Worthington was leading a protest in Miles Platting calling for more social housing in Manchester. See: "Social Homes for Miles Platting Now", *Community Savers,* 31 October 2023.

Conclusion: Militant Particularism in the Rentier City

1   "Left behind in one of Hulme's last tower blocks, the 'community of ghosts' facing a tidal wave of change", *Manchester Evening News*, 27 March 2021.

2   Massey, "Living in Wythenshawe", 467.

3   *Ibid.*, 466.

4   Greenwood, *Love on the Dole*, 14-15.

5   "Bev Craig's first year, dirty sites, and moving targets", *Place North West*, 1 December 2022.

6   David Harvey and Raymond Williams, "Militant Particularism and Global Ambition: The Conceptual Politics of Place, Space,

and Environment in the Work of Raymond Williams", *Social Text,* 42 (1995), 83.

7   *Ibid.,* 84

8   This argument emerges in the work of David Featherstone, see *Solidarity*, and his article "Towards the Relational Construction of Militant Particularisms: Or Why the Geographies of Past Struggles Matter for Resistance to Neoliberal Globalisation", *Antipode*, 37:2, 2005.

Index

Acknowledgements

Thanks to the Repeater team: Tariq Goddard, Rhian Jones, Josh Turner and my editor Carl Neville, who was a joy to work with. Additionally, to Owen Hatherley, Alex Niven and Tim Lawrence for helping me get the project off the ground, and to the team at *Tribune* — Marcus Barnett, Ronan Burtenshaw and Francesca Newton — for providing the space to write about some of the early ideas.

Many people read parts of the draft, and the final text is far better for their input. Thanks to Nick Bano, Lily Gordon-Brown, Rich Goulding, Jacob Mukherjee, Jon Silver, Paul Watt and Dan Whittall. Also, thanks to everyone I interviewed or spoke to. They are: Thirza Amina Asanga-Rae, Ekua Bayunu, Roy Bennett, Kate Bradley, Dave Carter, Sally Casey, Ben Clay, Allan Cochrane, Sam Fairbrother, Jamil Keating, Vicky Leigh, John Nicholson, Justin O'Connor, Irfan Rainy, Kath Robinson, Nilofar Siddiqi, Amanda, Nick (aka Lousy Badger) and an anonymous member of the Moss Side Tenants Union. Thanks to the family of John Clegg and to Annette Wright for allowing me use of the interview she did with John before he passed.

Much of the impetus for this book came out of my involvement with the housing justice movement in Greater Manchester, and I thank the other members of the organisations I have been a part of: the Greater Manchester Tenants Union, Greater Manchester Housing Action and Block the Block. Special mention must go to Debi Blanchard, Tina Cribbin, Thirza and Sally, who are among the most inspirational people I have ever met, and to Ekua and Nigel de Noronha of GMTU's anti-racism committee — I have learned, and continue to learn, so much from both of you. Additionally, I would like to thank the union's central Committee as well as my colleagues for supporting me in this endeavour, including granting time off work for its completion.

Two other central features of my time in Manchester ought to be mentioned. First, those of us who coalesced during the time of Corbyn's leadership of the Labour Party in Manchester Momentum and Salford Community Theatre, particularly Beth, Alice, Sarah, Steph, Hamish, Billy, Charlie, James, Scarlet and Poppy — thank you for that shared commitment. Second, the Do One / Community crew, who each month show us that there is an alternative to the corporate whitewashing of the city: Irfan, Joe, Blu, Nuuradiin, Simon, Yusra, Shannon, Tara, Dave, Tom, Brad, Luke, Paula.

Thanks to Martin, for giving me that most precious of things, cheap rent; to Sam, for his friendship, faith in this project and the maxim "how can one possibly write a play in a city with so many cranes" which became an unofficial analytic principle for the book, and to my dear friend Siobhán, whose work in the tenant movement has, for so many years, been an inspiration to my own.

To my family, Jo, Richard, Anna and Matty, thank you for your consistent support and love, and to Lydia, thank you for your unerring commitment to justice and for showing me that you can never truly love a city until you fall in love with someone in it.

REPEATER BOOKS

is dedicated to the creation of a new reality. The landscape of twenty-first-century arts and letters is faded and inert, riven by fashionable cynicism, egotistical self-reference and a nostalgia for the recent past. Repeater intends to add its voice to those movements that wish to enter history and assert control over its currents, gathering together scattered and isolated voices with those who have already called for an escape from Capitalist Realism. Our desire is to publish in every sphere and genre, combining vigorous dissent and a pragmatic willingness to succeed where messianic abstraction and quiescent co-option have stalled: abstention is not an option: we are alive and we don't agree.